The Twenty-First-Century Firm

The Twenty-First-Century Firm

CHANGING ECONOMIC ORGANIZATION
IN INTERNATIONAL PERSPECTIVE

Edited by Paul DiMaggio

PRINCETON UNIVERSITY PRESS

PRINCETON AND OXFORD

Library of Congress Cataloging-in-Publication Data

The twenty-first-century firm : changing economic organization in international
perspective / edited by Paul DiMaggio ; with contributions by Paul DiMaggio . . . [et al.]
p. cm
Includes bibliographical references and index.
ISBN 0-691-05851-2 (alk. paper)
1. Organizational change. 2. Industrial management. I. DiMaggio, Paul.
HD58.8.T89 2001
658.4′06—dc21   2001021988

*I dedicate this book with love and
with appreciation for their support
and encouragement to my parents,
Joseph J. and Cecelia DiMaggio.*

Contents

The Twenty-First-Century Firm

Introduction: Making Sense of the Contemporary Firm and Prefiguring Its Future

Paul DiMaggio

A GLANCE at the covers of contemporary business periodicals reveals that many people believe the corporation is changing so dramatically that we need a new lexicon to describe it. On a recent trip to my local book superstore, I found eleven titles that sought the right word to characterize the company of the future in a time of dizzying change. Some of these—*The Boundaryless Organization* (Ashkenas et al. 1998), *The Centerless Organization* (Pasternack and Viscio 1998), *The Clickable Corporation* (Rosenoer et al. 1999)—seized upon the greater permeability of organizational borders as the central image. Several others—*The Collaborative Enterprise* (Campbell and Goold 1999), *The Horizontal Organization* (Ostroff 1999), *The Self-Managing Organization* (Purser and Cabana 1998)—emphasized the flattening of hierarchy and a putative shift toward more cooperative forms of management. Still others—*The Minding Organization* (Rubenstein and Firstenberg 1999), *The Learning Company* (Pedler et al. 1991), *The Learning Organization* (Garratt 1994), *The Knowledge-Creating Company* (Nonaka 1995)—emphasized the central role of creativity, learning, and knowledge in the effective organization of the future.

Once observers of companies get down to specifics, the ways in which they characterize these changes are astonishingly disparate. Are contemporary firms recognizing the importance of their human assets, integrating employees into decision making as never before, investing in staff and workers, and defining them as "stakeholders"? Or are they treating workers as commodities, wringing the last ounce of commitment and energy from their employees, demanding give-backs from unions, and breaking implicit "lifetime-employment" contracts with managers in waves of ruthless downsizing? Is the "new firm" small and flexible, engaged in a web of collaborations with other small enterprises, each specialized to perform at peak capacity? Or is it an ever-expanding global leviathan, bloated with acquisitions after a decade of unprecedented merger activity? Does the

I am grateful to Peter Marsden, David Stark, and Charles Tilly for helpful comments on an earlier draft of this introduction.

future belong to flexible networks of cooperating companies—or to increasingly intense rivalry between leaner and meaner competitors? Do contemporary enterprises craft strong identities, motivating employees with meaningful corporate cultures and an intensely shared sense of mission? Or has the firm become a mere "nexus of contracts" (Fama and Jensen 1983a) that induces contributions with stock options and other financial incentives in a world in which company boundaries are porous and identities indistinct?

Although the tropes and images used to understand change in the business world are diverse and contradictory, their proliferation presents no mystery. For contemporary businesses are buffeted by a unique combination of change-inducing forces. The rise of the global economy has entailed unprecedented capital mobility, hastening the shift from manufacturing to service industries in the advanced economies, while requiring that companies everywhere develop the capacity to compete in a global marketplace. Changes in information technology expand the capacity of firms not only to monitor their workers and production processes but also to engage more employees in processes of product design and organizational change, to bring more information into the company, and to get products out to consumers in ways that dramatically alter cost structures and organizational designs. Expansion of educational levels in much of the world, and the combination of economic pressures and increased opportunities that have led more and more women into the marketplace, have reshaped the workforce. In the West, changes in technology and law, and in the philosophy and behavior of investors, have honed the market for corporate control and made company managements more responsive to the bottom line. In Asia, cycles of boom and bust have called into question distinctive ways of organizing that in the 1980s were hailed as models that could save Western competitors. And nowhere has change been more momentous than in the former socialist world, where nation-states privatized vast waves of factories and other enterprises, and business people and governments alike had to improvise "capitalist systems" that were far more complex and ambiguous in practice than they had been in prospect. Not since the industrial revolution have so many dramatic transformations coincided with such force. No wonder, then, that the categories people have used for the past century to think about the corporation appear inadequate, and no wonder that so many are trying so hard to find new ones.

Despite the variety of perspectives being offered, most commentators agree on a few fundamentals. For one thing, many agree that companies are interacting with one another differently than in the past. Throughout the world, the strong boundaries that once separated firms have become less distinct, while traditional arms-length market transactions have become more intimate. New forms of coordination—"relational contracting"—

have emerged that entail much less commitment and control than bureaucracy, but more binding ties than simple market exchange. Moreover, business alliances—groups of legally independent companies knit together by such factors as ownership by one extended family, mutual shareholding, or strong, enduring collaborations—achieved new visibility when the economies they dominate entered the world's center stage (as in the cases of Japan, and then in Taiwan and Korea), or emerged anew in response to institutional volatility in the wake of regime change (as in Russia and Hungary).

Within corporations, consultants, pundits, and new MBAs are telling seasoned managers to violate helter-skelter the rules they learned in business school. In the sphere of employment, less secure internal labor markets, more fluid job definitions, and more ambiguous reporting relationships replace the rules of clarity and commitment. In the realm of production, the "Fordist" system of disciplined assembly-line work using expensive, dedicated machinery to achieve a sharp division between execution and design is being replaced. Companies increasingly opt for flexible production using cheap and/or multi-use technology, with conceptual effort controlled in some firms by technical experts, but in others delegated to re-skilled production employees or distributed among teams drawn from many parts of the organization (Kelley 1990). In supplier relations, multiple competitive sourcing and the maintenance of large inventories—the conventional strategies by which companies protected themselves from exploitation—have in many instances yielded to long-term, sole-source relational contracts and just-in-time delivery. Company/customer relations are being redesigned as collaborations that challenge the traditional boundaries of firms: whereas firms once created attractive products first and then marketed them widely, clients now participate actively in the design of sharply differentiated products tailored to particular markets.

Management writers and business scholars have identified these developments at the same time throughout much of the world, and many have been quick to identify and label them as new forms. To be sure, the ubiquity of change—and the apparent affinity among several dimensions of change observed throughout the business world—*is* striking. But the nature and long-term implications of change are as yet dimly perceived.

For one thing, the literature is far richer in striking examples of purported trends than in careful empirical studies documenting the scope and incidence of change. It is one thing to read about a firm—or a half dozen firms—that have changed dramatically their way of doing business. We rarely have the information needed, however, to distinguish between eccentric companies, or industries facing idiosyncratic competitive environments, and harbingers of long-term organizational and economic change.

Even when trends—such as downsizing middle management and engaging in long-term relationships with suppliers—are documented, we lack a clear analytic understanding of the connections among them. Are trends that coincide connected by logical necessity? Is their simultaneous appearance merely coincidence? Or are they intrinsically unrelated elements united discursively into a package promoted by business consultants and academic management programs?

Moreover, there is little consensus about the relative importance of particular developments. Books targeted at the business trade market often focus on just one trend, making lavish claims and employing an unacknowledged synecdoche by which a single element of change substitutes for careful consideration of a hazily specified whole. Even serious scholars find it difficult to apprehend the full horizon of organizational change, due to academic specialization. No one person, no matter how gifted or industrious, could possibly be an expert on every facet of global enterprise: like the blind men and the elephant, researchers' perspectives on change are often restricted to particular places, industries, or business functions. Careful analyses that take into mutual account business firms (other than the largest multinationals) in different regions of the globe are especially rare.

This volume is an effort to bring some order to the chaotic tumble of diagnoses, labels, and descriptions that characterize the field. We make no effort to find a single trope to capture the variety of developments described herein, nor do we try to paint a single portrait of the corporation of the twenty-first century. Forms of business enterprise are much too diverse, and the currents of change are rushing forward too swiftly, for anyone to predict the future. Our goal, instead, is to take account of what we *do* know, to sweep aside commonly held misapprehensions, to provide a clear picture of the main directions of change and the possible alternative futures to which they lead, and to articulate clearly the major puzzles that remain. As such, this volume aims to be both a stock-taking and an exercise in historical imagination.

Our strategy has been to draw on the strengths of leading scholars from several perspectives and to induce a conversation among them. The authors of the three chapters that follow this introduction—Walter W. Powell, David Stark, and D. Eleanor Westney—are regional experts who have devoted most of their professional lives to understanding, respectively, economic organization in the United States and Western Europe, the former socialist societies of Eastern Europe, and Japan and East Asia. Their contributions report in a systematic way on what we know about change in corporate structure, strategy, and governance in the places they have studied, separating fact from fiction, established trend from extravagant extrapolation. The authors of the four commentaries that follow—Reinier Kraakman, David Bryce and Jitendra Singh, Robert Gibbons, and Charles Tilly—are experts in economic organization who are specialized by analytic perspective rather than region. Their chapters integrate the regional accounts and interpret the trends the regional authors describe, from the standpoints, respectively, of legal scholarship, evolutionary theory of the firm, organizational economics, and the comparative historical study of the nation-state. Together, the two sections of this book produce an overview unusual in its combination of depth, balance, and insight.

THE TWENTIETH-CENTURY MODEL

Until relatively recently, social scientists and historians viewed the corporation through the serviceable lenses of theories developed during, or shortly after, the industrial revolution. The period that saw the rise of the factory system in England and its diffusion to the United States and Europe witnessed changes in organization and production, and in the social relationships and community structures that sustained them, even more striking than those we experience today. And like the current era of change, the late nineteenth century was a period in which social thinkers worked overtime to give form to and grasp the significance of the transformations occurring before their eyes.

The twentieth-century view of the firm was shaped, above all, by two thinkers of uncanny, if hardly infallible, prescience. One of them, Max Weber, wrote an essay on "bureaucracy" at the turn of the last century that crystallized understanding of the organizational structure of the firm (and of government agencies and large nonprofit organizations as well) for several generations. The other, Karl Marx, writing several decades earlier, located the capitalist enterprise in the larger political economy in a way that influenced historians and social thinkers throughout most of the twentieth century.

Weber on Bureaucracy

Weber ([1924] 1946) presented his model of bureaucracy as an "ideal type"—not a literal description of concrete bureaucracies (though it was certainly influenced by the major examples he had before him, those of the Prussian armies and the major capitalist firms), but a simplified account of the central dimensions of a new technology of human control and of the logic that knit these dimensions together.

As Weber observed, methods of control based on the kinds of informal social networks in which every society abounds were poorly suited to an age of unprecedented military and economic competition. In both war and business, victory would come not simply to those with the biggest armies or the newest technologies, but to large-scale organizations that could harness the energies of their members to a common goal. The key, according to Weber, was to render irrelevant people's ordinary social ties, to structure organizations so that employees would leave their family connections and personal identities at the factory gate.

Weber's famous essay on bureaucracy provides a complex account of the form's features and internal organization, but for present purposes we can focus on only a few key dimensions. First, bureaucracies are governed by "calculable rules"—rules that are open, widely understood, and fairly applied—rather than by persons. The most important of these rules establish a hierarchy of offices, prescribing who can communicate with (and give orders to) whom. Another set of rules governs the admission of persons to the organization, describing clearly the accomplishments that make persons eligible for employment and articulating standards for advancement when vacancies arise. A third set of rules establishes routines for the performance of work: what tools are to be used to repair a machine, how many people must be in the cockpit to fly a plane, how many hours one can drive a truck without sleep, or how to fill out a purchase order for new supplies. Rules dictate who in the organization may do certain kinds of work: they tell us, for example, that only a radiologist may interpret a CAT scan or that only a union-certified electrician may repair a short circuit. And rules specify behaviors that are *un*acceptable—pilfering wallboard from a construction site, importuning employees for personal favors, promoting one's cousin over more qualified candidates—ordinarily because such actions put an employee's interests above those of the organization. These examples, like many of Weber's observations about bureaucracy, seem obvious today. But that simply goes to show how successful the bureaucratic form of organization was, because few if any such rules could be found in most organizations before the nineteenth century.

Rules, Weber argued, are beneficial for several reasons. For one thing, they prevent employees from using organizations to enhance their own welfare rather than contributing their services to advance the organization's ends. Most important, they reduce what we now call "transaction costs"—the costs of deciding, haggling, arranging, and coordinating—in two ways. First, by making everyday activities repetitive and predictable, they reduce uncertainty and permit bosses to give most of their attention to the relatively few decisions that deal with matters too unusual or complex to be reduced to a formula. Second, by specifying fixed procedures for the allocation of both rewards and punishments that apply to everyone, they increase the likelihood that employees will receive fair treatment (at least compared to one another) and limit the amount of time devoted to quarreling about horizontal equity.

After reliance on rules, a second essential feature of Weber's model of bureaucracy is what he called "the separation of person and position": the existence of fixed, well-defined roles specifying the rights and obligations of every organization member (except those at the top of the hierarchy, who remain free to do as they like unless they are constrained by rigid custom or by laws imposed by the state). The modern bureaucracy, with formal job descriptions and a formal organization chart, reduced transaction costs by making duties clear and eliminating the need for members to negotiate about the allocation of routine tasks. Equally important (in an age in which most people, if they could get away with it, regarded their workplace as an extension of their personal domain), bureaucracies required that participants interact with one another in terms of their formal work roles rather than their personal identities (mandating separation of personal and official business, evaluating workers on the basis of role performance, forbidding superiors to make demands on their subordinates unrelated to the latter's job description, and so on). In so doing, bureaucracy eliminated the source of much of the conflict that helped to make prebureaucratic forms of large-scale organization notoriously unwieldy.

A third feature central to Weber's model of bureaucracy was the proliferation of written communication and formal records, which had several functions. For one thing, it collectivized memory, which had previously been inseparable from (and therefore a source of considerable power to) persons. A filing system enabled many aspects of organizational history and routine to be written down and retained for the use of the occupants of relevant roles, whoever they might be. Moreover, files enhanced calculability and control, both of employees (whose performance could be tracked according to explicit criteria) and expenses, through the use of double-entry book-keeping, which enabled enterprises to discern fraud and control costs more effectively than in the past.

Finally, bureaucracies possessed a unique way of rewarding employees that created a coincidence of interest between worker and firm. By offering employees lifetime job security and making compensation and advancement depend on how well each worker fulfilled his or her official role, bureaucracy gave employees the strongest possible long-run motivation to please their superiors. Moreover, the likelihood that employees and superiors would advance through the hierarchy at unequal rates, and that employees would therefore have a variety of superiors over the course of their careers, provided an incentive for workers to gain the boss's esteem by performing well in their official capacity rather than doing personal favors that another superior would have no reason to reward. Here, for once, Weber was wrong, in the sense that formal job tenure rights have been limited largely to government service and to those professions where novices are admitted to a collegium (partnership in a law practice, tenure at a university) after several years of acceptable service. In practice, however, informal lifetime employment has often characterized large, market-insulated corporations as well, either for all employees (as in Japan's core firms) or for the white-collar labor force (as in the United States before the 1980s).

The key dimensions of Weber's model of bureaucracy—fixed hierarchy; separation of person and position through formal job descriptions; clear, numerous, universally applied rules; long-term employment within the enterprise; and reward based on a combination of merit and seniority—remained central elements of organizational design through most of the twentieth century and, indeed, in comparison to preindustrial forms of organizing, they characterize most large organizations today. Yet, as we shall see, contemporary managers, consultants, and academics are challenging some of the key tenets of this highly effective formula to an unprecedented extent.

Marx on the Capitalist System and the Post-Marxian Synthesis

It may seem odd in the twenty-first century to hail Karl Marx as prophet. But while aspects of his historical vision were sharply flawed (and the socialist state systems that others developed in his name have been roundly discredited), Marx, like Weber, captured key dimensions of the changes that buzzed around him, systematizing new developments into a comprehensive and compelling analytic framework. But whereas Weber (who, to be sure, benefited from having a half century longer than Marx to observe the contours of change) identified the blueprint of bureaucracy with uncanny accuracy, the Marxian account of the capitalist system was amended and supplemented by latter-day scholars trying to understand why Marx's big historical predictions had not panned out.

Marx himself deserves credit for identifying the logic of capitalism as a system, and the centrality to capitalism of the factory and the large-scale firm. Better than any of his contemporaries, Marx understood the endemic antagonism between boss and worker as the product of an economic logic built around inexorable competition among profit-seeking firms. And he described the implications of this conflict for the organization of the labor process with exceptional insight ([1867] 1887).

Where Marx's analysis failed (or, at least, proved premature), and where the neo-Marxists of the second half of the twentieth century sought to bail him out, was in his prediction that the capitalist system would come to a crashing demise amidst economic depression and workers' rebellions, as the rate of profit declined to zero. For a while, this prognosis appeared plausible: between 1870 and 1940, the United States, for example, suffered through repeated cycles of economic boom and bust, the latter accompanied by violent confrontations between labor and management. But after World War II, the ferocity of economic cycles declined, labor relations stabilized, and several decades of unprecedented prosperity (marred by rising inequality in the United States and high unemployment in much of Europe) ensued.

Why, asked political economists, did workers not revolt? How, they wondered, were companies able to avoid the ruinous competition that Marx had predicted? The numerous ways in which commentators answered these questions provided much occasion for vigorous disagreement, but in the end many observers—not just neo-Marxists, but liberal economists and sociologists as well—came to accept a story with six basic elements.

First, Western firms and Western workers benefited from the military subjugation of less-developed countries to the economic interests of the advanced capitalist nations. By exploiting the Third World's masses through gunboat diplomacy and political manipulation, Western companies could afford to exploit their domestic employees less (Lenin 1939).

Second, companies grew in size through merger and acquisition until only a few large players were left in many of the major industries. These big "oligopolists" (an "oligopoly" is an industry controlled by a small number of producers) were able to use tacit understandings to avoid serious competition and therefore to charge monopoly prices and earn monopoly rents, part of which they used to pacify their work forces (Baran and Sweezy 1966).

Third, this new system of "monopoly capitalism" generated its own form of workplace organization. Workers in the earliest factories (and in marginally profitable manufacturing industries that remained competitive) earned low wages and suffered under the thumb of coercive foremen, who disciplined them brutally and fired them if they complained. By contrast, workers lucky enough to find jobs in large postwar companies experienced more carrot and less stick. Many rules that governed their work were invisible because they were built into high-powered machines. The pace might be grueling but high wages, decent benefits, and job security (often guaranteed by labor unions that bargained tough on compensation but deferred to management on issues of workplace control) made up for it. The coercion Marx viewed as endemic to capitalism yielded to "bureaucratic control" (Edwards 1979) through formal rules administered by systems with which workers had little personal contact.

Fourth, not all workers fared so well. Employees in the industrialized nations' "competitive sectors" (and a *fortiori* those in the Third World), received few if any of the advantages awarded employees of "primary-sector" firms that were buffered from the competitive marketplace. Lacking union representation or job security, with few protections from labor law and few benefits beyond a meager wage, competitive-sector workers (drawn disproportionately from among immigrants or racial and ethnic minorities) served as shock absorbers for the larger system (Gordon et al. 1982).

Fifth, large monopoly-sector companies were willing to share the wealth with their workers, rather than distribute all of the surplus to shareholders, because of changes in company governance that shifted control from owners to professional managers. Whereas vigorous owner/entrepreneurs once strove to maximize profits, their heirs absented themselves from corporate governance, which they entrusted to salaried managers. In some versions of this argument (Galbraith 1967; Burnham 1941), companies became so complex that headquarters could no longer control middle managers, who ran their fiefdoms as they liked. In other versions, the diffusion of stock ownership and the rise of passive, pro-management, institutional shareholders meant that individual shareholders were too disorganized to exercise effective control (Berle and Means 1932; Drucker 1976). In any case, professional managers were said to prefer growth, increased market share, labor peace, and financial stability to the high profits that shareholders cherish.

The sixth and final component of the post-Marxian synthesis was the state, which Marx had dismissed as the "executive committee of the ruling class" ([1852] 1973). Yet the New Deal challenged the political power of business, supported union organizing efforts, passed protective legislation, and enhanced the status of federal employees with rights and benefits programs that became models for the private sector (Baron et al. 1986). After World War II, European social democracies increased the scope and generosity of social welfare programs and, in many cases, accepted trade unions as partners in both corporate and societal governance. Some neo-Marxists contended that such benefits represented a divide-and-conquer technique whereby the "ruling class" sapped the workers' revolutionary fervor. Other more perceptive observers viewed such reforms as products of the interests and convictions of political leaders, but questioned whether government revenues could sustain them in the long run (O'Connor 1973). Nonetheless, many believed that the capitalist social democracies had found a potentially stable trade-off between growth, profits, and welfare, anchored in an alliance between the liberal state and the bureaucratic, oligopolistic firm, with trade unions as junior partners.

The twentieth-century model of the firm, a view of enterprise based jointly on the analytic frameworks of Weber and of Marx and his successors, did more than structure our perceptions of the firm for half a century or more. It also identified the key factors—at the organizational level, bureaucracy, and at the level of the economy, free-market legal and political institutions—that constituted the modern industrial order. All working advanced market systems rest on an institutional base that accomplishes two things. First, legal and government institutions (contract law, securities law, consumer regulations, and so on) enable partners in market transactions to be confident that they will get what they paid for, or have effective avenus of appeal if they do not. Second, a range of institutions—insurance companies, government agencies, limited liability forms, and much corporate law—limit uncertainty by pooling risk at more inclusive levels than was possible in simpler societies, which relied upon such means as informal mutual-assistance networks, rotating credit associations, and community work-sharing norms. The legal and economic institutions of capitalism created an environment in which the large-scale bureaucratic enterprise could function so successfully that it dramatically reduced the scope of other forms of organization throughout the industrial economies (Chandler 1977; Tilly, this volume). And the capacity for control that the bureaucratic model afforded made it possible for both state-sector and financial-sector trust-producing institutions to exercise their responsibilities effectively and with considerable credibility (Carruthers 1996; Horwitz 1977; North 1990; Zucker 1986).

In effect, Weber's model of the bureaucratic firm and the post-Marxian model of the advanced capitalist political economy were twin perspectives on the same corporate entity. The first captured the structure of the firm itself. The second described the company's relationships to its work force, its competitors, and the state. Although these models were primarily analytic rather than prescriptive, the texts used to train management students affirmed their tenets, impressing upon future managers the need to reduce uncertainty (March and Simon 1958), buffer their organizational core to maintain stability at all costs (Thompson 1967; Pfeffer and Salancik 1979), and design competitive strategies that preserved company autonomy while keeping price competition to a minimum (Porter 1980). As late as 1980, these depictions of the firm constituted a serviceable conventional wisdom for academics and managers alike.

The Twentieth-Century Model Questioned, then Besieged

The framework I have described served as a loose paradigm, a conceptual model and set of rarely articulated presuppositions that structured perceptions of researchers and practitioners alike, shaping the questions they asked and the solutions that appeared sensible and attractive. At the turn of the new century, we see this paradigm losing its power, not just (or even primarily) in the more refined reaches of academic and business thought, but in the popular imagination as well, as authors of books and magazine articles search for ways to characterize what they believe is a fundamentally different order. Whether or not they are right—which is, of course, a central question addressed by each of this volume's remaining chapters—the change in tone is striking, and the rapidity of the change suggests that it is not merely a passive reflection of corporate practice.

One thing is sure: before they break down, paradigms begin to show wear. Well before the 1990s' sea change in conventional wisdom, scholars chipped away at aspects of the bureaucratic and neo-Marxian models, exposing anomalies that would eventually combine to undermine fundamentally those models' grip on our perceptions of the firm.

Challenges to the Bureaucratic Model

Elements of the bureaucratic model came under both normative and analytic assault. Three prominent lines of questioning are relevant here. First, from the 1930s on, critics noted that although bureaucracy was an unprecedentedly effective means of insulating organizations from personal and familial social networks, such insulation was never complete. Management theorists advocated schemes to make informal networks work *for* the firm, while sociologists warned that companies could not be understood unless networks of informal social relations—networks that intruded from the larger community and grew like ivy around firms' formal structures—were taken into account.

Second, from the 1950s on, empirically oriented organization theorists questioned whether the several components of Weber's ideal-type model of bureaucracy (clear and numerous rules, strong career incentives, extensive written records, and so on) were all essential. Critics suggested that they were not, and that distinct variants of bureaucracy, high on some components and low on others, were better suited for, and more likely to be found in, particular types of firms.

Third, from the 1970s on, economists, sociologists, and management theorists actively questioned whether bureaucratic firms were the best way to organize the production of goods and services after all. They suggested that the control advantages of bureaucracy should be (and, in practice, were) traded off against the flexibility afforded by markets, with the appropriate choice depending on the precise characteristics of the transactions that production entailed. By the 1980s, this work took an even more radical turn, as new scholarship suggested that the choice of form was not dictated in any simple way by production or organizing costs or technological factors, but was instead shaped within wide boundaries by a complex interaction of institutions, politics, and cultural understandings.

THE TENACITY OF INFORMAL SOCIAL RELATIONS

The genius of bureaucracy, as Weber described it, was its capacity for control, its ability to harness the activity of masses of employees to the goals of the executives of a corporation or a state. The genius of Weber was to see that control depended on the organization's ability to convince members to leave their ordinary social ties at the firm or bureau's door and to do their jobs without reference to the complex personal and family networks of reciprocal obligation in which they were otherwise embedded. Based on a painstakingly thorough reading of history, Weber appreciated the fact that an executive cannot control complex social activities simply because he or she is the emperor or the boss, or is strong and powerful, or possesses weapons and is willing to use them brutally. Weber analyzed perspicaciously the rise and fall of empires and the endemic failure of their executives to sustain control over the long run. He saw that in prebureaucratic systems might was never enough and power often evaporated more quickly than it could be accrued. He also observed that leaders relied for sensitive matters either on those to whom they were personally tied by kinship, or on staff members whose own kin networks were for some reason dramatically attenuated (for example, eunuchs or priests); and that nonkin groups were most effective in commanding loyalty over the long haul when, like monastic orders, they forced their members to renounce other social ties.

Weber was not alone in identifying the extraction of organizations from dense webs of informal social relations as the key to the problem of control. Even before Weber wrote his classic essay, an American engineer named Frederick Winslow Taylor developed a system called "scientific management" by which bosses, working with a new class of scientific industrial engineers, could dictate workers' every movement, eliminating every ounce of employee discretion in the interest of control. Although the Taylor method was rarely if ever adopted in its pure form, it powerfully influenced the organization of factory work, and was employed (with much attenuation) in service organizations and government units as well (Taylor [1911] 1947; Callahan 1962; Nelson 1980).

Beginning in the 1930s, this perspective was under siege. First, a set of management scholars and psychologists from Harvard University called attention to the "informal social system" of relationships among factory workers, illustrating their arguments through an extensive program of research in Western Electric's Hawthorne Plants near Chicago (Roethlisberger and Dixon 1961). Although the Hawthorne researchers focused on the purportedly irrational blue-collar work force, Chester Barnard, a telephone company executive who encountered their work when he took time off to study at Harvard, extended their focus on the "informal system" to all levels of the organization. In his influential text, *The Functions of the Executive* ([1938] 1975), Barnard contended that one of the executive's most important roles was to ensure that the informal social system worked *for* the organization and not against it.

Beginning in the 1950s (and continuing through the present), sociologists joined the debate with a series of intensive case studies of real-world organizations which demonstrated that informal networks were ubiquitous within business firms, and that such networks often worked successfully to frustrate the intentions of top executives or the interests of shareholders. Some of these informal networks emerged out of the division of labor, as department chiefs used "connections" to boost the size of their budgets and their staffs (Ritti and Goldner 1979) or to gain approval for projects they wished to pursue (Thomas 1994). Other informal networks linked the firm to the community around it: for example, Dalton (1959) reported that one had to be a member of the Masons in order to get ahead at Milo Manufacturing, and Gouldner (1954) described the deep embeddedness of the gypsum plant he studied in every aspect of community life.

Such examples by no means indicate that the Weberian model was "wrong," for Weber was comparing bureaucracy to premodern approaches to organizing states and enterprises and, compared to these, bureaucracies do indeed buffer organizational behavior from the informal networks of loyalty and identity in which it is always embedded. But such informal ties remain important nonetheless, and scholars who called attention to them set the stage for the more comprehensive assessment of networks that would follow.

VARIANTS OF BUREAUCRACY

A second line of criticism, based on statistical analysis of surveys aiming to measure the elements of bureaucracy at the organizational level, challenged Weber's model for misspecifying the relationship among the characteristics he believed bureaucracies would possess. Some scholars suggested that the link among the attributes of bureaucracy was weaker than Weber had indicated. For example, in an influential article, Udy (1959), analyzing data on organizations in preindustrial societies, demonstrated that formal hierarchy was not statistically associated with meritocratic reward systems and other aspects of the bureaucratic model (see also Blau and Scott 1962; Hall 1963). Others contended that there were different kinds of bureaucracy that varied in the extent to which they relied upon different forms of control, such as rules, hierarchy, commitment to a common purpose, or solidary incentives (Etzioni 1964). Still others, associated with what was called "structural contingency" theory, argued that organizational structures—including those aspects of structure to which Weber had called attention—varied substantially depending on the tasks the organizations had to perform. In this view, the more routine the tasks the greater the extent to which an organization can rely on a fine-grained division of labor governed by rules and a hierarchical chain of command. By contrast, formal organizations that must deal with individualized cases rather than mass or continuous-flow production need to give frontline workers more discretion. Such organizations find it rational to supplement hierarchy with more collegial forms of coordination (Perrow 1967; Woodward 1958; Thompson 1967).

A persistent theme in this literature was the argument that knowledge workers—highly educated professionals whose assignments demanded creativity and initiative—required (and, indeed, could tolerate) fewer rules and less constraining hierarchy than workers engaged in more routine undertakings (Scott 1965; 1992, 253–56). Burns and Stalker (1959), for example, distinguished the "organic" structures appropriate for nurturing firms' research and development function from the "mechanical" bureaucratic structures suitable for nearly everyone else (see also Lawrence and Lorsch 1969; Kornhauser 1962). Indeed, Weber left his model open to this criticism by failing to resolve a tension intrinsic to it. Bureaucracies, he argued, were rational instruments of both coordination and control; moreover, they drew on educated labor to an unprecedented extent, promoting employees on the basis of merit and harnessing their expertise to organizational ends. What critics noted was that the bureaucratic structures most effective for coordinating the work of educated employees committed to the organization's objectives were rather different from the bureaucratic structures equipped to control the behavior of employees who might prefer to pursue their own objectives. Indeed, if firms could solve the agency problem—that is, if they could motivate highly educated staff to adopt the interests of shareholders as their own—conventional bureaucracy might not be the best form at all.

BUREAUCRACY AND THE MARKET AS ALTERNATIVES

In the 1970s, building on the work of Coase (1937), Oliver Williamson devised an approach to the organization of business enterprise that portrayed bureaucracy (or "hierarchy," as he called it) and market exchange as fungible organizational alternatives. In Williamson's view, economic actors choose whether to purchase goods and services on the market or to produce them internally based on relative costs. Firms arise when the "transaction costs" associated with contracting exceed the fixed costs of establishing and maintaining a bureaucratic structure (1985).

The transaction-cost approach did not in itself challenge Weber's model; in fact, some critics felt that it overestimated the extent to which the executives of bureaucratic firms could exert frictionless control (Perrow 1986). But, in placing bureaucracy and the market within a common analytic compass, Williamson set out a broadly useful framework for a comparative social-scientific approach to organizational forms that viewed bureaucracy as just one of several ways to organize production and exchange.

At the same time, a resurgence of empirical studies of business enterprises likewise called attention to the fact that organizational forms were more diverse than the bureaucratic model might suggest. In the United

States, observers noted the rise within bureaucracies of matrix structures, which violated the bureaucratic tenet of unity of command by placing project teams under the joint control of both divisional and functional authorities (Davis and Lawrence 1977). They found a few large firms that boosted productivity among technical and production staff by freeing them from hierarchical constraints (Kanter 1983). They also witnessed the efforts of large companies to "internalize markets" by establishing factor pricing across divisions, a practice that led to a range of curious hybrids (Eccles and White 1988).

At the same time, historical sociologists called into question the magisterial work of Alfred D. Chandler, Jr. (1962, 1977), which depicted the modern multidivisional firm as the logical and optimal response to the challenges posed by industrial growth and diversification. Chandler drew on painstaking archival research to describe how captains of industry first created simple Weberian bureaucracies and later devised more complex multidivisional entities in response to practical problems created as by-products of their pursuit of successful business strategies. According to Chandler, in those industries where capital costs were high and competition was sharp, firms had to seek growth, integration, and structural differentiation in order to prosper.

By the 1990s, several sociologists took Chandler to task for painting what they believed was an unduly functionalist, economistic, and triumphalist picture of the contemporary firm. Four lines of attack have been particularly prominent. First, while not denying that entrepreneurs and managers tried to pursue their interests in a rational manner, critics argued that what was "rational' depended on the legal and social institutions that defined and protected property rights, secured trust, and regulated capitalization and exchange (Dobbin 1994; Roy 1997). Second, critics have emphasized the role of state policy in determining the form of these legal and social institutions and, in many cases, the role of political power in the policy determination process (Perrow 1991; Roy 1997). Third, critics have emphasized the role of cultural and cognitive factors in shaping the way in which managers understand rational action and the strategies they choose (Fligstein 1990; Dobbin 1994). Drawing both on cross-national case studies (Dobbin 1994) and formal statistical analysis of large numbers of U.S. firms (Fligstein 1990), they have argued persuasively that no single best corporate structure dominates all others, even within a particular technology or product market. Even economists have increasingly come to endorse these two powerful ideas: that institutions matter (North 1990); and that, in the language of game theory, there are multiple winning strategies or equilibrium solutions (Gibbons, this volume). Neither position, by the way, would be at all foreign to Weber. But they are devastating to those of his followers who believed that a particular version of the bureaucratic corporate form would dominate cross-nationally and over the long run.

As the U.S. and British economies stagnated in the early 1980s, scholars traversed the globe in search of alternative models. The ones they found deviated sharply from conventional templates. In the industrial districts of Italy and Germany, researchers discovered congeries of firms making apparel or ceramics that cooperated so intensely that they seemed to blur the line between market and organization. Using flexible-production methods to tailor products to rapidly fluctuating demand, these companies worked together on a routine basis, sharing workers, outsourcing to one another during times of high demand, even loaning machinery as the situation required (Sabel and Zeitlin 1996).

As Eleanor Westney notes in her chapter, the most jolting blows to the conventional model came from Japan, to which students of business flocked in the wake of Japanese successes in product development and trade. What they found there staggered the imagination: major companies that guaranteed their workers lifetime employment; reunited conception and execution through "quality circles" in which shop-floor employees routinely suggested changes in technical process and work design; maintained intimate relationships with suppliers and customers, working closely with them to schedule shipments to the day and meet rigorous production standards. Most remarkably, Japanese companies did all this with a mere fraction of the employees of their U.S competitors, and with flat hierarchies and relatively few middle managers.

Many scholars greeted these reports of exotic organizational forms with the excitement of seventeenth-century naturalists perusing the journals of New World explorers. Although many theorists (e.g. Williamson 1985) initially regarded such forms as "hybrids" locatable on a continuum between market and hierarchy, others viewed them as one or more entirely new species—"network forms of organization," in Walter Powell's felicitous phrase (1990; see also Gibbons, this volume). For all their diversity, the firms to which researchers called attention shared several notable features: greater suppleness than their more traditionally bureaucratic counterparts, a greater willingness to trust employees and business partners, a preference for long-term "relational contracting" over short-term market exchange for many transactions, a commitment to ongoing technological improvement—and an apparent renunciation of central features of Weber's model. Confronted by flatter hierarchies, more ambiguous job descriptions, fewer rules, and an increase in the ratio of oral to written communication, many observers concluded that in many sectors of the corporate world Weberian bureaucracy had yielded to a new way of organizing business enterprise.

Challenges to the Post-Marxian Synthesis

At the same time that changes at the organizational level called the Weberian model of the bureaucratic enterprise into question, new developments and new discoveries at the system level challenged earlier understandings of the relationship between capitalist firms and their shareholders, between companies and their workers, and among the firms themselves. First, just as growth- and stability-oriented managers seemed decisively to have secured their control of the firm against the authority of profit-minded shareholders, an antimanagerial counterrevolution turned the tables (Useem 1996). Second, as newly empowered investors and the globalization of markets provoked more vigorous economic competition, many companies became more aggressive in their stance toward unions and less indulgent in their treatment of managers. At the same time, observers of high-technology companies and immigrant enterprise in the United States, and of business organizations in Europe and, especially, Asia, began to notice the importance throughout the world of business groups or alliances (Granovetter 1993; Gerlach 1992). What they saw led them to reconsider the imagery of interfirm relations in Western management writing and, more radically, raised fundamental questions about the nature of firm identity and agency in evolving capitalist systems.

THE REASSERTION OF SHAREHOLDER CONTROL

After the 1980s, resurgent investors wound back the managerial revolution, reestablishing control over sluggish oligopolies in all the major industries, assertively in the United States and more tentatively in Europe. According to the managerial revolution thesis, this was not supposed to happen. Managers were to have been protected because they monopolized information, because shareholding was diffuse and shareholders were thus difficult to organize, and because the largest shareholders (institutional investors like insurance companies, pension funds, and mutual funds) passively observed "the Wall Street rule": Don't argue, sell your shares. Indeed, no less a pundit than Peter Drucker (1976) pronounced that "pension fund socialism"—his term for the rising share of equities controlled by institutional investors—would render managerial control unassailable.

So what happened? The antimanagerial counterrevolution reflected concurrent changes of several kinds—economic, political, and ideological. The importance of ideology should not be underestimated. Economists in the field of "agency theory" put forth a compelling new image of the firm that very quickly shaped the thinking of investors, legal scholars, and managers alike (Fama 1980; Eisenhardt 1989). Their perspective had three significant tenets. First, they rejected the image, in their view sentimental, of the "soulful corporation"—the large company as an institution of intrinsic value, bearing obligations to its employees and to the communities in which it operates, as well as to its shareholders. Instead they portrayed the firm as a mere administrative convenience, a "nexus of contracts" equipped to handle productive arrangements too complex or risky to be left to the market. This imagery entailed a heady view of management's power, indeed obligation, to reconfigure the firm as the balance of costs and benefits shifts between internalizing functions or purchasing them on the marketplace. Complementing this perspective was a new "finance conception of the firm" (Fligstein 1990) as a "portfolio of activities," to be assessed and revised regularly. In this view, companies are not bound to any particular business. Instead, the executive is a portfolio manager whose major responsibility is to analyze the performance of each of the company's divisions or "profit centers," and to sell off any that are underperforming relative to alternative investments. Third, the new finance economics defined the relationship of the manager to the shareholders as that of "agent" to "principal." As in any principal/agent relationship, the former should expect the latter to try to shirk their responsibility, and therefore should design systems to prevent that from occurring.

By the 1980s, investors were ready and able to assert their rights. As Michael Useem (1996) has explained, throughout the 1970s and, especially, the 1980s, shareholding became increasingly concentrated in pension funds, mutual funds, and insurance companies. To be sure, share ownership was spread across the millions of Americans whose funds these entities managed; but the power to vote the shares lay in the hands of a relatively small set of institutions. Two consequences followed. First, institutional investors owned so many shares that often they could not easily dispose of them, thus making the "Wall Street rule" of exit over voice increasingly impractical. Second, because institutional investing concentrated shareholding even in the largest companies, and because the major players knew one another, large investors could mobilize to challenge managers on their home turf. Thus the very development that Drucker (1976) believed would render managers all-powerful was to become the instrument of managerial capitalism's destruction.

Investors used several means to focus management's attention on profits during the 1980s. They were helped by the fact that the "liberal state" that the post-Marxian synthesis had taken for granted was governed in much of the West by conservatives like Ronald Reagan and Margaret Thatcher, who rejected most liberal orthodoxy. The new climate favored the ambitions of business interests, who organized politically to pursue the deregulation of financial markets, which in turn made it easier for investors to hold managers responsible for their performance and for managers to restructure firms (Vogel 1989).

First, newly empowered investors and their allies designed management compensation packages that tied executives' rewards to their firms' short-term financial performance through the generous deployment of stock options and bonuses. Second, during the 1980s a dramatic rise in the number of hostile takeovers (as well as quieter, behind-the-scenes coups), spearheaded an unprecedentedly vigorous "market for corporate control." By the end of the decade, managers realized that even if they could dominate their boards of directors, their companies could be sold out from under them. Third, by the 1990s, many managers had acceded to the new order, taking major investors into their counsel and pursuing many of the value-enhancing policies they recommended (Useem 1996).

The results of these developments were wide-ranging. One consequence with broad ramifications was a shift in the calculus of "make or buy" from the former to the latter, as firms tried to do fewer things more effectively and purchase the inputs and services they needed from other companies. Many companies were more willing to take relational risks, such as investing in new enterprises or developing ongoing commitments that made them more interdependent with suppliers. Firms focused on their core competencies, reevaluating the portfolio of businesses in which they were engaged. Often they sold divisions to other enterprises, or "spun them off" as new enterprises, sometimes (as in the case of Lucent Technologies, once the research and development arm of AT&T) with strong ties to the old.

THE SOCIAL CONTRACT RENEGOTIATED

A second set of consequences of the antimanagerial counterrevolution entailed dramatic, ongoing cost-cutting efforts. Such efforts reduced the size of the corporate labor force, challenging the expectations of managers and workers alike. Pushed by investors (and, in many cases, by an increasingly global marketplace) to compete more aggressively, many companies reduced the size of middle management, shifted tasks from full-time employees to contingent workers and took back some of the advantages once associated with primary-sector jobs. Companies' ability to do more with fewer full-time workers was enhanced by developments in information technology that increased productivity and made it easier to monitor and control off-site employees.

These developments need not detain us long, for Walter Powell describes them thoroughly in chapter 2. For present purposes, three points are worth making. First, although the post-Marxian synthesis held that the rapprochement between trade unions and big firms in the United States and Western Europe represented a long-term solution to labor/management conflict, many U.S. business leaders had always regarded unions as unwelcome intruders and viewed worker's compensation packages in primary-sector manufacturing as a deplorable drag on company profits. For such executives, increased competitive pressure from shareholders and the global market represented an excuse to accomplish what they had wanted to do all along.

Second, progressive management theorists had advocated a shift to team work and flatter organizational structures, and had called attention to exemplary firms that experimented with these approaches (Kanter 1983), well before the more widespread shifts in business practice that Powell describes. Management theories and organizational practices interact in complex ways. Management writers identify companies that employ innovative organizational designs that appear to embody principles they value; they promote these designs as models, but adoption is halting until and unless the business environment changes in ways that make companies search actively for alternative modes of organizing.

Third, the changes that occurred in employment relations, like the changes in company governance, posed a serious challenge to the post-Marxian synthesis. Suddenly, the "historic compromises" between European management and labor appeared less stable and conclusive; and the notion that the U.S. federal government colluded with leading business enterprises to preserve a mutually beneficial arrangement with the trade unions began to seem fanciful.

INTERFIRM ALLIANCES

The third challenge to the post-Marxian synthesis was an indirect result of the international search for models instigated by the Western industrial economies' prolonged slump in the late 1970s and early 1980s, and of the light that globalization of enterprise shed on industrial systems outside Europe and the United States. Just as Western observers first found the Japanese employment system exotic, but then, once they adjusted their conceptual lenses to take account of what they observed, began to perceive elements of it in their own societies, so the discovery of complex interfirm alliances in Japan and the "little tigers" of East Asia led Westerners to perceive for the first time the presence of networks in their own economies (Powell 1990; Granovetter 1993).

Whereas the rise of investor capitalism and concomitant revision of conventional understandings between primary-sector firms and their employees challenged specific tenets of the post-Marxian synthesis directly, the discovery of interfirm networks posed an even more radical challenge. The fact that many economies included groups of associated enterprises in which no single dominant firm could call the shots—and, *a fortiori*, of business networks in which corporate legal structures were draped lightly over underlying networks based on ties of consanguinity or shared ethnicity— raised fundamental questions about the nature of the firm itself, casting into doubt assumptions about identity, agency, and legal personality that had long been taken for granted.

As is often the case, it was easier for Western observers to perceive a new form in a culture very different from their own. As Eleanor Westney explains in chapter 4, Western management writers began to explore the political economy of Japanese enterprise—and, in particular, the central role of vertical and horizontal business alliances, or *keiretsu*—only after concluding that the Japanese employment and production systems rested on too distinctive a foundation to be adopted in toto by Western firms. Westerners read with wonderment accounts of the then remarkably successful Japanese business system's complex interfirm networks (Gerlach 1992), and the ongoing relations with government that encouraged, supplemented, and sustained them (Dore 1986; Johnson 1982), all in the apparent absence of a functioning market for corporate control. Even more striking were the comparative studies that followed of Korean and Taiwanese variants: for, whereas, in Japan, the units that networks comprised were bureaucratic firms, elsewhere in East Asia the companies themselves seemed almost like epiphenomenal outgrowths of densely woven kinship networks (Orrù et al. 1997).

Once the logic of the intercompany group became explicit, such networks became visible throughout the world. Students of European capitalism had long noted the weakness of antitrust laws throughout that continent, and the absence of prohibitions, like those in the United States, of bank ownership of industrial concerns. Consequently, financial institutions played a greater role in the governance of economic life in much of Europe than in the United States, knitting companies together in what some viewed as bank-centered networks (Scott 1987). Moreover, political scientists had long recognized that European companies collaborated actively in the political arena through various kinds of industry associations that states regarded as legitimate negotiating partners (Streeck and Schmitter 1985).

Studies of "small-firm networks" (Sabel 1992) reported a different kind of business network—involving more reciprocity than bank-centered groupings and far more commitment than political associations—in the industrial regions of Northern Italy. Unlike the *keiretsu* of East Asia, these networks comprised small enterprises working together locally. As with the East Asian interfirm groups, relations with government were often close and supportive, but almost exclusively at the local level.

At the same time, scholars in the United States began to notice networks in that country's economy. The earliest research on interorganizational networks (aside from the copious but highly focused literature on interlocking directorates) concentrated on cooperation among philanthropists or nonprofit service agencies, both of whom, in contrast to for-profits, were *supposed* to be mutually supportive (Warren 1967; Turk 1970; Galaskiewicz 1985). By the 1990s, scholars began to document interfirm networks in the for-profit sector as well (Powell 1990). At first, researchers described networks of small enterprises in atypical settings, especially immigrant communities in which entrepreneurs lacked ready access to capital and other benefits of the formal economy (Portes 1998; Waldinger 1986). Skeptics might dismiss such systems as anomalous and transitional accommodations to a particular economic niche. But other studies identified similar sets of stable relationships, sometimes entailing substantial long-term commitment, among long-established firms in competitive-sector industries like apparel (Uzzi 1997); and by the 1990s, as Powell notes in chapter 2, researchers found collaborative interfirm networks at the heart of the most vigorously entrepreneurial sectors of the U.S. economy (see also Aldrich 1999).

The terms "industry group" or "interfirm network" cover phenomena ranging vastly in the kinds of companies that participate, the number of firms and the amount of assets involved in the collaboration, the scope and duration of relationships, and the types of ties with which business partners are bound. As Kraakman points out in chapter 5, the Japanese vertical *keiretsu*, with its strong interfirm hierarchy, clear leadership role, and management dominance, raises few problems for the post-Marxian synthesis. By contrast, horizontal alliances of the kind that David Stark describes in his chapter are more startling in their implications, suggesting in some cases a reckless disregard (at least by the old rules of economic organization) for company autonomy, and in others a virtual mutation of conventional forms of agency, as hydra-headed interfirm networks replace corporations as the key actors in significant economic sectors.

Taken together, the assault on managerial capitalism changes in terms of employment for both managers and blue-collar workers, and the worldwide discovery of the role of interfirm networks and company groups set the post-Marxian synthesis on its head. Stable accommodations among independent companies, and between such companies and their workers and national governments, appeared to be breaking down, as new developments augured sharpened competition among new types of business entities.

The Organization of This Volume

The challenges to the twentieth-century model of the firm—to Weber's model of the bureaucratic enterprise and to the post-Marxian account of the systemic logic of advanced capitalism—have yielded a range of contradictory characterizations rather than a clarifying new synthesis. On the one hand, hierarchical bureaucracy is said to be yielding to more empowering and commitment-inducing systems of management. On the other, jobs and firms are becoming decoupled, with workers experiencing unprecedented career insecurity. At the same time that observers note a renewal of economic rivalry they also describe unprecedented forms of collaboration throughout the world's economies. Clearly the trends observers have discerned do not all point in the same direction, nor are contemporary corporations marching in lockstep along a single trajectory.

It is the aim of this volume to summarize what we know about the twenty-first-century firm—about its structures, strategies, and forms of governance—and to clarify the issues at stake. Each of the next three chapters describes contemporary change in business enterprises in one part of the world. These are followed by four commentaries that assess the first three authors' accounts in the light of particular theoretical perspectives.

In chapter 2, Walter Powell describes how firms in the United States and Western Europe—especially firms in the most technologically intensive and rapidly developing sectors of the economy, but also companies in traditional manufacturing sectors stung by global competition—have altered their management structures, labor relations, and forms of collaborating with other companies. Powell, whose paper "Neither Market nor Hierarchy" (1990), did much to define the current debate, contends that we are witnessing "the outlines of a fundamental change in the way work is organized, structured, and governed," a nascent new logic rooted in "a growing institutional infrastructure of law, consulting and venture capital firms." Throughout much of the economy, and especially among new firms, hierarchies are flatter, headquarters staff smaller, and collaborations more numerous than in the past, as firms compete for rich payoffs in high-tech "learning races." Companies use more contingent workers as projects replace "jobs" as the basic unit of work, and people's careers increasingly span business units and firms. Networks of relations among firms are thicker: small firms cohere into "virtual firms" whose success depends on the quality of their networks; while large companies, aiming to remain focused on core competencies, spin off and maintain close relations to enterprises that once would have been corporate divisions. Although Powell believes that fundamental changes are taking place, the ultimate destination of such change is still uncertain. Some companies, he suggests, will take the "low road" of simple integration, switching contractors based on cost considerations at a moment's notice and demanding much of their employees while offering little. Others will take the high road, maintaining long-term networks, the relationships in which become significant corporate assets, and fostering worker empowerment by offering ongoing training and commensurate rewards for the deeper engagement and greater accountability demanded of workers. The balance between them, and the ultimate impact of these changes, will depend in part on political choices about the extent to which governments will invest in their citizens and maintain credible "social safety nets" to soften the impact of economic change.

In chapter 3, David Stark describes the transformation of economic structures in post-socialist Hungary and the Czech Republic, as managers work with institutional resources and interpersonal networks left by socialism to improvise capitalist economies in a period of rapid change and political instability. The most striking feature of the postsocialist landscape is the multiplicity of institutional logics (principles of organization and legitimacy) competing for dominance. Stark warns against premature efforts to converge upon a single model, and praises the nurturance of ambiguity as a strategy well suited to the uncertainty and multivocality of the Eastern European economies. The entrepreneurs he studied draw on many assets, models, and discourses to cobble together companies through a process he describes as "recombinant bricolage." The firms that result, like those of Western high-technology industries, are decentralized, with interdependent departments, much lateral communication, and flexible business strategies. The processes used to privatize state enterprise throughout the socialist world have led to the emergence of complex, heterogeneous networks, knit together by cross-shareholding among firms. Stark characterizes these "complex network[s] of intersecting alliances" as "heterarchies," or "complex adaptive systems" that "interweave a multiplicity of organizing principles" to adjust to multiple environments. These heterarchies, he argues, are the real economic actors in Eastern Europe, sharing assets, discovering strategies through action, and retaining options during an era of rapid change. The challenge they face is to combine the suppleness that is their great advantage with the accountability that investors and regulatory agencies will require. Like Powell, Stark believes that a new kind of enterprise system is emerging, and that its precise form will depend on government policies, especially the ability of the state to develop a suitable framework for regulating the new economic entities.

In chapter 4, Eleanor Westney describes emerging trends in Japanese firms. Japan was the model for many aspects of the flat, flexible, high-commitment, collaborative organizational structures that Powell describes in the West; and Stark's Hungarian business networks bear a notable likeness to some kinds of Japanese *keiretsu*. Westney distinguishes among several aspects of the Japanese system. The Japanese employment system, which governs the work lives of primary-sector male employees, is based on lifelong employment, rewards for seniority and collective performance, and ongoing training. In the Japanese production system, a learning system focused on continual improvement, jobs are defined broadly, with workers assigned to task-oriented "activity clusters" organized to harness the knowledge of all employees. Firms maintain close relational contracts with suppliers, whom they integrate into product design and production, and work continuously with customers in order to produce frequent product changes in response to market demand. Finally, the Japanese governance system entails both vertical and horizontal company groups, or *keiretsu*, linked by copious flows of capital, personnel, and communication, which both enhance economic coordination and buffer managers from the market for corporate control. Ironically, just as aspects of the Japanese model gain acceptance throughout the world, Japan itself, which has suffered from more than a decade of sharp economic recession, is suffering a crisis of confidence. At the onset of the millennium, writes Westney, "the Japanese firm looks more like the apotheosis of the firm of the twentieth century, not the harbinger of the next." Japanese companies face intense pressure to adopt aspects of the Western model, especially those that increase accountability to shareholders and reward employees according to individual performance. Westney believes that Japanese firms will accommodate these demands without relinquishing their dependence on strong networks, creating a different and still distinctive form of capitalism.

The second of the book's two major sections contains four essays that reflect on the arguments of the three regional chapters from distinctive analytic perspectives. In chapter 5, Reinier Kraakman, a legal scholar whose work spans the boundary between law and economics, takes a skeptical view of the argument that the firm of the twenty-first century will differ fundamentally from its twentieth-century counterparts. "The corporation as we know it," he contends, "is too useful to disappear, or even to change all that much." Kraakman argues that the key aspects of the corporate form—legal personality, ownership by investors who are residual claimants, centralized management and governance by a board, limited liability, and transferability of shares—are direct responses to the need for firms "to raise capital, control agency costs, facilitate decision making, and allocate risk," and are thus unlikely to be supplanted. Vertical groups may play limited roles when a lead company can exercise effective authority, and autonomous firms may collaborate through informal networks to pursue their individual goals. But Kraakman believes that interfirm relationships that diffuse responsibility or separate ownership from control—for example, Japan's horizontal *keiretsu*, or the cross-shareholding arrangements of Hungary's multi-firm networks—will yield to increasingly standardized securities laws that will converge cross-nationally in response to business's interest in minimizing the cost of capital.

In chapter 6, David Bryce and Jitendra Singh comment upon the three regional contributions from the standpoint of evolutionary theory. Based on a taxonomic approach that distinguishes organizational forms on the basis of goals, authority relations, technologies, and markets, they argue that, despite apparent similarities, Western "alliance networks," the interfirm groups of Hungary and the Czech Republic, and Japan's vertical and horizontal *keiretsu*, are distinctive forms, adapted to quite different selection pressures. Moreover, they note that each form will experience different national selection environments, with variation in the stability of free-market legal institutions especially consequential. They also call attention to the fact that different units of selection are nested within interfirm networks, and that actors at each level always attempt to shift both risk and selection pressures upward or downward. Thus vertical *keiretsu* use low-status affiliates as shock absorbers for the core firm, and high-technology alliances shift risk from participating firms to the more fragile network and to contingent workers outside the firm. From an evolutionary perspective, convergence of organizational forms requires convergence of environments. Bryce and Singh describe many factors that may make business environments more similar in different countries, but argue that persistent, path-dependent institutional differences make the international convergence of capitalist forms extremely unlikely.

In chapter 7, Robert Gibbons comments on the regional chapters from the perspective of the economics of the firm, focusing on the circumstances under which cooperation between a firm and its suppliers is preferable to integration. Like Bryce and Singh, Gibbons calls attention to the differences among the "network forms" that Powell, Stark, and Westney describe, and argues that the prevalence of networks of companies bound by relational contracts depends on complex sets of contingencies. Gibbons argues that companies decide whether to make or buy a product—and whether to engage in long-term cooperative relationships with suppliers or to keep them at arm's length—on the basis of the relative costs of these arrangements after all parties have taken into account the risks associated with each. From this perspective, then, the design problem is one of "optimizing the boundary of the firm." Consistent with Powell, Stark, and Westney's arguments, Gibbons suggests that rapid economic and technological change creates an economic calculus that favors relational contracting over integration, whereas stagnation or stasis shifts the balance in the opposite direction. Given the delicacy of this balance and its dependence on the details of particular markets, it seems unlikely that costs will shift sharply enough to lead to wholesale restructuring of the corporation, although continual incremental change in the firm's boundaries is to be expected.

Finally, in chapter 8, Charles Tilly, a sociologist whose work spans the fields of comparative history, comparative politics, and the study of labor markets and inequality, takes the long perspective on organizational change, and suggests that the twentieth-century firm was a historical anomaly, based on a unique convergence of organizational form and state structures. Bureaucratic firms, argues Tilly, need strong states to establish and protect a legal framework for exchange. Strong states have relied on productive organizations (in the West, market enterprises) for economic stability, tax revenues, and other types of support. This alliance was fine while it lasted, but it is faltering today due to the increasing weakness, and declining ability to secure their boundaries, of nation-states throughout the world. As the state system declines, writes Tilly, so will the impersonal bureaucratic corporations that have relied on it. Instead, entrepreneurs of the future, like entrepreneurs throughout most of human history, will rely on "trust networks" based on kinship, ethnicity, propinquity, or culture to get things done. In his view, the "network forms" of enterprise described by the authors of the three regional chapters, and especially the network forms of Eastern Europe with its weak nation-states and underdeveloped legal frameworks, are harbingers of an uncertain future. Or, as Tilly succinctly puts it in the title to his essay, "Welcome to the Seventeenth Century."

In chapter 9, I identify common themes and key differences among the contributors' essays and articulate some questions that may repay researchers' attention. I begin by arguing that the "network form" is really several forms, rarely mutually exclusive, and suggest that change must be monitored at the level of national economies and industries as well as at the level of the firm. Nonetheless, there are common themes in the chapters that may be integrated to create a model of the "twenty-first-century firm," about which I raise several questions. First, how strong is the evidence for its component parts at the levels of the organization itself (for example, labor relations, the division of labor, customer-supplier relations) and of the system as a whole (for example, the role of networks in economic agency and governance)? Second, in so far as there is evidence that particular developments are, in fact, taking place, what reason is there to believe that they together constitute a new form of organizational and system logic—that is, that these changes cohere into a system of mutually implicated parts? Third, in so far as a new logic of organizing is emerging, what are the prospects for cross-national convergence around this new model of the firm? Finally, what is the relationship between practice and ideology in these developments? To what extent are we witnessing actual changes in corporate practice, and to what extent is the revolution primarily in the categories and scripts we use to perceive and comprehend corporate structures and behavior?

At this point, no one has all the answers. But by providing deeply informed accounts of the main lines of organizational change in significant portions of the world, and by holding these accounts up to the light of several theoretical traditions, the essays in this volume both aggregate current understandings and bring the questions into sharper focus.

PART ONE

Portraits from Three Regions

CHAPTER 2

The Capitalist Firm in the Twenty-First Century:

EMERGING PATTERNS IN WESTERN ENTERPRISE

Walter W. Powell

THE PAST decade was a confusing period for citizens, policymakers, and pundits alike. The pace of economic and technological change appears relentless, but the direction is unfamiliar. Joseph Schumpeter (1934) was one of the first analysts to observe that innovation brings with it the winds of creative destruction, but few were prepared for the gales of the 1990s. Consider just a few of the discordant trends in the U.S. and global economy.

Alongside the tremendous upsurge of startup companies, created in the United States and abroad as well, we see the creation of global giants in a number of key industries. The startups are regaled for their swiftness, their impressive array of new products and services, and their new business practices. But in banking, oil, autos, and telecommunications, we see the making of global corporate behemoths, the product of mergers such as Exxon and Mobil, Travelers Group and Citibank, Vodaphone Group and Air Touch, and Daimler Benz, Chrysler, and Mitsubishi, which are among the largest deals in history. And corporations continue to acquire and grow even as evidence accumulates that the hoped-for synergies and integration are seldom achieved. Moreover, many of the startups continue the founding and acquisition cycle. In the e-commerce field, the dream of many founders has been to grow large enough to be noticed and bought up. Of course, some startups eventually grow large, and companies like America Online, Microsoft, or Cisco Systems have acquired hundreds of other firms along the way.

But which companies represent the old economy and which ones the new? Cisco Systems had only 250 or so employees back in 1989, but by January 2000 it had more than 26,000 and a market capitalization in excess

I very much appreciate comments made by Paul DiMaggio, Neil Fligstein, Charles Tilly, Barry Wellman, and especially Steven Vallas, whose critical remarks were invaluable. I also benefited considerably from feedback given by seminar participants from the Sociology Department at the University of North Carolina, the Department of Business Studies at Uppsala University, the Strategy Workshop at MIT's Sloan School of Management, the Social Orga-

of $320 billion, one of the largest of any company in the world. Cisco is a designer and maker of computer networking equipment, much of which it sells to traditional companies that are developing Internet services. In so doing, Cisco makes the lines between the new and old economy much blurrier. And the growing reshaping of corporate purchasing through business-to-business e-commerce renders the distinction between the old and the new economy even less meaningful.

Are the new-economy companies in computers, wireless communications, electronic commerce, the life sciences, and genomics creating a new industrial transformation or just a phenomenal amount of speculative excess? *Red Herring* magazine and its Web site, one of many new business publications that has grown fatter and fatter with dot-com ads, routinely warns that Internet company valuations are completely unrealistic even as it touts a new company or the latest technological application. Thus the speculative frenzy increases, and even though caution is warranted, people everywhere are afraid of being left out of the game, falling behind as others make their fortunes, and getting stuck in the "old world" as the "new world" companies ascend. People know that most of the new ventures are unrealistic, but the problem is they do not know which ones are and which ones are not.

Wages and employment offer another puzzle. Unemployment is presently at a thirty-year low, but job security appears tenuous to many employees. Despite impressive performance, many U.S. companies continue to revamp jobs and organizational structures as if the economy were in a tailspin. More jobs were lost to downsizing in 1999 than in any previous year during the 1990s.[1] On the upside, nearly twenty-two million new jobs were created in the United States in the 1990s.[2] Some organizations now complain about the lack of corporate loyalty as employers have become buyers in a seller's market, forgetting that it was their practices of downsizing and contracting out that eroded worker loyalty. Consequently, both voluntary and involuntary departures from jobs have increased (Bernhardt et al. 1998; Capelli et al. 1997; Farber 1996; Osterman 1999, ch. 2).

Despite economic growth, productivity gains, and tight labor markets, there is widening income disparity as growth in the incomes of the winners far outpaces the modest wage gains of others. Moreover, the success of the winners is more and more tied to the fluctuations of the stock market. Industry sources estimate that 48 percent of the U.S. population now has money invested in stocks or stock funds, and roughly ten million workers

---

nization Seminar at the University of Arizona, and the History, Technology, and Society Program at the Georgia Institute of Technology.

[1] Reported in "Career Evolution," *The Economist* (29 January 2000): 89–92.

[2] Reported in "The Great American Jobs Machine," *The Economist* (15 January 2000): 25.

hold equity in their own companies.[3] But for those whose jobs do not offer such opportunities, the gap grows wider. Silicon Valley is the epitome of these contradictions. In Palo Alto, the local mantra in 1999 was that sixty-four millionaires were created daily, and this success drove the cost of housing to stratospheric levels, making it harder and harder for policemen, school teachers, fire fighters, and assistant professors, not to mention administrative or service workers, to be able to afford to live in the valley.

Finally, consider the emerging political resistance that has coalesced against the specter of globalization and international economic integration. The amalgam of left and right that has brought together environmentalists and dockworkers, French farmers and American steelworkers, has highlighted a backlash against economic change. Anxiety and uncertainty are growing at the same time that more newcomers, from Ireland to Finland to Israel to Bangalore to Taiwan, prosper from the internationalization of production. In sum, economic change has been so rapid and so profound that few seem to understand its dynamics and shape, and much traditional social science is hard pressed to measure its scope and consequence.

The core claim of this chapter is that, behind the confusion and divergent trends of recent years, we can discern the outlines of a fundamental change in the way work is organized, structured, and governed. This transformation, I suggest, is sufficiently far-reaching that looking back from the twenty-first century to the end of the twentieth, many will view the struggles of the 1990s as a disruptive and costly period of adjustment to a new logic of organizing. Just as the shift to the era of the assembly line, vertical integration, and mass production brought with it a great transformation, so will the change to what today we inarticulately term the "new economy" or decentralized capitalism.

This new logic of organizing involves changes in the standard recipes for jobs, organizations, and industries. I will next offer a description of the architecture of a work world in which jobs disappear and projects ascend, and design and production become simultaneous processes rather than orderly sequential steps. The boundaries of many firms have become so porous that to focus on boundaries means only to see trees in a forest of interorganizational relations. The core competence of a firm, to use the new argot, is based on knowledge production and building a sustainable advantage that can be leveraged across products and services, thus enmeshing firms in all manner of different relationships and markets that were traditionally called industries. Power, to be sure, remains crucial, but it is employed to enhance reach and access and to compete in high-speed learning races. These new innovations are inherently fragile because they

---

[3] Reported in Carolyn Lochhead, "Old World Discovers New Economy's Money," *San Francisco Chronicle*, 12 December 1999, sec. A1, p. 23.

are premised on obtaining deeper engagement and participation from "core" employees and more collaboration and mutual involvement among ostensible competitors. But employees toil in a context of greater labor market volatility and interfirm cooperation coexists with rivalry among competing networks.

To appreciate better the key features of this emergent model, we need to understand where it came from, the forces triggering and sustaining it, and its contrast with the dominant post–World War II model of organizing work. I begin, then, with an outline of the system of organizing that typified large U.S. firms for most of the second half of the twentieth century, followed by a brief consideration of the forces that caused the old system to fray and possibly crumble. I consider whether this is a one-time change, and consequently things will eventually settle down, or whether change and uncertainty have become ubiquitous, injected into nearly every aspect of corporate organization. I sketch the elements of a new form of organizing and examine whether it is more suited to a world of change and tumult. I stress that this new logic is still nascent; we see its outlines in restructured mature firms, and its fuller operation in emergent industries that were never wedded to the older system, and in a growing institutional infrastructure of law, consulting, and venture capital firms that are potent carriers of these new recipes.

At the outset, I need to offer several strong cautions. First, mine is neither a normative argument nor a determinist one. The chapter is by no means a manifesto for the new system, nor an argument that it is inevitable. Politics always looms large in shaping the organization of work. But I do want to suggest that we spend too much time lamenting the demise of the old system and make too insufficient an effort talking and theorizing about new forms of organization, leaving to the sidelines discussions of much-needed accompanying social and political adjustments. In the United States, we all too typically equate the public good with market outcomes, and considerations of justice, equality, and solidarity are silenced. These concerns are, however, extremely salient issues in a new era of decentralized capitalism. Finally, I resist the view that all advanced industrial countries are converging on common ways of organizing economic life. Instead, I argue that different forms of capitalism—each characterized by particular national ensembles of practices, institutions, and political cultures—have both distinctive advantages and liabilities. Rather than see hybrid amalgams of best practices forming, we will witness divergent national institutions shaping differential responses.

In addition, a comment about evidence and sources is in order. This chapter is written as a synthetic essay, in which I borrow freely from scholarly sources and journalistic accounts by authors who are much more expert than I on particular topics. My aim is a broad, suggestive survey, not a definitive treatment or a thorough, bibliographically comprehensive essay. Thus one goal of the essay is to set an agenda for subsequent research; the other primary aim is to aid readers in seeing the organization of work in a different light. Mine is only one voice in an emerging chorus that includes the new growth theorists in economics, business scholars pursuing a knowledge-based theory of the firm, geographers who study regional agglomeration processes, and economic sociologists who analyze the role of networks in economic exchange. My own expertise stems from a decade of empirical research on the biotechnology and pharmaceutical industries. I emphasize that I do not believe the experiences of these research-intensive fields are generalizable to the entire economy. I do recognize, however, also that these global industries are exemplars of late-twentieth and early twenty-first century white-collar forms of knowledge-intensive work.

The "Old" System of Organizing Work

To understand the magnitude of the current transformation we need to recall the broad outlines of how work was structured in a "typical" large U.S. corporation throughout much of the postwar era, running from 1950 to around 1985. The most salient feature was a sharp division in responsibilities and rewards between management and labor. Managers did the "thinking," making key decisions regarding long-range planning and the setting of short-term goals. Workers did the physical work necessary to execute management's decisions. The employment relationship was guided by standard objective criteria, most notably seniority, and merit or performance was rarely measured. Most workers and nearly all managers did not face serious risk of layoffs. Pay was also secure, with cost of living increases a routine part of union labor contracts. Pay was even more secure for managers. In the auto industry, for example, MacDuffie (1996) notes that mid-level managers lived in a paternalistic culture that produced virtually automatic annual pay increases.

Work was structured around the principles of scientific management, with each job specified in an explicit description and tasks clearly differentiated across jobs. Work was organized into departments, with each department corresponding to a key business function (e.g., production, sales, research and development, human resources). Most workers and managers spent their careers within a single functional area. Workers often entered a firm in unskilled entry-level positions and over time worked their way up the blue-collar ladder, with some moving into supervisory and lower or even middle management. Managers were recruited out of college or business schools, joining the firm at the lower end of the management ladder, and working their way up the managerial ranks over the course of a career. There was steady growth in the numbers of managers too, reflecting both growth in organizational scale and the reliable maxim that managerial pay rises with the size of the unit reporting to a manager.[4] The overall picture of the firm was one of order, predictability, and hierarchy; in short, a well-coordinated machine with a fixed repertoire of routines.

During the 1940s, '50s, and part of the '60s, the bulk of a company's activities were carried out in a single industry. Moreover, firms often operated in stable markets, where the winds of competition were gentle. As firms grew, there was expansion into related products, but generally the identities of a firm and its industry were intermingled. There was also a clear separation between managers and shareholders, with the latter bearing the risks associated with business and the former responsible for smoothing out ups and downs in performance and reducing uncertainties. In contrast to today—where business leaders are widely visible public figures, business news competes with politics and entertainment for the limelight, and business reporters are celebrities—this was a quiet world. Business leaders were not well known to the public at large. Stockholding in a large corporation was not a widespread phenomenon, nor was the daily performance of a firm on the stock market closely scrutinized.

With corporate growth and diversification, the organization of work became more complex, but the basic tenets of stability held fast. The rise of conglomerates and unrelated diversification turned some firms into large holding companies, in which finance became the lingua franca for comparing and uniting far-flung activities. Of course, the move into different products and markets was initially seen as another way to ensure steady performance and avoid short-term perturbations in particular markets. And even in those firms whose activities remained in related industries, the tightly organized bureaucracy was changing at the margins, with senior managers now possessing some cross-departmental experience and periodic task forces bringing together teams from different departments. In firms with a core technology that could be utilized for a range of different products, such as 3M or Corning, and in firms with expanding global operations, efforts were afoot to develop dual reporting relationships, and matrix-like structures became common. On the surface, these changes seemed gradual and evolutionary, the basic core strength of corporate bureaucracy was being amended, but certainly not graying or under challenge.

Several caveats are, naturally, in order. Clearly this is a broad-brush portrait; the organization of work varied across industries and between union-

---

[4] Gordon (1996) shows that over the post–World War II period, U.S. firms have been much more managerially intensive than companies in other industrialized nations, attributing this fact to a need for greater control and more intensive supervision. But this pattern is no doubt also related to the higher rate of college graduation in the United States, and fits as well with ethnographic accounts of the desire for managerial fiefdoms (Kanter 1977; Jackall 1988).

ized and non-unionized settings. And few small and medium-sized companies could either afford or have need for all of the elements sketched above. Moreover, this was a U.S. model, or perhaps an Anglo one, with certain broad similarities found in the United Kingdom, Canada, and Australia as well. This system was also neither natural nor necessarily optimal. The social organization of work is molded by history, and evolves through bargaining and conflict. This form of organizing was very much embedded in a postwar, suburban, middle-class culture. Moreover, this "Fordist" model grew in response to the demands of mass production for a continuous, reliable labor force and as a reaction to labor strife, especially to the growing prewar political power of labor unions. The growth of internal labor markets and tightly specified jobs replaced the earlier "drive" system, in which foremen ran production, often in a highly capricious manner, and in which effort was continually negotiated and turnover was high. The focus on well-defined jobs reflected both a desire for predictability and a labor-management truce in a postwar era that yearned for routine and regularity. The accommodation between labor and management, dubbed "job control unionism," protected workers from management whim but relinquished worker control and autonomy.

The triumph of the large firm displaced other forms of enterprise, so that even though the majority of workers toiled in small and medium-sized organizations, the large corporation was the dominant force in business activity. Not only did large-scale corporate enterprise dominate other forms of enterprise, it influenced the larger culture of everyday life as well. The expectation of most employees of the large firm was that they would spend their life slogging away or climbing the ladder within a single firm. Seniority, security, and status were all tied to one's employer, and community life was inextricably shaped by the large firm as well.

In a relatively short period of time, little more than the ten-year period from 1985 to 1995, this model of organizing work underwent considerable change. Just how much change is hard to say. At a minimum, a number of key features—job security, routine pay increases, narrowly defined jobs, and considerable distance between managers' and shareholders' interests—have been eroded. What is unclear is whether the entire system is fragmenting, to be replaced by an altogether different organizational model or whether the current period of ferment will, at last, settle down and a reformed model will emerge, pieced together out of remnants of existing practices and a partial set of new arrangements. Building entirely new models of organizing entails steep transition costs, and certainly many would point to the past decade as just such a period of tumult. But a decade is a relatively short period of time, and some skeptics note that while the bonds between employer and employee have been weakened, they have not been broken

(Neumark 2000). Still, I argue that the scope of the multi-level changes in the organization of work, firms, and industries has been dramatic.

Causes and Consequences of the Reshaping of Work and Organization

There is considerable debate over what factors are responsible for the demise of the post–World War II accommodation between management and labor, and much debate over the consequences of these changes. One explanation points to the large firm and argues that rampant corporate downsizing and restructuring along with an incessant drive for flexibility brought the system down. A second argument stresses global economic interdependence, highlighting lower-wage foreign competition. A third account suggests that there is a serious mismatch between the skills of older and less-educated workers and the job requirements of a new information-technology era. Running through each account is the suggestion of greater wage polarization, and the emergence of a "winner-take-all" ethic. Each argument captures some salient features of the past two decades, but each is also partial and incomplete, and in some respects inaccurate. The evidence is worth reviewing, however, because it aids us in seeing how a large systemic change is unfolding.

Downsizing and Restructuring

Unquestionably, one of the most dramatic changes of the past fifteen years has been the willingness of large corporations to downsize, shedding themselves of thousands of formerly "safe" white-collar employees. Although downsizing was first regarded as a response to the economic downturn of the late 1980s, it continued throughout the 1990s even as the economy surged. And companies that had long histories of employment security joined the trend. For example, back in January of 1996, on the first business day of the new year, AT&T—a highly profitable company that was known for its job security—announced it would lay off forty thousand employees. The Vice President for Human Resources at AT&T, James Meadows, subsequently opined to the *New York Times* (13 February 1996) that

> People need to look at themselves as self-employed, as vendors who come to this company to sell their skills. In AT&T, we have to promote the concept of the whole work force being contingent [i.e., on short-term contract, no promises], though most of our contingent workers are inside our walls. Jobs are being replaced by projects and fields of work, giving rise to a society that is increasingly "jobless but not workless."

In tandem with the downsizing wave has been a rapid increase in various forms of contingent employment. Benner (1996) dubs temporary employees the shock absorbers of the flexible economy. Various forms of contingent employment have grown rapidly (Barker and Christensen 1998; Carnoy, Castells, and Benner 1997). The idea that workers should be employed only when there is immediate need for their services is hardly new, but clearly the use of this practice grew considerably over the 1990s. Just how rapidly is hotly contested and very much contingent on how one defines the employment practice. Does the term include part-time work, self-employment, contract work, home-based work, temporary-help service employment, or a job without long-term security? Regardless of definition, the expansion of such temporary employment firms as Manpower Incorporated is ample proof to many observers that employees are increasingly regarded as another factor in the process of just-in-time production.

There is little doubt that downsizing has exerted a considerable toll on employees and communities. But just how potent a force is it and is the quest for labor-force flexibility the driving force behind organizational change? Despite the headlines, David Gordon (1996, ch. 2) marshals data suggesting that the proportion of managers and supervisors in private nonfarm employment has not shrunk. Moreover, throughout the 1980s, he tells us, the proportion of managerial and administrative employment was more than three times as high in the United States as in Germany and Japan. U.S. management structures, many analysts claimed, were top-heavy, flabby, and redundant.

Osterman (1996) concurs with Gordon that managerial ranks are not shrinking rapidly in the United States, but provides a more nuanced picture of changes in the terms of managers' employment prospects. Middle-level managers are experiencing distress from restructuring, he argues. His analyses show a fairly dramatic decrease in rates of management retention, greater than that experienced by blue-collar employees with comparable job tenure (Osterman 1996, 9). In an excellent study of the insurance industry, Elizabeth Scott et al. (1996) finds a substantial flattening of the structure of firms. This "delayering" is accomplished by cutting several levels of middle to lower management, and greatly upgrading and expanding the role of claims adjusters through the use of expert systems and intensive monitoring. In a careful analysis of a nationwide survey of displaced workers, Farber (1996, 33) documents that "older and more educated workers, while continuing to have lower rates of job loss than younger, have seen their rates of job loss increase more than those of other groups." Moreover, he finds that job loss due to position-abolished reasons, as opposed to layoffs or plant closings, has increased, largely among more educated workers. Thus the number of management jobs may not be declining, but job security clearly has lessened.

Similar complications abound concerning contingent employment, and much of the debate turns on what is meant by routine and nonstandard work, and whether labor-market circumstances are voluntary or involuntary.[5] Standard work has long been thought to be continuous, secure, on a preset schedule, and full-time. In return for satisfactory performance and loyalty, the employer provided benefits and abided by government regulations of employment, in particular protection from hazardous conditions and unfair discrimination, and provided some array of benefits for retirement and health care. These benefits in turn are buttressed by government through social security and unemployment insurance. Nonstandard work, which was the most typical form of work probably until the middle of this past century, comes in many guises, ranging from independent contractors (e.g., plumber, storefront lawyer, seamstress, or computer consultant) to part-time shift workers to temporary employees. All such arrangements purportedly involved weak attachment between a worker and a firm.

The basic analytical problem is whether such agreements are voluntary or involuntary, and whether weak attachment is an apt description. Clearly the labor force includes some people who do not choose to seek full-time jobs and others who would prefer them but can find only contingent work. Has the recent surge in downsizing increased the number of people with involuntary contingent work? The available evidence suggests yes, with women and minorities most likely to be rendered worse off by these new circumstances. (For excellent surveys of the issue and some of the best available evidence, see Carnoy, Castells, and Benner 1997; and Kalleberg, Hudson, and Reskin 2000).

We need to be careful, however, that we do not remain fixed on an image of a mythical workplace. Harriet Presser's (1995) work reminds us that the stylized model of the standard workday no longer holds: less than one third of employed Americans over age eighteen worked the "traditional" Monday-through-Friday, nine-to-five workweek in 1991. Consider too that not all temporary work is low wage. Contingent employment now covers every position up to chief executive. Manpower Incorporated placed 750,000 people in temporary jobs in 1995; high-technology was their fastest growing segment. The growth is fueled by a thirst for high-tech specialists

---

[5] Indeed, estimates of the size of the contingent workforce vary widely. In 1995 the Bureau of Labor Statistics reported that "contingent and alternative" employment represented five percent of the U.S. work force. The National Association of Part-Time and Temporary Employees, taking a very broad view and including full-time workers employed by temporary agencies and permanent part-time workers, estimates that twenty-four percent of the work force is contingent. (Reported in Elena Bianco, "Temporary Workers Gaining Market Share, Statistics Show," *Los Angeles Times*, 31 December 1996, p. A5.) And whatever the "correct" size of the contingent labor force, there has been another key change: many more workers now pass through temporary agencies on their way to permanent jobs.

whose wages range from $15–50 an hour and who work on short-term projects averaging thirty-six months. Moreover, whose situation is more contingent—an employee who does the same job but over the course of several years sees considerable turnover in her coworkers and supervisors, or an independent contractor or temporary worker with a long-term, stable clientele?

In a poignant series on "The Downsizing of America," the *New York Times* (3–9 March 1996) emphasized the dislocation and sacrifice that has resulted from this profound remaking of employment. In a segment on the job losses accompanying the merger of Chase Manhattan and Chemical Bank, entitled "Farewell, Mother Chase," the reporters described a thirty-five-year-old bank employee who had previously spent several years as an itinerant pianist in New York:

> He never sought security in corporate work, and thus the merger doesn't especially throw him. He has embraced Chase's career assistance and thinks he has sharpened his abilities, become a resilient worker. His background has given him an emphatically 90s outlook on work. "I feel my job is to do the best that I possibly can, but my whole area could look totally different in five years through no fault of Chase. I can't imagine any corporate entity owes anyone a career.
>
> By virtue of his background, Matt Hoffman is perhaps the archetypal corporate man of the future. His introduction to the world of work was a terrain where his paycheck depended on how well he sold himself each day. Nothing was guaranteed past tomorrow.
>
> He has imported that mindset into banking and currently, into Chase, and he has found the fit to be all too perfect. For an odd reality of the new work environment is that the turbulent world of the freelance classical pianist is more like than unlike the world of the corporate employee. He, too, has to sell himself every day, and he, too, doesn't know if the gig will be there tomorrow. (New York Times, 4 March 1996).

The reporter conceptualized this new form of employment as a game of musical chairs, an aberrant alternative to a steady, life-long job with clear career prospects. But perhaps the fact that working for a bank now resembles the challenges of "gigging" practiced by freelance musicians is no longer aberrant and instead represents a labor practice that is becoming the norm. Sociologists have long studied "craft-based work" in which workers labored on short-term projects and were paid for specific performances (Stinchcombe 1959; Eccles 1981; Faulkner and Anderson 1987—see the review of this literature in Powell 1990, 306–9).[6] But we treated work in

---

[6] Recall the arguments made by Stinchcombe (1959) and Perrow (1967): When work involves products that are customized, the work process depends to a considerable degree on

such fields as construction and the film industries as exceptions to a more "standard" organizational structure in which jobs and careers were tied to a single organization. I next argue that the set of social arrangements we label a job are fast disappearing as work is being packaged in a different form and the conditions that once gave rise to a career of performimg repeated tasks for a single employer are now disappearing.

For now, three observations seem salient. First, if jobs as a way of organizing work are no longer adaptive, then cutting jobs is not necessarily an effective response. Downsizing reduces head count and creates turmoil, but seldom addresses the idea that work no longer needs to be organized into neat packages called jobs. Consequently, downsizing efforts fail to deliver on expectations, often leading to even further cuts, which in turn leave gaps in corporate memory, diminished reputation, and dissatisfied customers. The American Management Association's survey of downsized companies reports few productivity enhancements in the wake of cutbacks and a host of problems; a *Wall Street Journal* cover story dubbed the trend "dumbsizing."[7]

Second, in companies where rapid technological change is commonplace and tightly defined job ladders are not viable, a project-based model for organizing work has evolved. These companies have the advantage of having never developed career structures and management systems that defined work as a steep vertical ladder, hence there are fewer transition costs to a new form of organizing. At Intel, the largest maker of microchips for computers, the corporate hierarchy is so flat that there are few upper positions to vie for. A horizontal employment model makes sense in areas of semiconductors where each new generation of microprocessors requires a different mix of skills. Intel invests more than $120 million a year on training, or nearly $3,000 per worker, with a goal to redeploy employees as fast as a new generation of chips emerges. The expectation is that workers will redeploy themselves, finding new jobs within the company. But if they are not successful, they are out of work.

Third, by holding fast to the idea of work organized around well-defined jobs and lamenting the loss of job security, we neglect to evaluate the range of options necessary in a world in which the focus should be more on employability and less on preserving dead-end jobs. Access to universal health coverage, portable pension plans, and a form of unemployment benefits for independent contractors and contingent workers are much-needed

---

tacit knowledge and craft-based skills, and organizations in these fields eschew bureaucracy in favor of more flexible, short-term arrangements.

[7] See "Fire and Forget?" *The Economist*, 20 April 1996: 51–52 for discussion of AMA survey; see "Call It Dumbsizing: Why Some Companies Regret Cost-Cutting," *Wall Street Journal*, 14 May 1996, pp. Al, A8.

steps in an environment where work is more likely to consist of short-term projects. A focus only on job preservation leaves workers alone to grapple with the risks of the new workplace. In the labor movement there are clear signs of recognition of these new circumstances. The Justice for Janitors campaigns in Silicon Valley reflect the development of new multi-employer collective bargaining strategies. Benner (1996) points to the Alliance of Motion Picture and Television Producers as one collective response to an industry based on flexible production, craft and technical work, and short-term contracts. The alliance takes on administrative functions formerly done by management and protects the income of "members" directly without necessarily protecting their jobs. Similar innovations are underway in the building and garment trades, where new efforts are afoot to respond to the competitive success of the industry as a whole. In sum, we need more creative responses to the fluidity of project-based work, arrangements possibly like guilds for independent contractors that provide opportunities for professional community and learning, as well as financial security.

Globalization

In the minds of many people, global competition costs workers in advanced industrial nations their jobs and contributes to financial uncertainty as capital flows freely around the globe. Citizens and politicians alike contend that foreign competition robs jobs at home. Corporations now locate their activities according to the logic of a global market. Moreover, fickle international financial markets have become the judge and jury of policymaking, and central banks no longer have the capacity to intervene and stabilize currencies. But is global economic interdependence actually responsible for job loss, declining wages, and changes in the organization of work? The evidence is much less compelling than the heated rhetoric suggests.

The great bulk of our trade imbalance is with Japan (about two-fifths of the total trade deficit) and with Western Europe. In both cases, hourly wages in manufacturing are higher than ours, in Japan by 25 percent and in much of Europe by 10 to 15 percent.[8] The sharpest impact of import competition is in manufacturing, but there has not been a steep decline in wages in this sector. In his analysis of wage decline between 1979 and 1994, Gordon (1996, 191) shows that production-worker wages fell most rapidly in mining, construction, transportation, public utilities, and retail trade—

---

[8] According to the United States Bureau of Labor Statistics, in 1994 dollars, manufacturing employees in the United States averaged $17.10 an hour, $27.31 in Germany, and $21.42 in Japan. The industrial nations with appreciably lower wages than the United States were Canada at $15.68 and the United Kingdom at $13.62 (Gordon, 1996, 29).

sectors not heavily exposed to competition from abroad. Indeed, immigration into the United States may be more responsible than global competition for wage stagnation in these sectors.

Viewed broadly, today's global economy is not even particularly new. Economic historians remind us that the half century before World War I was roughly comparable in economic integration (J. Williamson 1995, 1996; O'Rourke, Taylor, and Williamson 1996). Trade in goods and services is only slightly larger now, as a fraction of gross world product, than it was in 1914. Measured against GDP, United States imports are somewhat bigger now (11 percent) than they were in 1880 (8 percent). But labor mobility was probably higher in the late nineteenth century. Migrants left Europe for Australia and the United States in extraordinary numbers and investment from the "Old World" followed labor into the New. We also forget that a substantial foreign corporate presence in the United States is not novel either. In 1913 the United States pharmaceutical business was largely German-dominated, and Bayer aspirin the most common medicine of the day. On the other hand, there was scant manufacturing located in the less developed world, and product markets were not global in the pre–World War I period.

What is different today, dramatically so, is the speed with which massive amounts of information can be transmitted and received, making it possible to react to shifts in demand faster. And the content of much of what is traded internationally has high value. The fields most influenced by global competition—accounting, banking, computers, construction, consulting, legal services, semiconductors—are high-wage industries. Thus, globalization does not appear to be the chief culprit for wage decline and job loss in the United States In a survey of the impact of globalization of wages, labor economist Richard Freeman (1995, 30) concluded that "we lack compelling evidence that trade underlies the problem of the less skilled."

Global economic interdependence is fundamental in an altogether novel respect, however. The speed with which information and certain commodities move around the globe reshapes production in powerful ways. A decade or two ago, new pharmaceutical drugs were initially released in the United States and Western Europe, and after a five- to even 10-year period of sales in the home market, they were sold abroad in less developed countries at cost, while newer medicines were released at home. Now there is demand for new medical interventions from all corners of the globe. Similar product life-cycle stories, with different time lines, could be told for such diverse industries as autos, electronics, or movies. Today, development times are vastly speeded up for almost every product, but especially for these regarded as innovative or fashionable. Whether we are talking about a new CD, cell phone, computer, or clothing, consumers in Mexico City, Helsinki, or Singapore want it at the same time. Sun Microsystems offers round-the-clock technical services at a single phone number, drawing on staffers around the globe who electronically hand work off as each shift comes on line. Such changes in demand press firms to recast their internal organization in a manner that stresses speed and learning. And when competition is based on ideas, the costs of creating additional copies of a conceptual product are low. The advantages of selling in many countries are considerable, provided that the firm is first to market.

The traditional multinational firm's strengths were its wealth and concomitant influence and the economies of scale it reaped in global production. But high tariffs, transportation costs, and local politics often necessitated that a multinational firm set up redundant "full-service" operations in most of the countries in which they sold products. Thus the economies of production were greatly offset by costs of administration. In contrast, an emerging focus on faster product development, combined with sensitivity to local tastes, rewards speed rather than sheer size. The model transnational firm today is no longer Coca-Cola, IBM, or Royal Dutch Shell, but Asea Brown Boveri (ABB), the Swiss-Swedish energy and engineering firm, organized as a "constellation" with more than 65 business areas, 1,100 companies, and 4,500 profit centers, coordinated by a corporate staff in Zurich of less than 200 (Taylor 1991; Bartlett and Ghoshal 1993).

In the United States, General Electric has evolved to a radically decentralized organization with thousands of parts connected not by centralized control but by a passionate commitment to organizational learning. Rather than standardization, GE relies on relentless efforts at knowledge transfer, of moving successful organizational practices and processes across highly disparate units. The aim, then, is diversification and local experimentation, complemented by rapid diffusion of new ideas.[9] These radically decentralized corporations are remaking both the geography of production and the administration of large-scale organization.

But ABB or GE are not here, there, and everywhere at once. They do not shift operations from one site to another in search of lower labor costs as do smaller global firms such as Nike. The United Nations Conference on Trade and Development, which keeps a watchful eye on multinational firms, distinguishes between simple and complex integration.[10] The Nike strategy of chasing cheap labor and switching production exemplifies the simple strategy. In contrast, firms like ABB or GE, which pursue the complex strategy, must rethink all of the activities and strategies that multinationals have long pursued. In trying to be both global and local simultane-

---

[9] Remarks of Steve Kerr, Chief Knowledge Officer, General Electric, at "fireside chat," Organization Science Winter Conference, Keystone, Colorado, 12 February 2000.

[10] See the discussion in the extremely valuable survey on multinationals in *The Economist*, (24 June 1995).

ously, these firms find that region matters more than ever before. To begin with, subsidiaries are no longer regarded as distant back offices, but may have responsibility for global functions or products. Thus, if the Canadian subsidiary masters cost competitiveness best, it is given the reins of that program throughout a firm's global operations. Or if Hewlett Packard decides the office products market is most appealing in Europe, it relocates responsibility for that business unit in France and serves the United States from abroad. In turn, European firms like Glaxo, Thomson, and Unilever migrate to the United States and set up primary operations here. Far from being oblivious to locale and in search only of low-cost labor, most multinationals are reorganizing into complex internal networks that compete with one another.

Region looms large in several other respects as well. Many of the recognized centers of excellence around the world are found in industrial districts—the Prato region in northern Italy for fashion and design, Seattle for software, Japan for electronics miniaturization, Hollywood for filmmaking, to name only a few. Companies in these industries have no choice but to locate in or have access to these centers in order to stay abreast and draw upon the best talent. Finally, most foreign investment still clusters around the home country—Western Europe moves into Eastern Europe, Japan into Southeast Asia, the United States, into Canada, Mexico, and South America. And the huge growth in many service industries, such as health care, day care, financial services, and the like, represent sectors that are not moveable. These fields must locate where the customers are.

In our research on the evolution of the global biotechnology industry, we have found that spatial agglomeration is critical in two respects. One, United States firms are located primarily in only a handful of regions—the Bay Area, San Diego, Seattle, the Research Triangle, Cambridge, and the suburbs of Washington, Baltimore, and Philadelphia. Spatial concentration is even more pronounced in Western Europe. In each case, the links between firms, research universities, prestigious research hospitals, and non-profit research institutes are exceedingly important. Two, despite talk about the mobility of capital, the most critical source of financing—first-stage venture capital backing for startup companies, is local. We have found that over 40 percent of the venture capital funding for U.S. biotech companies in the late 1990s was between a venture firm and a biotech located within twenty-five miles of each other. Thus, despite much popular talk about globalization location still matters a great deal.

Technological Change

Another common explanation for recent workplace changes is that technological innovations have failed to deliver dramatic increases in productivity and instead have replaced workers rather than enlarged their skills. In this respect, 1990 was a watershed year—one in which, according to the U.S. Department of Commerce, capital spending on the information economy (i.e, computers and telecommunications equipment) was greater than on all other aspects of the country's industrial infrastructure (Zuboff 1995, 202). By 1996 the information technology sector—defined as including computing and telecommunications but not semiconductors or electronic games—was the largest industry in the United States, according to Commerce Department data, employing 4.3 million people and generating 6.2 percent of the nation's output.[11] Has there been a related substitution of machines for hands and minds? Chrysler, for example, produced 1.72 million cars in 1995, the same number as in 1988, but with seven thousand fewer workers. Former Secretary of Labor Robert Reich frequently argued that there is a mismatch between the skills Americans have and the skills the economy requires. Wages are falling for various categories of workers, so the argument goes, because they have become technologically obsolete. Obviously, computing capability once viewed as astounding is now trivial. My son's Nintendo 64 runs on a higher performance processor than the original 1976 Cray supercomputer, which was accessible back then only to an elite team of physicists. Surely, then, one answer to why organizations are restructuring is that there is a mismatch between worker skills and organizational needs.

But not so fast. Hasn't the increase in computing power also allowed workers to produce more? Bound and Johnson (1995), two influential proponents of the skills mismatch view, recognize that evidence in favor of the argument that technology has rendered classes of workers obsolete is "largely circumstantial." Perhaps, then, the explanation is not a misfit in worker skills but a disconnect between organizational form and the new technologies. The canonical twentieth-century bureaucracy was designed to meet the business needs of increasing throughput and lowering unit costs. As Alfred Chandler (1962, 1977) has shown in his magisterial studies of the rise of first a functional hierarchy, then a multidivisional structure, the proliferation of mass production entailed a detailed division of labor and the simplification and delegation of administrative tasks. The role of a manager "evolved as guardian of the organization's centralized knowledge base" (Zuboff 1995, 202). Dramatic gains in computing power were initially harnessed to reinforce hierarchical, centrally controlled organizational structures—to watch, control, detect, and duplicate. Managers fought hard to hold onto the information on which their power rested,

---

[11] The study, "Cybernation: The Importance of the High-Technology Industry to the American Economy," was reported in Steve Lohr, "Information Technology Field Is Rated Largest U.S. Industry, *New York Times*, 18 November 1997.

even as the new information technologies opened up novel possibilities for broad distribution of information. The organization of General Motors in the 1960s was a complicated analog of a mainframe computer. But, as I later argue, the economy today resembles a web, not a hierarchy, and to force technologies that enhance "networking" into a pyramidal form serves only to constrain their effectiveness. If there is a mismatch, then, I contend it is between the capabilities of information technology to handle information and problems whenever and wherever necessary, and the older organizational arrangements that force decisions to be made by a central managerial hierarchy (see also C. Freeman 1994; Zuboff 1995).

The coevolutionary process by which technologies and institutions adapt to one another entails experimentation and learning, therefore it takes time for fundamentally new technologies to be debugged, widely diffused, and become productive. Thus the long-expected gains in productivity from information technology do not flower until older, centralized organizational arrangements are abandoned and new ways of organizing are institutionalized, and until new methods of measuring productivity, which capture gains in speed and innovation, are developed. Consider how slowly we are adjusting to a world in which companies low on physical capital but extraordinarily high on intellectual capital are in ascendance. We still measure the economy with indicators created for a mass production era. Intellectual assets do not appear anywhere on a balance sheet. The ability to generate new discoveries, to make dramatic improvements in design, service, or customization are not easily measured. But we are moving to a regime where the speed at which individuals and organizations learn may prove to be the only sustainable advantage. The evolution and spread of new information technologies that enhance collaborative work hold the possibility for remaking work practices in radical ways (Brynjolfsson et al. 1994). Achieving results from investments in intellectual capital, that is, winning in a learning race, requires new organization arrangements that allow information to flow freely.

A "Winner-Take-All" System?

There is considerable evidence of a growing disparity in income, in which people in the top one-fifth of the income distribution have grown much wealthier, while those in the lowest fifth have become poorer, and those in between have largely failed to keep pace with inflation.[12] Moreover, the

[12] The scholarly literature on growing earnings inequality is considerable, and debate over the causes is extensive. But the observation that wage inequality has widened by race, by level of education, and by industry has been well documented (see Levy and Murname 1992; Danzinger and Gottschalk 1993, 1995; Freeman and Katz 1994; Harrison 1994, ch. 9; Tilly

real wages of many blue- and pink-collar workers did not increase in tandem with the economy's resurgence in the 1990s. Thus, to many, capitalism has grown both leaner and meaner, exacerbating social inequality. Wall Street investment banker Felix Rohatyn puts the case vividly, arguing that "advanced capitalism" and its harsh and cruel climate "imposes stringent discipline on its participants." "What is occurring," he claims, "is a huge transfer of wealth from lower skilled, middle-class American workers to the owners of capital assets and to a new technological aristocracy with a large element of compensation tied to stock values."[13]

Bennett Harrison (1994) is more direct, arguing that the global economy is increasingly dominated by large firms that have become skilled in "lean production," which utilize cross-border alliances and extensive networks of subcontracting to maximize their advantage. "Dressed in new costumes—and armed with new techniques for combining control over capital allocation, technology, government relations, and the deployment of labor with a dramatic decentralization of the location of actual production—the world's largest companies, their allies, and their suppliers have found a way to remain at the center of the world stage" (Harrison 1994, 12). Dubbing the process "concentration without centralization," Harrison argues that firms that have mastered global network production have four key components: (1) core-ring structures, typified by the auto industry's lean manufacturing process, in which there is a center of high-paid, high-skill employees and the rest of production is relegated to a lower-paid periphery; (2) new uses of computerized manufacturing and information management to coordinate far-flung activities according to principles of "just-in-time" production; (3) extensive use of subcontracting and strategic alliances, especially across national borders; and (4) attempts by management to elicit more active collaboration on the part of their most expensive-to-replace employees. Harrison is deeply concerned that these practices exacerbate labor market inequality and free firms from oversight and regulation by national governments.

Critics agree that a new and more flexible mode of organizing has been adopted by many capitalist firms, but they maintain that this new form is a concerted effort to differentiate sharply workers and managers with different levels and types of skills. The much-vaunted lean production

---

and Tilly 1998, ch. 10). The Center on Budget and Policy Priorities, a Washington, D.C.–based research group, released a state-by-state analysis showing that the gap between the rich and the rest of the U.S. population had grown since the 1970s (reported in Richard Perez-Peña, "New York's Income Gap Largest in the Nation," *New York Times*, 17 December 1997). Spiers (1995) provides an account of the labor market in Albuquerque that illustrates the squeeze in the middle and the growth in jobs at the top and the bottom.

[13] In a speech entitled "Requiem for a Democrat," delivered at Wake Forest University, 17 March 1995, quoted in Simon Head (1996, 47).

system, developed by Japanese automakers, "dramatically lowers the amount of high-wage effort needed to produce a product . . . , and it keeps reducing it through continuous incremental improvement" (Womack et al. 1990, 260). In a similar vein, Vallas and Beck's (1996) research on the introduction of programmable control systems and new process technologies in the paper-making industry shows that these innovations undercut the experience of established manual workers and contributed to the hegemony of well-educated engineers as production decisions came to be based on engineering criteria. More broadly, the massive upsurge in reengineering efforts places considerable power in the hands of those who control the relevant software and computer technologies that guide workplace reorganization.

Changes in the design of work, in tandem with growing reliance on outsourcing and contract manufacturing, have indeed altered the landscape of work. Semi-skilled, decent-paying jobs in manufacturing and transportation have fallen sharply, and this decline has been especially devastating for low-skilled African-American men at the end of the employment queue (Bound and Freeman 1992; Kasarda 1995; Wilson 1996). Combined with the shrinkage in the size and clout of organized labor in manufacturing and the overall evaporation of job security, there has been an erosion in the kind of jobs for blue-collar workers that used to provide a steady, reliable income. Employees who have fallen from semi-skilled positions into low-wage and/or temporary jobs find not only that their incomes and benefits have dropped, but that their work conditions have worsened as well. No longer is work predictable and routine. Even those who secure employment find themselves treated like yo-yos, yanked from part-time work to full-time and back, from the day shift to the night shift.

But treating the labor supply like a spigot to be turned on and off as market conditions dictate is by no means unique to the United States. In West European nations, where the greater power of labor unions makes wholesale restructuring less of an option for employers, more and more manufacturing has moved to the model of the "breathing factory," in which work and hours expand to meet rising demand and contract when conditions slacken. The transformation of production to a system that responds much more rapidly to changes in markets is a global phenomenon. Why, then, is growing income-polarization more pronounced in the United States?

The answer turns on a combination of political, institutional, and technological factors. The comparative weakness and decline of the United States labor movement vis-à-vis its relative strength in West European nations (and the broadly diffused system of seniority-based wages in Japan) means that in those industries most affected by economic changes, managers in the United States dominate labor to an extent unprecedented in

n of time clocks into the workplace. Hounshell (1984, 259) captured
slocation wrought by the innovations of Henry Ford and his far-
ng mechanization of work in this quote from a letter to Ford written
housewife of an assembly-line worker:

chain system you have is a *slave driver! My God!*, Mr. Ford. My husband has
e home and thrown himself down and won't eat his supper—so done out!
't it be remedied? . . . That $5 day is a blessing—a bigger one than you know
b they earn it.

emerged in the late ninteenth and early twentieth centuries as a way
kage work in settings where the same task was done repeatedly. But
ve consider as work today is evolving in terms of how it is conducted,
is changing into short-term projects often performed by teams. Con-
ntly, the future organization of work is likely to be much less fre-
y honeycombed into a pattern of highly specified jobs. To be sure,
lways represented rigid solutions to solving tasks. The ubiquitous
"that's not my job" captured the reality that formal structures did
readily into a field of work. But in the postwar system, new opportu-
and new statuses were typically treated as occasions to create more
tegories. Efforts at job-rotation or cross-training were responses to
oliferation of job categories, but such efforts were piecemeal when
red with emerging forms of work organization.

rk is more and more commonly organized around a team or work
charged with responsibility for a project. Sabel (1994) terms this
s of joint exploration "learning by monitoring." The activities of
eams are coordinated by a process of iterated goal setting. General
ts, such as the design of a new car, are initially determined by thor-
study of best practices and prospects for competing alternatives.
broad plans are in turn successively decomposed into tasks for work
s. The goals are subsequently modified as work groups gain experi-
a executing the required tasks. Through these revisions, changes in
rts lead to modifications in the conception of the whole, and vice
The same procedure of monitoring decentralized learning, more-
llows each party to observe the performance of the other collabora-
osely enough to determine whether continued reliance on them, and
tion of resources to the joint projects, are warranted.

s form of production integrates conception and execution, with de-
d production running on parallel tracks. With concurrent design
velopment, participants constantly evaluate one another's work. If
groups decide who supplies their inputs, they need not choose the
nal internal unit but instead may turn to outside suppliers if they
e better value. This reconceptualization of work is designed to re-
d expose fixed costs, to make the expenses of all units dependent

the latter half of the twentieth century. Moreover, wage inequality is but one key component of overall inequality. The sparseness of the U.S. social safety net—unemployment, retraining, and welfare—and the more general reliance on the private sector rather than on government for health care and pensions means that changes in the private sector exacerbate inequalities.

But there is a reverse side to the structural change that the United States is undergoing. The United States has been in the forefront of economies creating new jobs and making the shift in its industrial structure to a high-tech, knowledge-based economy. The very dynamism and flexibility that creates volatility and renders groups of workers less employable also fosters the development of new industries and new companies that spur job growth. In many of these new fields, pay and other benefits are tied directly to company performance, and so successes result in even greater rewards. The very success of the high-tech sector, however, generates inequality by widening the gap between winners and losers, by closing off opportunities to those experienced in the older system and who are unable to make the transition, and by narrowing the points of entry for unskilled workers.

The shift to the so-called "new economy" widens polarization in several other respects as well. There is, clearly, a dramatic difference between the extraordinary success of a relatively small number of employees at a firm like Microsoft, who are millionaires many times over from their gains on stock options, and the larger number of workers left with only low-wage options. Successes at Microsoft or throughout Silicon Valley contribute to a growing winner-take-all ethic (Frank and Cook 1995), in which success creates increasing returns; that is, the capabilities, skills, and experiences of those who have prospered rebound such that they are vastly better positioned and qualified than those left behind. This reinforcing cycle is virtuous for the winners, vicious for the losers. Moreover, an added consequence of this transformation is that labor conflict has been altered. Unlike the traditional antagonisms between management and labor, conflicts generated by new forms of production disperse laterally: between full-time and part-time workers, between insiders and outsiders, and between knowledge workers and the unskilled. But it is wrong, I believe, to argue that the new system is just a kind of decentralized Fordism or a wolf in sheep's clothing. We are undergoing a period of "creative destruction," in which the established practices of one regime are being replaced by new ones. Income polarization is a clear outcome of the turbulent transition from one system to another, but it is not at all clear that these inequalities are a necessary component of the new form. I have argued previously that the contradictory pulls of integration and disintegration, of collaboration and cut-throat competition, are built into the very nature of how network forms of organization grow and develop (Powell 1990). How these combinatory possibilities are realized depends largely on social and political relations and on the trajectories inherent in particular technologies.

I turn now to a fuller analysis of this emergent system, beginning at the level of what used to be called a job, moving to the firm, and then industry level. My aim is not a detailed account of all the components; rather I want to stress how jobs are increasingly constituted as projects, firms as networks, and industries as capabilities, and sketch just how interconnected these changes are.

A New Logic of Organizing

New systems of organizing production do not arrive on the scene ready-made and announce their availability. The historian David Hounshell (1984) showed how the model of mass production emerged piecemeal in the United States in the latter half of the ninteenth century, beginning with the use of interchangeable parts in rifles made at the armories. Subsequently, the manufacture of sewing machines and then bicycles, and later meatpacking and beer brewing all played a critical role in the eventual development of the assembly line by Henry Ford. Similarly, what I term a new logic of network production has emerged incrementally, in fits and starts, but is now visible in a variety of guises.

We need a language to describe profound institutional change. The unraveling of the older system of bureaucratic employment in the large firm is now widely recognized, but how do we ascertain whether a new set of understandings about the nature of work and organization has emerged? In their superb study of the transformation of health care in the Bay Area, Scott, Reuf, Mendel, and Caronna (2000, ch. 6) identify a set of factors that are key components of institutional change. Scott et al. (2000) stress the multidimensional nature of organizational change, noting that governance structures, organizing logics, and the key actors involved shift in tandem with one another. They stress that institutional change is both multilevel and discontinuous, involving new mechanisms of governance, as well as new types of actors. Novel meanings are developed to account for behaviors, and new relationships are forged among key participants. A core aspect of strategic management now involves leading and assessing the various probes in which organizations are engaged, as they explore new technologies, new partners, and new markets (Eisenhardt and Brown 1999). Consequently, the boundaries of organizations are redrawn and the status order of fields is remade. Measured against these metrics, it is possible to talk about a new logic of organization. The developments I discuss next are thoroughly multilevel in nature, involving a transformation in the ordering of work at the point of production, a profound change in the linkages among organizations, and a remaking of relations with competitors.

These developments are discontinuous, I argue stopping point in the process and no road ba Performance is replacing seniority as the conditi ing and speed are replacing quantity as the metr tions. These shifts bring new actors and identiti to the fore, and push aside incumbents. Entrepr capitalists, IPOs, new products, new search en ment, network managers, information technolo come the talk of the day.

More concretely, empirical research shows boundaries of organizations, most notably in the opment (R&D). A recent National Research in industrial R&D reports that the innovatio significant transformation in the past decade, stantial" in magnitude and consequential to ec rill and Cooper 1999). There are four compo R&D: (1) a shift in the industries and sectors t new emerging technologies and nonmanufactu in the time horizons of R&D, with industry term development and relying more on univer a change in the organizational structure of R& tion of research activities and increased relian collaboration among firms, universities, and g (4) changes in the location of R&D, with suc dependent on geographic proximity to cluster companion National Research Council surve posefully diverse in character and technology b notes that common to each industry is an incr nal sources of R&D as universities, consort tories; and greater collaboration with domestic well as customers, in the development of r (Mowery 1999, 7).

Thus I think it is possible to theorize abou the outlines of which we see in three key inte of my goals is to illuminate the connections an and to flesh out how each contributes to an e

From Jobs to Projects

For much of the last half of the twentieth ce rangements that constituted work as a job la the enormous effort and power it took to o Thompson (1971) vividly illustrated the man

on their contribution, and to fuse the knowledge housed in different parts of the organization.

In its most naked form, the new system approaches a form of pay for productivity, with little recourse to loyalty or seniority—in essence, a modern variant on the old putting-out system. In a cover story on the new labor concept, *Fortune* magazine (13 June 1994, p. 44) described the changes bluntly:

> There will never be job security. You will be employed by us as long as you add value to the organization, and you are continuously responsible for finding ways to add value. In return, you have the right to demand interesting and important work, the freedom and resources to perform it well, pay that reflects your contribution, and the experience and training needed to be employable here or elsewhere.

These new arrangements are deeply corrosive of the old system of sequential steps, linear design, and vertical integration that provided worker and manager alike with security. Hence workers are increasingly the authors of their own work. These new methods, designed for a world of rapid changes and product customization, utilize technologies to speed product development in a manner that greatly enhances the contribution of frontline technical workers. Employees forced to transfer their talent from project to project, however, also find they can move readily from employer to employer. In these new circumstances, managers constantly fret about the devolution of their control, worrying that project groups may pursue their own interests rather than those of top management. But, then, when the goals are shaped by success in pushing a technology frontier, whose goals are the appropriate ones? Barley and Orr (1997) refer to work groups that specialize in technically skilled, project-based work as "communities of practice," recognizing the extent to which both work and organization structures are increasingly guided by initiative and skill, and signaling that loyalty to a professional or technical community may be stronger than attachment to a firm. This broadened conception of knowledge and the locus of innovation remakes not only work but organizations as well.

Some commentators initially saw in the merging of conception and execution a renaissance of an earlier craft tradition of organizing work. But as Sabel (1994) points out, this imagery does not do justice to the continuous efforts at exploring new possibilities and the subsequent formalizing of these efforts so that they can be perfected and communicated to others. The combination of methods and tasks, that is, the use of benchmarking, various error-detection correcting systems, just-in-time inventory, and very short product cycles involving intricate steps renders it impossible to rely on the older craft system of informal coordination of work. And it is precisely on this point that critics charge that the new system is really just hyper-Fordism, obscured behind participatory language, resulting in more intensive and stressful work (Pollert 1988; Kenney and Florida 1993; Sayer and Walker 1992). Job intensification, these critics assert, does not constitute the remaking of work.

The various criticisms of the new system are on target in several key respects, as I will soon discuss, but they are wide off the mark in failing to see just how autonomous many work teams are. In terms of the scope of their efforts and responsibilities, Sabel (1994) points out that some teams approximate the effective rights of independent firms. Teams can determine their own internal organization, communicate horizontally within the organization instead of up a hierarchy, and build close relationships with suppliers, sharing information rather than hoarding it. Teams choose, within broad parameters, the necessary tools, services, and inputs needed to execute a task. Teams intensively monitor their own activities, thus in a key respect, they are self-managed. Critics, however, are right when they point out that supervision, responsibility, and even discipline, is often shifted from managers to peers, without any parallel increase in compensation or security. Thus in many situations, workers are asked to do much more without any increase in pay.

My aim is not to resolve whether this new flexibility is liberating or imprisoning; clearly elements of both are present, and which aspect is more potent depends on specific political and social conditions at the workplace. Instead, I want to highlight how sharply the conception of work has changed from a focus on narrow and specific tasks carried out by individuals, constrained by rules and procedures, to a collective effort conducted by teams with diverse skills, working with considerable discretion, judged on results and outcomes. The hallmark of the old was the compartmentalization of jobs; the core features of the new are interdependence and involvement. A key consequence of the remaking of the division of labor is that important tasks no longer need be performed inside the boundaries of the organization. This change remakes not only the organization of work but also the work of organizations.

Flattening of Hierarchies, Spread of Networks

Just as the changed conception of work, as organized around project teams, transforms firms internally, the growing involvement of firms in an intricate latticework of collaborations with "outsiders" blurs the boundaries of the firm, making it difficult to know where the firm ends and where the market or another firm begins. The former step redraws internal lines of authority, while the latter spreads the core activities of the firm across a much wider array of participants, with an attendant loss of centralized control. Astute observers of these developments, such as Richard Rosenbloom and William Spencer (1996), suggest that industrial competition today resembles less a horse race and more a rugby match in which players frequently change uniforms.

Various forms of interorganizational collaboration have grown rapidly in recent years (Hergert and Morris 1988; Hagedoorn 1995; Gomes-Casseres 1996; Doz and Hamel 1998; Mowery and Nelson 1999). So intensive are these partnering efforts that it may be more relevant to regard the interorganizational network as the basic unit of analysis. To be sure, collaboration does not dampen rivalry but instead shifts the playing field to sharp competition among rival networks with fluid membership. But changes inside the large corporation in the United States, and Europe as well, go way beyond simple agreements to pursue research and development in new fields or to pursue joint ventures to tap new markets. The growth of alliances and partnerships entails novel forms of complex collaboration with suppliers, end-users, distributors, and even former competitors.

The motives for the upsurge in collaborations are varied. In one form, they are an effort to reshape the contours of production by relying more on subcontractors, substituting outside procurement for in-house production. The subcontractors work under short time frames, provide considerable variety of designs, spend more on R&D, and deliver higher quality, while the "lead" firm affords reciprocal access through data-sharing and security through longer-term relationships (Helper 1993; Dyer 1996a and b). There is no natural stopping point, however, in this chain of decisions to devolve centralized control. Thus fixing the boundaries of an organization becomes a nearly impossible task, as relationships with suppliers, subcontractors, and even competitors evolve in unexpected ways. As these network ties proliferate and deepen, it becomes more sensible to exercise voice rather than exit. A mutual orientation between parties may be established, based on knowledge that the parties assume each has about the other and upon which they draw in communication and problem solving. Fixed contracts are thus ineffectual, as expectations, rather than being frozen, change as circumstances dictate. At the core, then, of this form of relational contracting are the "entangling strings" of reputation, friendship, and interdependence (Macneil 1995).

A revolution in the organization of supply chains, such that Chrysler can be considered to have formed its own *keiretsu* (Dyer 1996a), is only one facet of the changes underway. Equally strong are efforts to access diverse sources of technological knowledge. Simply put, companies have awakened to the idea that the best sources of ideas are no longer located internally. Access to relevant centers of knowledge is critical when knowledge is developing at a rapid pace. In attending to dispersed sources of knowledge, firms try to enhance their "absorptive capacity" (Cohen and Levinthal 1989, 1990; Powell et al. 1996). A firm with a greater capacity to learn becomes more adept at both internal R&D and external R&D collaboration, thus enabling it to contribute more to a collaboration and to learn more extensively from such participation.

A good portion of sophisticated technical knowledge is tacit in character (Nelson and Winter 1982)—an indissoluble mix of design, process, and expertise. Such information is not easily transferred by license or purchase. Moreover, passive recipients of new knowledge are less likely to appreciate fully its value or be able to respond rapidly. In our research on biotechnology, an industry rife with all manner of interorganizational collaborations, we have argued that learning is closely linked to the conditions under which knowledge is gained (Powell 1996; Powell et al. 1996). Thus regardless of whether collaboration is driven by calculative motives, such as filling in missing pieces of the value chain, or by strategic considerations to gain access to new knowledge, network ties become admission tickets to high-velocity races. Connectivity to an interorganizational network and competence at managing collaborations have become the drivers of the new logic of organizing.

We have shown that centrality in the biotech industry network enhances a firm's reputation and generates access to resources. Firms so positioned attract new employees, participate in more new ventures, and develop deeper experience at collaborating with other parties. Put colloquially, a firm grows by becoming a player; it does not become a player by growing. Growth and financial success result from centrality in industry networks (Powell, Koput, Smith-Doerr 1996; Powell, Koput, Smith-Doerr, and Owen-Smith 1999). And once firms experience initial success, they typically restart the process by pursuing new avenues of collaborative R&D and deepening their ties to their partners. By developing more multiplex ties with individual partners, either through pursuing multiple collaborations or expanding an existing R&D partnership into clinical development or manufacturing, biotech firms increase the points of contact with their collaborators. When relationships are deepened, greater commitment and more thorough knowledge-sharing follow. Organizations with both multiple and/or multifaceted ties to others typically develop better protocols for the exchange of information and the resolution of disputes (Powell 1998).

This new knowledge-based conception of a firm (Brown and Duguid 1998; Grant 1996; Powell et al. 1996) views organization and networks as the vehicles for producing, synthesizing, and distributing ideas. The core task of both firms and networks is to access sources of knowledge rapidly and turn the "partial, situated insights of individuals and communities" into tangible products (Brown and Duguid 1998). In tandem with this new model for organizing innovation, a dense, transactional infrastructure of lawyers, financiers, and venture capitalists has emerged to facilitate, monitor, and adjudicate network relationships. These professional-service firms have become the "Johnny Appleseeds" and marriage counselors for relational contracting. In law, these firms deal with intellectual property and dispute resolution more than perform litigation. In venture capital, investors provide money, counsel, and managerial experience to early-stage companies. They offer information and advice, monitor performance, arrange connections, and lend enhanced credibility to small firms (Lerner 1995; Black and Gilson 1998; Gompers and Lerner 1999).

Venture capitalists and financiers have become extremely savvy about valuing the worth of different network ties. Indeed, there is experimentation with altogether different financial conceptions of a firm. To wit, an established biotech company may spin off as a separate entity a promising research team in a newly emerging therapeutic area. Were this group to remain inside the existing firm, its steep R&D expenditures would cause the firm's financial picture to look bleak. But by setting the operation up as a separate legal entity, while retaining partial control, the firm enables the new organization to compete for federal research grants, issue stock, attract new investors, and raise capital much as a startup firm would. The established firm is also buffered in terms of legal liability, as the new entity's assets are treated separately if any legal issues arise. In short, these subsidiary spin-offs are a network alternative to the multidivisional firm, with attendant financial and legal advantages. And by holding the subsidiary's "feet to the fire," its activities are closely tied to both the relevant technical communities and the marketplace. The arms-length relational tie means the new entity must succeed on its own, but with considerably more assistance than if it were a stand-alone operation.

Thus we see the growth of interfirm networks driven by a variety of motives and pursued by a diverse array of organizations. Large firms are relying on more nimble, smaller companies for key components or critical R&D. Large firms ally with other large firms to take on projects too risky or expensive for one firm to pursue alone. And clusters of small firms collaborate, cohering into a production network to create what no single small entity could on its own. In sum, firms are coming to resemble a network of treaties because these multistranded relationships encourage learning from a broad array of collaborators and promote experimentation with new methods, while at the same time reducing the cost of expensive commitments. These developments do not mean that competition is rendered moot. Instead we find that the success of firms is linked to the nature and depth of their ties to organizations in diverse fields.

Cross-fertilization among Industries

At the industry level, one consequence of the blurring of organizational boundaries is increased effort to deploy competence with a key technology or skill across a range of fields. For example, Microsoft builds on its expertise with computer operating systems to sell software, consumer electronics, corporate-information systems, and news broadcasting. Honda employs its skill with power trains to build lawn mowers, motorcycles, and autos. While efforts to leverage skills across industries are hardly new, what is unusual are the evolving patterns of friend and foe: a competitor in one market is often a collaborator in another. As the rules of competition shift (Powell and Smith-Doerr 1994, 385–91), customers become competitors and vice versa. Thus one does not seek to vanquish opponents, but to outrace them.

At times, the growing fertilization across industries seems all too trendy. The fascination of bankers with neural network models and genetic algorithms seems fanciful and far-removed from the world of customer service, mortgages, and currency exchange. But consider the example of Silicon Graphics, ostensibly a company formed to develop computer-aided lasers, in which Defense Department funding for the Star Wars project led to the special effects of the film *Jurassic Park*. Contract work for the Defense Department, NASA, and the CIA enabled Silicon Graphics to develop technology used in medicine to create virtual surgery for medical training purposes, as well as new "intelligent" designs for such manufacturers as Ford, GM, BMW, Volvo, and Boeing. One of the company's biggest successes has come in the entertainment field, with Nintendo, LucasArts, and Time-Warner, where cutting-edge knowledge has been employed to create vivid special effects for video games and movies. Certainly this was not the intended effect of Star Wars funding, but perhaps a former movie-star-turned-President would approve. The idea is simple: leverage distinctive capability across fields. The execution—compete and collaborate with a dazzling array of rivals and partners—is complex indeed. Beneath the interdependencies, however, are a myriad of new and mixed motives—learning, positioning, supply, and distribution, all bundled together in a process of cooperative competition. Again, my aim at this point is not to comment on whether these developments are harmful or positive for consumers or creators. We cannot address these questions adequately until we recognize how radically the units of analysis, the firm and the industry, have changed.

On the Scope of the Network Form:
Toward Convergence or Diversity?

The argument as presented thus far has been largely adaptationist: new competitive pressures, along with changed economic conditions and emergent business ideologies, have given rise to new forms of organizing. In our empirical work on interorganizational collaboration, my colleagues and I have attempted to specify the conditions under which network arrangements arise, arguing that the more rapidly knowledge develops, and the more diverse its sources, the more firms will turn to relational contracting and collaboration (Powell et al. 1996). Such contingency-based arguments imply an unusually high freedom of choice, however. I have argued that the origins and development of network forms of organizing seldom reveal a simple causal story (Powell 1990). The immediate causes, to the extent that they can be discerned, reveal a wide variety of reasons for the proliferation of relational contracting practices. Strategic considerations—efforts to access critical resources or to obtain skills that cannot be produced internally—loom large. But so do concerns with cost minimization, speeding up work, and increasing productivity. And in a world of sharper competition, more vigilant investors, and enhanced efforts and ability to measure just about everything, intensive search efforts are triggered to find ways to cut product development times. Given this constant experimentation, new ideas and new models are readily generated.

The reception and diffusion of these new models, however, is a much more complex story. In some cases, the formation of networks anticipates the need for this particular form of exchange; in other situations, there is a slow pattern of development that ultimately justifies the form; and in still other circumstances, networks are a response to the demand for a mode of organizing that resolves exigencies that other forms are ill-equipped to handle. The evolutionary development of network practices is a complicated and contingent process, one that is also tempered by adjustment to social and political conditions. To account for the diffusion of this new logic, I begin at the level of firms and industries, focusing largely on the United States. I offer an initial assessment of where the new logic of organizing has most firmly taken hold, discuss the difficulties faced by established organizations in responding to new challenges and models, and analyze the role of carriers of management practice in the diffusion process. I then briefly mention several counter trends that either delay or retard diffusion. I then turn to the nation-state, and discuss cross-national responses. The central questions are clear: will each nation find its own accommodation to a new logic of organization, modifying alliance capitalism to its own institutional milieu? Or will some nations more rapidly embrace the new form, while others resist such change? Answers to these questions are much contested. I cannot resolve them here; instead I offer several propositions concerning which nations will be more or less receptive to new forms of organizing.

Diffusion across Firms

There is wide variation across firms and industries on the three dimensions of change identified above. With respect to changes in the nature of jobs,

Osterman (1994) reports that many large corporations in the United States have altered their work practices, but just how deeply these changes go is a matter of contention (Applebaum and Batt 1994). In a series of studies of work practices in the mid-90s, Osterman (1999) finds evidence that a range of reforms, including forms of profit-sharing and greater employee involvement, have been adopted by high-performing firms. Similarly, most large firms are now increasingly reliant on subcontractors, strategic alliances, and joint ventures for one or more key business functions, but again the evolutionary consequences of these collaborative activities are not well understood. Firms also differ in their involvement in multiple industries based on the extent to which their key technologies or capabilities can be exploited in different domains. And in regard to all these dimensions, separating cause and consequence is difficult.

But rather than look cross-sectionally among firms and industries, a better measure of the changes underway comes from a longitudinal view that examines changes over time in established organizations, the emergence of a new cohort of firms and industries, and the development and articulation of new ideas and models of business practice. Viewed in this fashion, the three sets of organizational changes are quite extensive. Consider what is now taught in business schools, recommended by the leading consultancies and discussed by the business press. These carriers of management practices (Engwall 1997) promote a new model of organizing today, one in which compensation is contingent upon performance and competitiveness is crucially dependent upon the development of core competencies and many basic organizational functions are either outsourced or done collaboratively with outsiders. The basic skeleton of a firm is different, too, with a model of a flatter organization, entailing very different relations with employees, now commonplace.

To be sure, what is championed by business schools, the media, and consultants can represent a good deal of hype, showcasing only the latest fashions from the salons of business couture. But this criticism misses the extent to which a new set of ideas and skills have become part of both managers' and employees' tool kits. The skills and knowledge base of relational contracting and project-based work are now part of this repertoire to an unprecedented degree. As those skills spread and become normatively sanctioned—built into a growing institutional infrastructure in universities, consulting firms, the financial community, and law and venture capital firms—a new model of organizing takes root. Consequently, current and future generations of managers are exposed to a very different set of ideas regarding what a firm should look like.

Simultaneously, as the economies of advanced industrial countries undergo a transition from a manufacturing to a service base, a new set of knowledge-intensive industries (in fields such as information technology, software, artificial intelligence, and biotechnology) become the leading-edge sites where these new ideas about organizing are developed, honed, and eventually transferred to other fields. These knowledge-based fields are either populated entirely by newly formed organizations, which are not tethered to older models of organizing, or by established firms undergoing significant-to-radical changes in their modus operandi.

For established firms, change entails considerable costs. The existing mode of organizing was at one time a recipe for success, and so there is both more resistance to new ways of doing things and greater difficulty in creating novel practices than in a new organization built from scratch. As a result, skepticism, bargaining, persuading, and confusion are often the order of the day. To be sure, Ford Motor Company does not come to resemble Dell, or IBM become like Yahoo, or Eli Lilly like Genentech. Measured in those terms, the extent of change in large, established organizations is only piecemeal and incremental. But much more dramatic is the simple fact that the reference groups for large firms have changed fundamentally. In this respect, established firms now borrow "best practices" from a much broader set of organizations than they did two decades ago. Again, the repertoire of practices and models has shifted. Moreover, the growing reliance of established firms in all industries on outside parties for nearly every stage in the research, design, and production process has become very strong. Indeed, the direction of change in established companies is as much external as internal. Recognizing that when products and competencies change, old skills may become obsolete, firms look externally for new capabilities and utilize outsiders for tasks that cannot be done effectively internally. The destructive part of this form of learning is the calculation by many firms that it takes too long to retrain and redeploy existing employees; it is cheaper and quicker to fire them and hire new ones.

In an important respect, the disposing of employees rather than redeveloping them may represent a contrary trend. In earlier work I stressed the distinction between the "low road" of cheap labor, usage competition, and costcutting, and the "high road" of reconstituting work and skills without rendering the employees the victim (Powell 1990). Outsourcing and subcontracting can represent a double-edged sword: on the one side, a move toward draconian cost-cutting and sweating labor; on the other, a step toward relational contracting in which trust and joint problem-solving are key. In knowledge-intensive fields, we have argued that the latter strategy is essential because the quality of what you learn externally is crucially dependent upon your internal "absorptive capacity" (Powell et al. 1996). If a firm outsources only in search of cheaper costs, it loses the ability to assess the quality of the services it has procured. But knowledge-based industries are only a part, albeit a highly significant one, of the overall economy.

Variation across Nations

Turning to cross-national comparisons, there are abundant reasons to expect that this new logic of organizing will diffuse globally. On the other hand, compelling rationales are also offered that suggest national-level institutions have a resilient quality that both refracts global competitive pressures and produces divergent responses. (See the essays in Berger and Dore 1996 for both viewpoints). The world of industry does display considerable uniformity because it develops through global connections: finance moves from country to country, firms set up operations in many lands, international organizations set standards, and consultants offer their counsel around the globe. Thus it is very hard to be immune to transnational developments. Yet there clearly are divergent national systems of production, or put differently, diverse models of capitalism. Recent political developments in France highlight these distinctions, with Prime Minister Jospin referring to "Anglo-Saxon" economics as "ultra-capitalism," and arguing that the French prefer security and equality to efficiency. But even as he speaks, French firms such as Renault and Parabis are undergoing extensive restructuring, and the chemical giant Rhône Poulenc's branch, Rhône Poulenc Rorer, is busy helping establish and bankroll a confederation among some thirty-odd competing, small gene-therapy firms in the United States in order to speed the advancement of this technology.

Still, there is abundant empirical evidence that national differences do matter. Research on the diffusion of lean production systems in autos finds important national-level differences in performance (Womack et al. 1990). Various studies of ostensibly successful companies in different nations making similar products with comparable technologies find that the organization of work is carried out in fundamentally different ways (Dore 1973; Maurice et al. 1986; Jaikumar 1986; Streeck 1992). Moreover, taking a very broad view, the advanced industrial nations appear to have distinctive competencies in quite different fields: German firms excel at high-quality engineering, Japanese at electronics and miniaturization, Italian at fashion and design, British at advertising and publishing, U.S. at software, biotechnology, and filmmaking.

These differences point to the importance of national systems of innovation (Porter 1990; Lundvall 1992; Nelson 1993; Freeman 1995). These systems provide the broad institutional context for economic organization, building on the influence of national education systems, industrial relations policy, technical and scientific institutions, government policies, and cultural traditions. Posed abstractly, these ensembles of institutional practices cohere in different ways. Thus, as Boyer (1996) suggests, while global economic pressures may signal common problems and create an impetus for change, economic forces alone do not provide clear clues about the pathways of change or which policies should be altered and which solutions implemented.

To account for the responses of different national systems to growing international economic interdependence, we need to theorize about the diffusion process in a manner that accounts for both receptivity and resistance. Drawing upon Whitley (1994), I offer a first approximation of the interaction of national-level factors and international influences. Consider, as a start, that the industrial democracies vary markedly in terms of their degree of internal institutional cohesion and interdependence. Thus, the more tightly integrated and cohesive the dominant institutions of the home country, the more resistant that nation will be to forms of organizing that are regarded as foreign. Similarly, strong interdependencies among dominant political, financial, labor, and cultural institutions will deter the spread of non-national forms of organizing. Conversely, the likelihood of adopting new models of organizing is increased to the extent that international organizations (be they financial, political, legal, or cultural) dominate national institutions. Moreover, the degree to which national institutions are fragmented rather than interdependent will render a nation more likely to be susceptible to external models. Finally, as I stressed earlier, new and emergent industries are considerably less dependent on traditional forms of organizing. Consequently, the centrality of new industries to national economies will be a critical factor in determining the pace of adoption of new forms of organizing. Thus the speed of industrial change in Finland and Ireland may seem startling, but the dominance there of the new fields of wireless communications and software, respectively, usher in new business models while stimulating rapid growth.

In sum, explaining the diffusion of a new logic of organizing requires understanding how various national-level practices (e.g., the role of financial markets, labor-management relations, and university-industry linkages), mesh with factors in the international system. Since few nations possess an identical combination of institutional practices and cultural legacies, the diffusion of a new mode of organizing is likely to be uneven and partial throughout the industrial democracies. Rather than convergence, I suggest that we will see distinctive strengths and weaknesses as national elements either combine with or fail to articulate key elements of the new model. But such variety is likely to be useful over the long haul, as each national system may flourish or lag under different economic and political circumstances.

SUMMARY AND CONCLUSION

I have argued that a series of changes are well underway in how work is constituted, organizations are structured, and competition is conducted. These changes are responses to different pressures, and stem from experimentation with divergent ideas. But I contend that they are converging to produce a distinctive and novel logic of organizing that is built around project-based work and team organization; flatter, more horizontal organizations that rely on long-term interdependent relations with external parties; and extensive efforts to leverage capabilities across a wide range of activities. One consequence is that the activities of many organizations are now more interdependent, and selection increasingly operates at the network level as rivalry shifts from firm-versus-firm to coalition-versus-collaboration. This system seems to combine the give and take of long-term relational contracting with a short-term focus on results and market discipline. The transition to this new system is rocky, and there are both considerable gains for the winners and steep losses for the losers. At present, it appears the flexibility of the new model is well suited to an era of rapid technological change. Whether the new system will prove adaptive for the long haul, or be as robust as the post–World War II system was for nearly four decades, is not clear. But what is apparent is how rapidly the social technology for organizing work has changed. Our shared understandings about how work and organization are to be carried out now involve fundamentally different recipes than existed previously.

We need, I suggest, to think much more deeply about the social and political consequences of this transformation. Richard Sennett (1998) has argued that there are considerable costs to individuals when attachment and loyalty are replaced by flexibility and constant change. Although he provides evidence mostly from older workers, he shows poignantly that connection to a larger purpose is hard to sustain in a world of projects and perpetual change. We need to ask who has been harmed the most by this transition, and what social policies might ease the burdens of the shift? What kinds of institutional supports—public, private, and civic—are needed both to cushion and sustain new forms of organizing? What actions might push more organizations to follow the high road of continuous learning for their employees rather than the low road of intensified and insecure work? A key transition is underway, and organizations have, in many respects, become much more productive and responsive. We now know a good deal about the organizational consequences of this transformation; but our understanding of its social ramifications is murky. This chapter is an effort to start these conversations by sketching the outline of the new system and arguing that our current thinking has not kept pace.

CHAPTER 3

Ambiguous Assets for Uncertain Environments:

HETERARCHY IN POSTSOCIALIST FIRMS

David Stark

I HAVE A tin can on my desk that I bought in Budapest in the autumn of 1989. It is considerably smaller than a standard tuna can and extremely light in weight. If you tap your fingernail on it, it gives a hollow ring. But the label, complete with a universal bar code, announces in bold letters that, in fact, it is not empty: *"Kommunizmus Utolsó Lehelete"*—"The Last Breath of Communism."

If I were so inclined, I could take my tin can as a facile metaphor for the transition in Eastern Europe. The last breath of communism marketed by a clever entrepreneur represents the irrepressible urge to truck and barter released by the fresh winds of the free market. Exhale communism, inhale capitalism.

But the conditions under which my tin can was actually manufactured carry another story: It was not produced in the garage workshop of a petty entrepreneur but right in the heart of a state-owned enterprise by a work team which, since 1982, had been taking advantage of legislation that allowed employees of socialist firms to form "intra-enterprise partnerships." As in many thousands of such intrapreneurial partnerships, this group of thirty workers in a large factory had been running factory equipment on the "off-hours" and on weekends, subcontracting to the parent enterprise and getting orders from outside firms. The limited batch run of "The Last Breath of Communism" was a good joke, but the venture had been a serious one.

The internal subcontracting partnerships of the 1980s were a curious mixture of public property and private gain. As they blurred organizational

The first version of this paper was completed in 1996 while I was a Fellow at the Center for Advanced Study in the Behavioral Sciences in Palo Alto, with financial support provided by the National Science Foundation Grant No. SES–9022192 and the U.S. Department of State Title VIII Funds Grant No. 1006–304101. The paper was first presented at the Annual Meetings of the American Sociological Association, New York City, August 1996. My thanks to Christina Ahmadjian, Penny Becker, Pablo Boczkowski, Luc Boltanski, Ron Breiger, László Bruszt, Andy Buck, Paul DiMaggio, Walter Fontana, István Gábor, Monique Girard, Gernot Grabher, Szabolcs Kemény, Bruce Kogut, John Padgett, Laurent Thévenot, and Eleanor Westney for helpful criticisms and suggestions.

boundaries, the partnerships were a form of organizational hedging: managers gained flexibility within the terms of state property, and workers gained higher incomes without losing the benefits of employment in the socialist sector. Within the subcontracting units, the partners allocated earnings and coordinated the production process through a mixture of evaluative principles from the logics of markets, redistribution, and reciprocity.[1]

Similar practices of organizational hedging, resulting in the blurring of public and private and the coexistence of multiple justificatory principles, characterize the bricolage of recombinant processes that are a key feature of the current postsocialist period.

The unopened tin can on my desk thus points to the emptiness of the toggle-switch theory of "market transition" that posits public ownership and state subsidies on one side and private property and markets on the other. And it signals a continuity of recombinatory practices in the repertoire of organizational innovation for actors at the enterprise level.

This paper examines the organizational strategies and the resulting structural features of East European firms in response to the extraordinary uncertainties of systemic transformation following the upheavals of 1989. My starting premise is that postsocialist Eastern Europe is a genuine social laboratory, not simply because researchers can use it to test competing theories, but because people there are actively experimenting with new organizational forms. Unlike scientists, their localized experiments are not "by design," nor should they be. The attempt to create and manage an entire economy by design was the colossal Leninist failure, and efforts to create capitalism by design would do well to learn from those mistakes. Instead, their experimentation is more like "bricolage": making do with what is available. But if they use existing institutional materials that are close at hand, they are not for that reason condemned to mimic the old. As Joseph Schumpeter (1934), Harrison White (1993), and biologists François Jacob (1977), Edgar Morin (1974), and John Holland (1992) have shown in very different contexts, combining old building blocks is one means to innovate: innovation through recombination.

Innovation in the postsocialist setting, it would seem, should be directed to adaptation, as firms adapt to the new market environment and national

---

[1] The partnership form was an organizational innovation that modified, for industry, organizational forms transplanted from agricultural cooperatives during the 1970s—a set of practices themselves borrowed from the "household plots" that had developed on state farms starting already with the demise of Stalinism in the late 1950s. For details on the politics of the "second economy," its relationship to the partnerships, and their functioning inside the socialist firm, see Stark (1989). For a case study of the multiple regimes of worth intertwined in the internal dynamics of a single partnership followed over a five-year time frame, see Stark (1990).

economies adapt to global markets. Without questioning the need for major restructuring, in the opening section of the paper, I argue that preoccupation with short-term adaptation can hinder long-term adaptability. In making that argument, I draw on the concept of "lock-in," the process whereby early successes can pave a path for further investments of new resources that eventually lock in to suboptimal outcomes. But must organizations and systems accept this fate? Are there organizational forms that are better configured to learn from their environments? Such organizations would need practices that recognize (re-cognize) new resources in an ongoing reconfiguration of organizational assets.

These challenges are hardly unique to the postsocialist transformations. Therefore, the subsequent section of the chapter makes explicit my assumption that the term "transforming economies" applies no less to the societies of North America and Western Europe than to those of Eastern Europe and the former Soviet Union. Firms in both types of economies now face extraordinary uncertainties, caused by the rapidity of technological change and the extreme volatility of markets in the former, and shaped by political and institutional uncertainties in the latter. The response to these uncertainties is an emergent, self-organizing form that I call *heterarchy*. In elaborating its features, I point to processes of lateral or distributed authority and explore how organizations can benefit from the active rivalry of competing belief systems.

Having outlined the characteristics of heterarchical forms, I then focus on the specific challenges facing the postsocialist economies with the new uncertainties of international trade, the new challenges of reading market signals, and the new dilemmas created by the simultaneous extension of property rights and citizenship rights. In the subsequent section, I describe in detail the recombinant practices of postsocialist firms[2] and the network properties to which they give rise, focusing on Hungary and the Czech Republic, with reference to several other postsocialist cases. By exploring two cases in depth, we gain an appreciation of some variation within the family resemblance of an emerging East European capitalism. In these subsections, I explicate recent Hungarian developments, chart their Czech counterparts, account for differences in broad network structures across the two cases, and give the reader a sense of the peculiar form of "portfolio management" that can be seen in contemporary postsocialism. The paper concludes with a discussion of the problems of accountability that accompany the relentless pursuit of flexibility.

---

[2] My analysis focuses on postsocialist firms (typically, large firms that already existed in the socialist period). An analysis of "the firm in postsocialist economies" would be a much broader study encompassing new private startups, small and medium-size firms, and the subsidiaries and greenfield investments of foreign multinationals.

THE ORGANIZATION OF DIVERSITY

Each evening during their hunting season, the Naskapi Indians of the Labrador peninsula determined where they would look for game on the next day's hunt by holding a caribou shoulder bone over the fire.[3] Examining the smoke deposits on the caribou bone, a shaman read for the hunting party the points of orientation of the next day's search. In this way, the Naskapi introduced a randomizing element to confound a short-term rationality, in which the one best way to find game would seem to have been to look again tomorrow where they had found game that day. By following the divergent daily maps of smoke on the caribou bone, they avoided locking in to early successes that, while taking them to game in the short run, would in the long run have depleted the caribou stock in that quadrant and reduced the likelihood of successful hunting. By breaking the link between future courses and past successes, the tradition of shoulder bone reading was an antidote to path dependence in the hunt.

Mainstream notions of the postsocialist "transition" as the replacement of one set of economic institutions by another set of institutions of proven efficiency are plagued by similar problems of short-term rationality that the Naskapi practices mitigated. As the policy variant of "hunt tomorrow where we found game today," neoliberal advisors recommend the adoption of a highly stylized version of the institutions of prices and property that have "worked well in the West." Economic efficiency will be maximized, they argue, only through the rapid and all-encompassing implementation of privatization and marketization. I argue here, by contrast, that although such institutional homogenization might foster *adaptation* in the short run, the consequent loss of institutional diversity will impede *adaptability* in the long run (see Grabher 1997). Limiting the search for effective institutions and organizational forms to the familiar Western hunting ground of tried and proven arrangements locks in the postsocialist economies to exploiting known territory at the cost of forgetting (or never learning) the skills of exploring for new solutions.

Recent studies in evolutionary economics and organizational analysis suggest that organizations that learn too quickly sacrifice efficiency. Allen and McGlade (1987), for example, use the behavior of Nova Scotia fishermen to illustrate the possible trade-offs of exploiting old certainties and exploring new possibilities. Their model of these fishing fleets divides the fishermen into two classes: the rationalist "Cartesians" who drop their nets only where the fish are known to be biting, and the risk-taking "Stochasts" who discover the new schools of fish. In simulations where all the skippers

[3] This account is drawn from Weick (1977, 45).

are Stochasts, the fleet is relatively unproductive, because knowledge of where the fish are biting is unutilized, but a purely Cartesian fleet locks in to the "most likely" spot and quickly fishes it out. More efficient are the models that, like the actual behavior of the Nova Scotia fishing fleets, mix Cartesian exploiters and Stochastic explorers.

James March's (1991) simulation in "Exploitation and Exploration in Organizational Learning" yields similar results: he finds that interacting collections of smart learners frequently underperform interactions of smart and dumb. Organizations that learn too quickly *exploit* at the expense of *exploration*, thereby locking in to suboptimal routines and strategies. The purely Cartesian fleet in Allen and McGlade's study, like the organizations of homogeneously smart learners in March's simulations, illustrate the potential dangers of positive feedback and the pitfalls of tight coupling. Like infantry officers who instructed drummers to disrupt the cadence of marching solders while they are crossing bridges, lest the resonance of uniformly marching feet bring calamity, I draw the lesson that dissonance contributes to organizational learning and economic evolution.

Restated in the language of the new economics of adaptive systems (Arthur 1994), the problem for any transforming economy is that the very mechanisms that foster allocative efficiency might eventually lock development in to a path that is inefficient, viewed dynamically. Within this framework, our attention turns from a preoccupation with adaptation to a concern about adaptability, shifting from the problem of how to improve the immediate "fit" with a new economic environment, to the problem of how to reshape the organizational structure to enhance its ability to respond to unpredictable future changes in the environment (Grabher 1997).

Sociologists within the tradition of organizational ecology have a ready answer to this problem. At the level of the economic system, adaptability is promoted by the *diversity of organizations*; that is, a system with a greater variety of organizational forms (a more diverse organizational "gene pool") has a higher probability of having in hand some solution that is satisfactory under changed environmental conditions (Hannan 1986, 85). From that viewpoint, the problem of socialism was not only that it lacked a selection mechanism (firms were not allowed to fail), but also that almost all economic resources were locked into one organizational form: the large state-owned enterprise. That form was formidable in achieving industrialization; but lacking capacity for innovation, it failed woefully in the subsequent competition with the West.

Similarly, the problem in the current period of transformation is that "success" that is achieved during the transition through forced homogenization toward the privately held corporation might suppress organizational diversity, thereby impeding adaptability in the next round of global competition.[4]

But where do new organizational forms come from? Understanding organizational change as taking place almost exclusively through the deaths and births of organizations, the organizational ecology perspective downplays organizational learning and neglects the possibilities of organizational innovations that result from the recombinations of existing forms.[5]

Because I put organizational innovation front and center, I argue that, in addition to the diversity of organizations within a population, adaptability is promoted by the *organization of diversity*[6] within an enterprise. Organizational diversity is most likely to yield its fullest evolutionary potential when different organizational principles coexist in an active rivalry *within the firm*.[7] By rivalry, I do not refer to competing camps and factions, but to coexisting logics and frames of action. The organization of diversity is an active and sustained engagement in which there is more than one way to organize, label, interpret, and evaluate the same or similar activity. Rivalry fosters cross-fertilization.[8] It increases the possibilities of long-term adapt-

---

[4] Diversity and variety allow evolution to follow at the same time different paths that are associated with different sets of organizational forms, thus reducing the risk that local maximization results in an evolutionary dead end. Two or more trajectories are able to cope with a broader array of unpredictable environmental changes than is the case with a single one. The reproduction of diversity depends on the ability of different levels of efficiency to coexist. On the one hand, evolution comes to a stop in cases where less efficient forms are eliminated immediately through selection: too little diversity, no evolution. On the other hand, however, the absence of any evolutionary selective comparison might turn diversity into "noise" in which none of the organizational forms would be able to influence the direction of any evolutionary trajectory: too much diversity, likewise, no evolution (Grabher and Stark, 1997; Lewontin 1982). The point at which organizational diversity in economic systems is too little or too much remains a question open for empirical, comparative research.

[5] Stated simply (and thus at the risk of creating misunderstanding if not caricature), despite all its (appropriately cautious and always distanced) adoption of biological metaphors, organizational ecology lacks sex. That is, it is relatively infrequent in the population ecology of organizations literature that we find cross-fertilization, mixing, or recombinations of "genetic" organizational materials.

[6] "[T]he sphere of complexity is that of organized diversity, of the organization of diversity" (Morin, 1974, 558).

[7] This shift from a preoccupation with variation within a population of organizations (characteristic of organizational ecology) to attention to the organization of diversity inside firms is broadly comparable to the difference between population biology and new work in computational biology on the origins of organization. "In contrast to the traditional approach, a constructive dynamical system specifies the interactions among objects not externally, but rather internally to the objects as a function of their structure. . . . A self-maintaining system is one which continuously regenerates itself by transformations internal to the system" (Fontana and Buss, 1993, 3). For a cogent discussion of the evolution of *variability* and genetic control of genotype-phenotype mapping, see Wagner and Altenberg (1996).

[8] "Recombination plays a key role in the discovery process, generating plausible new rules from parts of tested rules" (Holland, 1992, 26). "Novelties come from previously unseen

ability by better search—"better," not because it is more consistent or elegant or coherent, but precisely because the complexity that it promotes and the lack of simple coherence that it tolerates increase the diversity of options. The challenge of the organization of diversity is to find solutions that promote constructive organizational reflexivity, or the ability to redefine and recombine resources. I call the emergent organizational forms with these properties *heterarchies*.

HETERARCHY

Heterarchy represents a new mode of organizing that is neither market nor hierarchy: whereas hierarchies involve relations of *dependence* and markets involve relations of *independence*, heterarchies involve relations of *interdependence*.[9] As the term suggests, heterarchies are characterized by minimal hierarchy and by organizational heterogeneity—a pair of concepts that I elaborate next, drawing upon studies of collaborative practices in high-tech Western firms and my own observations in interactive media firms in New York City (Stark 1999). Subsequent sections further specify the applicability of the heterarchy concept in the postsocialist cases.

Heterarchy's twinned features are a response to the increasing complexity of the firm's strategy horizons (Lane and Maxfield 1996) or of its "fitness landscape" (Kauffman 1993). In relentlessly changing organizations where, at the extreme, there is uncertainty even about what product the firm will be producing in the near future, the strategy horizon of the firm is unpredictable and its fitness landscape is rugged.[10] To cope with these uncertainties, instead of concentrating resources for strategic planning among a narrow set of senior executives or delegating that function to a specialized

---

association of old material. To create is to recombine" (Jacob 1977, 1163). Or, in Harrison White's (1993) terminology, "values mate to change."

[9] As a more general process, heterarchy refers to a process in which a given element—a statement, a deal, an identity, an organizational building-block, or sequences of genetic, computer, or legal code—is simultaneously expressed in multiple crosscutting networks. My discussion here focuses on heterarchy as an organizational form. While this paper was going to press, Eleanor Westney pointed me to a fascinating paper by Hedlund (1993), who employs the term in an analysis of multinational corporations.

[10] A smooth fitness landscape is highly regular and single peaked, reflecting a single optimal solution possessing a higher fitness value than any other potential solution. A more complex or "rugged" fitness landscape, by contrast, is not amenable to linear programming models (e.g., lower unit costs through economies of scale) because the topography is jagged and irregular, with multiple peaks corresponding to multiple optimal solutions. On the use of genetic algorithms designed to explore initially unpromising paths and thereby avoid the danger of "climbing to the nearest peak," which might simply be the highest point in a valley surrounded by yet higher peaks, see Holland (1992). On adaptation in rugged fitness landscapes, see Kauffman (1989).

department, firms may undergo a radical decentralization in which virtually every unit becomes engaged in innovation. That is, in place of specialized search routines in which some departments are dedicated to exploration while others are confined to exploiting existing knowledge, the functions of exploration are generalized throughout the organization. The search for new markets, for example, is no longer the sole province of the marketing department, if units responsible for purchase and supply are also scouting the possibilities for qualitatively new inputs that can open up new product lines.

These developments increase interdependencies between divisions, departments, and work teams within the firm. But because of the greater complexity of these feedback loops, coordination cannot be engineered, controlled, or managed hierarchically. The results of interdependence are to increase the autonomy of work units from central management. Yet at the same time, more complex interdependence heightens the need for fine-grained coordination across the increasingly autonomous units.

These pressures are magnified by dramatic changes in the sequencing of activities within production relations. As product cycles shorten from years to months, the race to new markets calls into question the strict sequencing of design and execution. Because of strong first-mover advantages, in which the first actor to introduce a new product (especially one that establishes a new industry standard) captures an inordinate market share by reaping increasing returns, firms that wait to begin production until design is completed will be penalized in competition. Like the production of "B movies" in which filming begins before the script is completed, successful strategies integrate conception and execution, with significant aspects of the production process beginning even before design is finalized.

Production relations are even more radically altered in processes analyzed by Sabel and Dorf (1998) as *simultaneous engineering*. Conventional design is sequential, with subsystems that are presumed to be central designed in detail first, setting the boundary conditions for the design of lower-ranking components. In simultaneous engineering, by contrast, separate project teams develop all the subsystems concurrently. In such concurrent design, the various project teams engage in an ongoing mutual monitoring, as innovations produce multiple, sometimes competing, proposals for improving the overall design.

Thus, increasingly rugged fitness landscapes yield increasingly complex interdependencies that in turn yield increasingly complex coordination challenges. In situations where search is no longer departmentalized but is instead generalized and distributed throughout the organization, and where design is no longer compartmentalized but deliberated and distributed throughout the production process, the solution is *distributed authority* (Powell 1996).

Under circumstances of simultaneous engineering where the very parameters of a project are subject to deliberation and change across units, authority is no longer delegated vertically but rather emerges laterally. As one symptom of these changes, managers socialized in an earlier regime frequently express their puzzlement to researchers: "There's one thing I can't figure out. Who's my boss?" Under conditions of distributed authority, managers might still "report to" their superiors; but increasingly, they are accountable to other work teams. Success at simultaneous engineering thus depends on learning by mutual monitoring.

The interdependencies that result from attempts to cope with rugged fitness landscapes are only inadequately captured in concepts of "matrix organizations" or in the fads such as treating the firm as a set of "internal markets" according to which every unit should regard every other unit in the firm as its "customer." These conceptions are inadequate because they take the boundaries of the firm and the boundaries of its internal units as given parameters.

First, as Walter Powell (1990, 1996, and chapter 2 in this volume) and others show, the boundaries of the firm, especially those in fast-breaking sectors, are criss-crossed by dense ties of interlocking ownership (Kogut et al. 1992) and complex patterns of strategic alliances. Where the environment is most volatile and uncertain, the real unit of economic action is increasingly not the isolated firm but networks of firms. As with the networks linking mental representations and physical artifacts in "distributed cognition" (Hutchins 1995), networks of strategic alliances create opportunities for distributed intelligence across the boundaries of firms.

Second, as it shifts from search routines to a situation in which search is generalized, the heterarchical firm is redrawing internal boundaries, regrouping assets, and perpetually reinventing itself. Under circumstances of rapid technological change and volatility of products and markets, it seems there is no one best model of organization. If one could be rationally chosen and resources devoted to it alone, the benefits of its fleeting superiority would not compensate for the costs of subsequent missed opportunities. Because managers hedge against these uncertainties, the outcomes are hybrid forms (Sabel 1990). Good managers do not simply commit themselves to the array that keeps the most options open; instead, they create an organizational space open to the perpetual redefinition of what might constitute an option. Rather than a rational choice among a set of known options, we find practical action fluidly redefining what the options might be. Management becomes the art of facilitating organizations that can reorganize themselves.

The challenge for the modern firm—whether it be a postsocialist firm coping with the uncertainties of system change or a digital technologies firm coping with unpredictable strategy horizons—is the challenge of building organizations that are capable of learning. Flexibility requires an ability to redefine and recombine assets: in short, a pragmatic reflexivity.

This capacity for self-redefinition is grounded in the organizational heterogeneity that characterizes heterarchies. Heterarchies are *complex* adaptive systems because they interweave a multiplicity of organizing principles. The new organizational forms are heterarchical not only because they have flattened hierarchy, but also because they are the sites of competing and coexisting value systems. The greater interdependence of increasingly autonomous work teams results in a proliferation of performance criteria. Distributed authority not only implies that units will be accountable to each other, but also that each will be held to accountings in multiple registers. The challenge of a new media firm, for example, is to create a sufficiently common culture to facilitate communication among the designers, business strategists, and technologists that make up interdisciplinary teams—without suppressing the distinctive identities of each.[11] A robust, lateral collaboration flattens hierarchy without flattening diversity. Heterarchies create wealth by inviting more than one way of evaluating worth.

Heterarchies are organizations with multiple worldviews and belief systems such that products, processes, and properties carry multiple "tags" or interpretations (Clark 1999; Clippinger 1999). Success in rugged fitness landscapes requires an extended organizational reflexivity that sustains rather than stifles this complexity. Because resources are not fixed in one system of interpretation but can exist in several, heterarchies make assets of ambiguity.[12]

This aspect of heterarchy builds on Frank Knight's (1921) distinction between *risk*, where the distribution of outcomes can be expressed in probabilistic terms, and *uncertainty*, where outcomes are incalculable. Whereas neoclassical economics reduces all cases to risk, Knight argued that a world of generalized probabilistic knowledge of the future leaves no place for profit (as a particular residual revenue that is not contractualizable because it is not susceptible to measure *ex ante*) and hence no place for the entrepreneur. And whereas the French school of the "economics of convention" (Boltanski and Thévenot 1991) demonstrates that institutions are social

---

[11] A young business strategist in a leading new media consulting firm in Silicon Alley grasped the problem intuitively. When I asked whether he can speak the language of the designers and technologists on his project teams, he responded that he frequently does. But then he paused for a moment and added, "But I don't always do so. If I always talked to the technologist on his own terms, then he would never understand *me*."

[12] In coping with highly uncertain organizational environments, heterarchies exploit the uncertainty of which regime of worth is operative. From ambiguity, they make an asset. In creating assets that can operate in more than one regime of worth, they make assets that are ambiguous.

technologies for transforming uncertainty into calculative problems, they leave unexamined the possibility of uncertainty concerning which institution ("regime of worth") is operative in a given situation. Knight's conception of entrepreneurship as the exploitation of uncertainty is, thus, here respecified in the heterarchy framework: Entrepreneurship is the ability to keep multiple regimes of worth in play and to exploit the resulting ambiguity (Stark 1998, 2000).

MAKING THE BEST OF ONE'S RESOURCES AS THE NEXT-BEST WAY TO CAPITALISM

While managers in advanced sectors are coping with volatile markets, rapid technological change, and the challenges of simultaneous engineering, policymakers in the postsocialist world must cope with a set of different, but equally complex, strategy horizons.

The restructuring of the postsocialist firm is taking place in the context of a dual transformation of politics and property: the twinned processes of democratization and privatization accompanying the collapse of Communism have simultaneously extended citizenship rights and property rights.[13] Indeed, this simultaneity marks the specificity of postsocialism. Several East Asian societies, for example, have embarked on the course of democratization, but, unlike Eastern Europe and the former Soviet Union, only after economic reforms had already opened their economies to world markets in a period of an expanding global economy. In Latin America, economic liberalization and political democratization were undertaken at the same time, but unlike Eastern Europe, economic reforms did not involve a fundamental transformation of property regimes.

Adept at mitigating the bureaucratic uncertainties of central planning, managers of the formerly socialist firms suddenly had to cope with an imposing set of uncertainties of a very different character: Trade relations would have to be reoriented with the collapse of the old Soviet-directed COMECON-CMEA (Council of Mutual Economic Assistance) trading partners; suppliers and customers were no longer hierarchically imposed but would now be regulated by contracts (of untested and therefore uncertain enforcement); and new legislation regulating accounting, bankruptcy, and corporate governance brought strange new professionals (accountants,

---

[13] The simultaneous emergence of newly propertied classes and newly enfranchised subordinate groups poses the central postsocialist challenge of how to restructure economies when those who perceive their interests to be threatened by economic change have the capacity to replace political incumbents. For a comparative study of this problem in four East Central European countries, see Stark and Bruszt (1998).

lawyers, and boards of directors) right into the heart of the firm. These new uncertainties in the firm's business environment, moreover, were compounded by new political uncertainties when startling rates of unemployment occurred among workers/citizens recently empowered with the capacity to replace political incumbents. Policymakers and enterprise decision-makers thus confronted a complex and unfamiliar strategy horizon. How should they reorganize economies and restructure firms in the face of these extraordinary uncertainties?

For many Western policy advisors who flew into the region (often with little knowledge of its peculiarities), the answers were straightforward, and two positions quickly dominated the debate. On the one side was the message of the neoliberals: the best way to restructure is to use strong markets. Markets, they argued, were not only the goals but also the means. Rapid privatization, trade and price liberalization, strict bankruptcy laws, and an end to government subsidies were key elements of their policy prescriptions. But the depth and rapidity of economic recession in the aftermath of 1989 dampened enthusiasm for the neoliberal agenda, and an alternative, neostatist, position entered the debate arguing that the neoliberal strategy confuses goals and means: To create markets, one cannot simply rely on markets; strengthening the market requires strong states.

At first, the choice seemed clear: strong markets versus strong states. The problem, however, was that the societies of the postsocialist world historically had lacked both developed markets and coherent states. The nonexisting starting points of the neoliberals and the neostatists recall the joke in which an Irishman in the far countryside is asked, "What's the best way to get to Dublin?" He thinks for a minute, and responds, "Don't start from here."

The irony of the answer would not be lost on East Europeans, for they are all too acutely aware that the *best* ways to get to capitalism started somewhere else. But those options are not available to our contemporary traveling companions. Accordingly, this essay adopts a different analytic starting point—the pragmatic, self-organizing starting point of the East Europeans themselves who, instead of the question "What is the best way to get to capitalism?" must ask, "How do we get there from here?" In place of the therapies, recipes, formulas, and blueprints of designer capitalism, postsocialist firms have had to adopt a different strategy: precluded from the best ways to get to capitalism, they are making the best of what they have.

With what institutional resources have they embarked? Postsocialist societies lack strong markets and strong states, but they have decades of experience with strong networks under socialism. These associative ties of reciprocity were unintended consequences of the attempt to "scientifically manage" an entire national economy. At the shop-floor level, shortages and supply bottlenecks led to bargaining between supervisors and informal groups; at the level of the shadow economy of gray market activities, the distortions of central planning reproduced the conditions for networks of predominantly part-time entrepreneurs; and at the managerial level, the task of meeting plan-targets produced dense networks of informal ties that cut across enterprises and local organizations.

Some of these network ties dissipate in the transforming postsocialist economic environment; others are strengthened as firms, individuals, banks, local governments, and other economic actors adopt coping strategies to survive (not all of them legal, and in some countries, many of them corrupt); and still others emerge anew as these same actors search for new customers and suppliers, new sources of credit and revenues, and new strategic allies. The existence of parallel structures in the informal and interfirm networks that "got the job done" under socialism means that instead of an institutional vacuum, we find routines and practices that can become assets, resources, and the basis for credible commitments and coordinated actions. In short, associative ties build new forms of association as the "ties that bind" shape binding agreements.

As interdependent assets, network ties are not the property of the isolated firm but are a "property" of relatively discrete business groupings based on interorganizational ownership ties constructed across the boundaries of enterprises. That is, in the analysis that follows we shift from thinking about *networks as property* (e.g., "social capital") to thinking about *the properties of networks*. This exploitation of the polysemic character of "property" is deliberate as we seek to understand the structural properties (characteristics) of interconnected properties (holdings). The phrase *network properties* thus has a multivocal character. In the parlance of property theory, it refers to the interdependence of assets across organizational boundaries; at the same time, in the parlance of network analysis, it refers to the properties of networks—varying, for example, according to such characteristics as their density, extensivity, centrality, and the patterns of their strong or weak (direct or indirect) ties.

This analytic shift has implications for how the categories of structure, strategy, and governance (so prominent in the field of organizational analysis) figure in this account. Once we think about different *groups* of firms constructing different network portfolios (of varying concentration/diversification and varying shapes, contours, and configurations), the very unit of strategic action changes: structure and strategy become emergent properties of groups. As such, this study is orthogonal to the problem of ownership and control that pervades the literature on enterprise governance. From questions about the role of property in the corporate governance of the postsocialist firm, it turns to implications about the structural properties of network ties for the governance of the postsocialist economy and subsectors within it. But network ties are only part of the story whereby postsocialist firms are attempting to restructure under difficult circumstances in which there are few new resources. Aid, credit, and direct investment have been paltry when compared to the magnitude of the economic and political transformation in the region. In this situation, one of the principal resources of the postsocialist firm is resourcefulness. Less design than improvisation, restructuring is often a process of bricolage: making do with what is available, redeploying assets for new uses, recombining resources within and across organizational boundaries. From the aggregation and recombination of existing building blocks emerge genuinely new structures and processes.

These recombinant practices have a special character in postsocialist societies where economies are undergoing a profound transformation in property regimes. Conventionally addressed under the rubric of "privatization" and understood as a straightforward transfer of property from public to private hands, much of the property transformation in postsocialist firms is in fact, neither a simple transition from public to private nor a clarification of property rights. Instead, the emerging new property forms blur the boundaries of public and private, erode the organizational boundaries of the firms, and multiply the operative evaluating principles with which the firm justifies access to resources. I refer to this ensemble of characteristics as *recombinant property*.

Recombinant property is a form of organizational hedging in which actors respond to uncertainty in the organizational environment by diversifying their assets and by redefining and recombining resources. In its extreme form, it is an attempt to hold and label resources that can be justified or assessed by more than one standard of evaluation. The overlap of a multiplicity of property regimes in the postsocialist circumstances does not simply mean that multiple owners are making different claims on the resources of the firm, but rather that the multiple regimes are providing multiple opportunities for the firm to make claims for resources. "Asset diversification" in such cases differs markedly from that of the mutual fund portfolio manager, whose strategy can be captured in the algorithm that expresses optimizing preferences across risk functions, short-term revenues, long-term growth, and the like. By contrast, the recombinant strategies in the postsocialist cases are practices that seek to manage asset ambiguity. Under circumstances of asset interdependence, some assets are most valuable precisely where property claims are least clarified; thus, under circumstances where multiple legitimating principles are at play, actors gain advantage if they can exploit the ambiguity of justifications for claims.

In this highly uncertain environment, therefore, enterprise survival can depend on skills that make assets of ambiguity.

RECOMBINANT PRACTICES IN HUNGARY

Immediately following the first free elections in the spring of 1990, the new democratic government of Hungary announced an ambitious program of privatization. Because this was intended to be a state-directed course of property transformation, the government created a large bureaucratic agency, the State Property Agency (SPA), responsible for every aspect of privatizing the productive assets of the Hungarian economy, some 90 percent of which had been held by the state. From its inception, the SPA adopted the official policy that privatization would be conducted on a strictly case-by-case, firm-by-firm basis. SPA policy never treated assets as interdependent across firms, or considered that firms might be broken up and their assets regrouped by economic agents with local knowledge of constraints and opportunities. Instead, it adopted a role as "Big Broker," attempting to match buyers to firms, and it sought to legitimate its activities externally by emphasizing the bottom line: revenues brought into the state treasury from the eventual sale of individual firms.

Enterprise directors took a different approach. While bureaucratic administrators in the agency debated the merits of auctions versus public offerings, and transaction officers in the agency scrambled to acquire some familiarity with the dozens of firms assigned to their supervision, enterprise management took advantage of several pieces of legislation to launch their own strategies of property transformation.

Although we typically think about owners acquiring firms, the peculiar circumstances of the economic transformation in Eastern Europe has placed extraordinary political and economic pressure on postsocialist firms to acquire owners. They do so, moreover, under circumstances in which the demand for owners greatly exceeds the supply. On one side, the demand for owners is high: the postsocialist firm is searching for new owners at precisely the same time that thousands of other firms are doing the same. On the other side, the supply of owners with adequate capital and interest is relatively low: the domestic population has savings that equal only a fraction of the value of the assets of the state-owned enterprises, while there are only so many interested foreign buyers. Politically compelled to find owners to adjust to the new political setting, and organizationally compelled to find owner-allies to address the challenges of the new economic environment, the postsocialist firms find each other. That is, they acquire shares in other firms and they make arrangements for other enterprises to become their new shareholders.[14] The results are dense networks of interlocking ownership ties that extend through and across branches and sectors of the economy, especially among the very largest enterprises and banks.

Network Properties

To assess the prevalence of such inter-enterprise ownership, we compiled a data set on the ownership structure of the largest two hundred Hungarian corporations (ranked by sales).[15] These firms compose the "Top 200" on the listing of *Figyelö*, a leading Hungarian business weekly. Like their Fortune 500 counterparts in the United States, the "*Figyelö* 200" firms are major players in the Hungarian economy, employing an estimated 21 percent of the labor force and accounting for 37 percent of total net sales and 42 percent of export revenues. The data also include the top twenty-five Hungarian banks (ranked by assets). Ownership data were obtained in the spring of 1994 and updated in the spring of 1996, gathered directly from the Hungarian Courts of Registry, where corporate files contain complete lists of the company's owners at the time of the most recent shareholders' meeting. Following the convention in the literature of East Asian business groups, analysis is restricted to the top twenty owners of each corporation.[16]

Who holds the shares of these largest enterprises and banks? Through its property holding agencies, the state remains the most prominent owner. In 1996 it was the sole and exclusive owner of 16.4 percent of these firms, and participated as one of the top twenty owners in 44.4 percent of the largest corporations and banks. Although whittled down, the state is not withering away. Only five companies (2.0 percent) in this population were owned exclusively by private individuals in 1996. Even by the least restrictive criterion—the presence of even one individual private investor among a company's major owners—individual private ownership cannot be seen as ascendant. In 1994, 102 individuals in the data set held ownership stakes in 8.5 percent of these largest enterprises and banks. In 1996, these figures actually declined, with only 61 individuals appearing among the twenty major owners of only 7.3 percent of the units in this population.

---

[14] Property transformation in Hungary thus bears some resemblance to Sabel's "simultaneous engineering" (Sabel and Dorf 1998). That is, firms began restructuring before design was finalized, and they did so in a collaborative way.

[15] My research partner in this data analysis is Szabolcs Kemény, a Hungarian Ph.D. candidate at Columbia University.

[16] In the Hungarian economy, where only thirty-seven firms are traded on the Budapest stock exchange and where corporate shareholding is not widely dispersed among hundreds of small investors, the twenty-owner restriction allows us to account for at least 90 percent of the shares held in virtually every company.

Intercorporate ownership, on the other hand, is increasing as the percentage of units with at least one corporate owner rose from 66.3 percent to 77.6 percent in 1996. Most notably, the number of units in which all the top twenty owners are other corporations increased from 35.6 percent to 40.2 percent. Many of these owners are themselves the largest enterprises and banks, the very firms for which we gathered the ownership data.

Property as an Emergent Property

Beyond confirming the prevalence of such inter-enterprise ownership, the data also allow us to identify the links among these large enterprises. These ties are dense and extensive, and they yield numerous networks of interconnected holdings. Figure 3.1 presents a typical network formed through these ownership ties. The numbered nodes represent specific firms or banks, and the lines indicate an ownership connection between them.

Direct ties among the largest firms, however, are only the most immediate way to identify relational properties in the field of interacting strategies. For, in addition to knowing the direct ties between two firms (e.g., Company A is a major shareholder of Bank B) we can also identify the patterns formed by their mutual shareholdings even when two firms are not themselves directly tied (e.g., Enterprises C, D, E, and F share a relation by virtue of the tie through Bank X, which is a major shareholder in each; or Bank X and Bank Z are "linked" by their mutual ownership in Enterprise M).

Incorporating this more complete ensemble of ties allows us to probe a concept that network analysts refer to as "structural similarity." To take a homely example, if all your friends are my friends, we are structurally similar even if we do not know each other. The notion of structural similarity gives a more robust view of the overall properties of the field because it provides a richer interpretation of proximity in a structural space: we might be indifferent to knowing precisely who is friends with whom if our question is to ask, who runs in the same social circles. The strategist for a biotechnology firm who is trying to anticipate the next moves of the competition might well want to know which firms tend to license identical patents, even when the competitors do not directly license patents from each other (e.g., where A's competitors B and C do not license each other's patents, but both tend to license patents from D, E, and F).

For our data set, two companies are structurally similar if their overall sets of relations, compared to all the other firms in the data set—that is, to all the possible owners as well as to all the units that can be owned—are nearly alike. We use a clustering algorithm to identify the major business

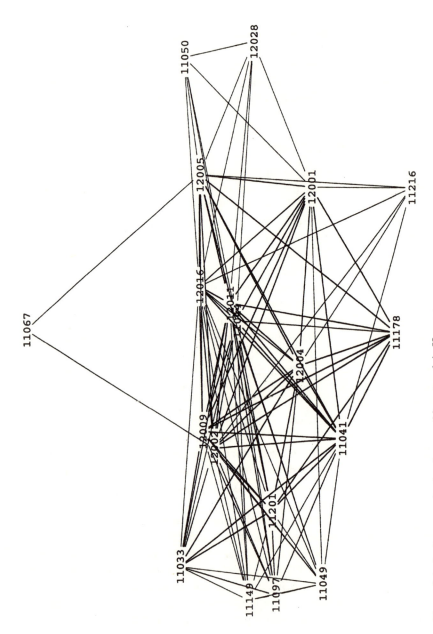

Figure 3.1. An interorganizational ownership network in Hungary.

groupings of the Hungarian economy formed through inter-enterprise ties. The results are depicted in figure 3.2.[17]

Whereas figure 3.1 represents a discrete network formed through direct ties, figure 3.2 takes a broader view to show the various "teams" and their proximity to each other in the whole field. To understand the representation, as a first approximation, think of each firm as having a portfolio of holdings (the other companies in which it holds shares) *and* as having a portfolio of owners (its shareholders). The eight business groupings shown in figure 3.2 result from the intersections of these twinned portfolios. Then think again, but this time instead of taking the individual firm as the unit of analysis, take the relatively discrete network of firms as the unit. That is, think about *property* as the network properties of a group of firms, and about a *portfolio* not as a feature of a single firm but as a property of the network. Once we think of each network as a distinctive portfolio, the very unit of strategic action changes. Firms do not disappear in the story, for it is their individual actions of shareholding, of making and breaking ties, that drive the process. But the whole is more than the sum of the parts. Or, more accurately, simply summing the individual portfolios yields the descriptive statistics of percentages held by this or that type of owner; while aggregating their relational properties yields new orders of phenomena above the constituent units. Restated in the language of Complex Adaptive Systems: *property* has emergent properties. The networks represented in figure 3.2 are not conglomerates or holding companies. They were not built by design, but emerged from the interacting ownership strategies of hundreds of enterprises. As examples of distributed intelligence, these emergent networks display a feature of heterarchy. A Hungarian business network is not a megafirm, it has no single decision-making center, and unlike the Japanese *keiretsu*, it has no distinctive emblem or flag through which affiliate members signal their collective identity. Too extensive to be called a single strategic alliance, it is a complex network of intersecting alliances.

More detailed analysis of the discrete networks indicates that their strategies of portfolio management are distinctive (for details, see Stark, Kemény, and Breiger [1998]). In some networks, structure derives from the role of key banks that own shares in manufacturing enterprises. In others, banks are also prominent, not as owners, but as mutually owned by

---

[17] Adopting a combination of cliquing and block-modeling procedures (for technical details see Stark, Kemény, and Breiger [1998] we use the CONCOR clustering algorithm to identify the business groupings. To plot them, we used KrackPlot (Krackhardt, Lundberg, and O'Rourke 1993), a software program for representing multidimensional scaling. Figure 3.2 presents the relative proximity of the groupings in the space of structural similarity, with the discrete network diagrams portraying the relative proximity of nodes (firms) and lines indicating ties between respective nodes.

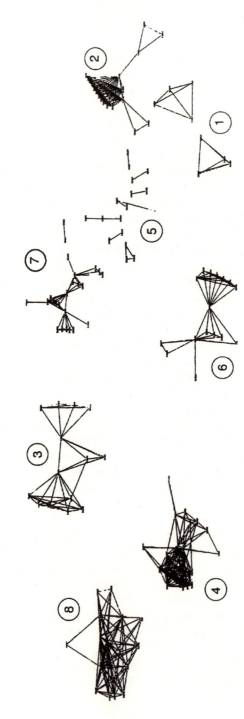

Figure 3.2. The field of Hungarian business groups.

the affiliated enterprises. Some of the networks span branches and sectors. Others group firms in particular sectors. Network 3, for example, contains the major bus, railroad, trucking, and airline firms, linked with three banks and six foreign trade companies; and the elongated configuration of network 7 corresponds to its character as an integrated commodity chain that links firms in petroleum, petrochemicals, chemicals, and pharmaceuticals.

But despite the distinctive shapes of their network properties, all of these major business groupings share an important feature of heterarchies: common to each is a strategy of combining heterogeneous resources. Each business network attempts a strategy of portfolio management that diversifies across the resources (and constraints) which derive from ownership by state agencies as well as from the new resources of multinational enterprises and other foreign investors. None is exclusively public nor predominantly private. Each regroups assets that allow it to operate across the playing field. All are poised to take advantage of continuing subsidies, exemptions from tariff restrictions, and state largesse in forgiving inherited debt, while benefiting from new sources of capital, access to markets, and technology transfers. In the postsocialist context, networked property is recombinant property.

Similarly recombinant strategies take place inside the postsocialist firm. With figure 3.3, we take a closer look at Heavy Metal, one of Hungary's largest metallurgy companies that remains predominantly state-owned. At the same time that it was participating in one of the inter-enterprise business networks shown in figure 3.2, Heavy Metal was spinning off its assets into limited liability companies (*korlátolt felelöségü társaság* or KFT). Limited liability companies are the fastest growing business forms in the Hungarian economy, increasing from 450 at the end of 1988 to 158,000 by the end of 1998. Some of these KFTs are genuinely private ventures. But many, like those shown in figure 3.3, are the corporate satellites of large enterprises. These satellites have more ambiguous property status.

Like Saturn's rings, Heavy Metal's satellites revolve around the giant corporate planet in concentric orbits. Near the center are the core metallurgy units, the hot-rolling mills, and the energy, maintenance, and strategic planning units, held in a kind of geo-synchronous orbit by 100 percent ownership. In the next ring, where the corporate headquarters holds roughly 50 to 99 percent of the shares, are the cold-rolling mills, wire and cable production, oxygen facility, galvanizing and other finishing treatments, specialized castings, quality control, and marketing units. The satellites of the outer ring are in construction, industrial services, computing, ceramics, machining, and similar activities, and are usually of lower levels of capitalization. Relations between the company center and the outer- and middle-ring satellites are marked by the center's recurrent efforts to introduce stricter accounting procedures and tighter financial controls.

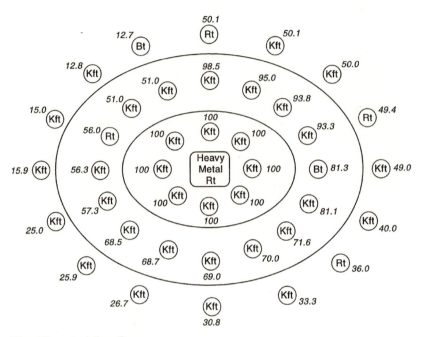

Rt = Shareholding Company
Kft = Limited Liability
Bt = Partnerships
Numerals in italics indicate Heavy Metal's ownership stake in a given satellite.

Figure 3.3. Corporate satellites at Heavy Metal. Source: Stark 1996.

These attempts are countered by the units' efforts to increase their autonomy, coordinated through personal ties and formalized in the biweekly meetings of the "Club of KFT Managing Directors."

These corporate satellites are far from being unambiguously "private" ventures, yet neither are they simply "statist" residues of the socialist past. Property shares in most corporate satellites are not limited to the founding enterprise. Top and mid-level managers, professionals, and other staff can be found on the lists of founding partners and current owners. Such private persons rarely acquire complete ownership of the corporate satellite, preferring to use their insider knowledge to exploit the ambiguities of institutional co-ownership. The corporate satellites are thus partially a result of the hedging and risk-sharing strategies of individual managers. We might ask why a given manager would not want to acquire 100 percent ownership in order to obtain all of the profit, but from the perspective of a given

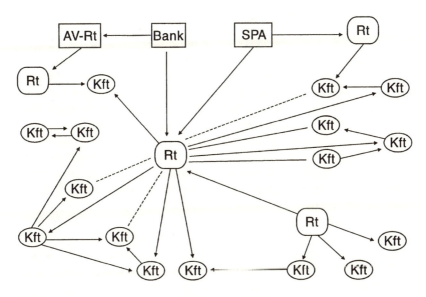

Figure 3.4. A Hungarian recombinet. Source: Stark 1996.

manager the calculus instead is "Why acquire 100 percent of the risk if some can be shared with the corporate center?" With ambiguous interests and divided loyalties, these risk-sharing owner/managers are organizationally hedging.

In some cases, ownership stakes of the corporate satellites include ties to and from other large enterprises and the limited liability companies spinning around them. As figure 3.4 illustrates for one such restructuring network, the resulting property form finds horizontal ties of cross-ownership intertwined with vertical ties of nested holdings.

Here we see that the limited liability companies that began as corporate spin-offs are oriented through ownership ties either to more than one shareholding company and/or to other limited liability companies. In these restructuring networks, actors recognize the network properties of their interdependent assets and regroup them across formal organizational boundaries. Such network restructuring thus opens the possibilities of increasing the value of existing assets through their recombination. This regrouping does not necessarily imply bringing interdependent assets under the common ownership umbrella of a hierarchically organized enterprise. Hungarian recombinant property thus provides examples of intercorporate networks that are alternatives to a dichotomously forced choice between markets and hierarchies.

RISK-SPREADING AND RISK-TAKING

These inter-enterprise networks are an important means of spreading risk in an uncertain environment. Firms in the postsocialist transformational crisis are like mountain climbers assaulting a treacherous face, and interorganizational networks are the safety ropes lashing them together. Such risk-spreading, moreover, can be a basis for risk-taking. Extraordinarily high uncertainties of the kind we see now in the postsocialist economies can lead to low levels of investment with perverse strategic complementarities (as when firms forgo investments because they expect a sluggish economy based on the lack of investments by others). By mitigating disinclination to invest, risk-spreading within affiliative networks might be one means to break out of otherwise low-level equilibrium traps.

This relationship between risk-spreading and risk-taking suggests that it would be premature in the postsocialist context to impose a rigid dichotomy between strategies of survival and strategies of innovation. Above all, we should not assume that firms will necessarily innovate even when survival seems to demand it, as if necessity in itself creates the conditions for innovation. Recent studies (Miner, Amburgey, and Stearns 1990; Grabher and Stark 1997) provide strong theoretical arguments that firms are more likely to undertake the risky business of innovation (exposing themselves to the "liabilities of newness" by engaging in unfamiliar routines), not when they are pushed to the wall, but when they are buffered from the immediate effects of selection mechanisms. They further demonstrate that interorganizational networks provide this buffering by producing the requisite organizational slack through which enterprises can find the available resources that make it possible to innovate. Thus, these studies suggest circumstances in which the simple imperative "Innovate in order to survive" is reasonably reversed: "Survive in order to innovate."

These insights have been independently confirmed in a recent study by Ickes, Ryterman, and Tenev (1995) who demonstrate, on the basis of rich survey data on Russian firms, that enterprises that are linked in inter-enterprise networks are more likely to engage in various forms of economic restructuring than similar firms that are not so linked. This finding, moreover, is robust: purely private enterprises are not more likely to undertake restructuring than firms in state ownership, or mixed property arrangements embedded in inter-enterprise networks. A related study on innovation in the Hungarian economy (Tamás 1993) found that firms with the organizational hedging strategy of "mixed" (public and private) ownership were more likely than purely private or purely state-owned firms to have innovated by introducing new technologies or bringing out new products. In short, when we abandon the forced dichotomy of survival *versus* innovation, we can see that there are circumstances in which survival strategies can be the prelude to strategies of innovation.

RECOMBINANT PRACTICES IN THE CZECH REPUBLIC

Postsocialist recombinant property is not a peculiarly Hungarian phenomenon. In Russia, a decree by President Boris Yeltsin in December 1993 authorized the creation of Financial-Industrial Groups (FIGs) involving the merger of the capital bases of enterprises and financial institutions (both state and private). Ratified by a law passed by the Russian Parliament in October 1995, officially registered FIGs are eligible for special state investment credits, loan guarantees, and favorable regulations such as accelerated depreciation of their assets. At the beginning of 1996 there were already 30 officially registered FIGs, containing over 274 member companies, including 69 financial institutions. By October 1999, their numbers had grown to 87, comprising over 2000 organizations and employing more than 4 million workers (Buck 1999). Meanwhile the number of unregistered, or unofficial, FIGs has soared into the hundreds (Kim 2000). Whereas large manufacturing firms typically occupy a central place in the FIGs and their assets are correspondingly specific to a particular industrial sector or branch (e.g., metallurgy), FIGs exhibit the predominance of financial over industrial capital and are frequently characterized by highly diversified assets. Large Russian banks have been purchasing shares in manufacturing firms since 1992, but more recently the unofficial FIGs have benefited from equity transfers of formerly state-owned assets through "loans-for-shares" privatization in which the state has auctioned majority stakes of voting stock of strategic enterprises in exchange for FIG-sponsored credits to the Russian government (Johnson 1997). The unofficial FIGs thus acquired strategic assets through closed auctions at a fraction of their market value.[18]

Recombinant property is also a prominent feature of the postsocialist Czech economy—perhaps surprisingly given that the initial ideology of its leading policymakers appeared so antithetical to recombinant strategies. The original vision of Vaclav Klaus (Finance Minister of postsocialist Czechoslovakia and later, after the "Velvet Divorce," Prime Minister of the Czech Republic) was determinedly neoliberal. As a central component of his strategy, a speedy if unorthodox privatization scheme would separate property from the state, from other stakeholders, and from any considerations other than caring for profitability. One of the goals of the privatiza-

---

[18] In Poland, Industrial Holdings (Dornisch 1997) are a further postsocialist example of megacorporate groupings that blur the boundaries of firms and the boundaries of public and private.

tion program was to create sovereign owners with clear property boundaries thereby avoiding the kinds of mixed property forms and blurred organizational boundaries so characteristic of the Hungarian experience. The much-vaunted voucher privatization scheme (in which state-owned enterprises were put on "auction" for "investment points" held by citizens) was to be the means to this end.

By transferring assets of the state enterprises through a voucher-auction, the Czech policymakers appeared to favor a kind of popular capitalism with millions of citizen investors and a clear separation of public and private property. Until just a few months before the first wave of computerized auctions, however, only several hundred thousand citizens had entered the privatization lottery by paying 1000 crowns (about $35) to register the investment points of their voucher coupon books. The problem of low participation was solved when "investment funds" (an afterthought in the initial program) began to promise citizens who signed over their investment points a 1,000 percent return, payable a year and a day following the transfer of their points into shares. The response from Czechs and Slovaks was conditiotned by years of socialism: Averse to risk, they were unwilling to play the investors' game, but they could recognize a guaranteed income when they saw it. Millions signed up.

The consequence of the voucher privatization was not to make popular capitalism but to make Vaclav Klaus popular.[19] Klaus was named Prime Minister following an election held just weeks after millions had registered their investment points by signing their names next to his signature (as Finance Minister) on their voucher coupon booklets. The outcome, moreover, has not been a people's capitalism but a peculiar kind of finance capitalism. During the first wave of privatization, only 28.1 percent of investible points were held by individual citizen investors; 71.9 percent were held by the 429 Investment Privatization Funds (IPFs). When we aggregate the voucher points obtained by the multiple IPFs founded by the same investment company, we find that 48.5 percent of all available voucher points in the first wave were held by the nine largest investment firms. That is, almost half of all the investment points were held by less than ten investment companies.[20] This concentration of investment points, moreover, still understates the predominant position of the largest investment companies because individual voucher holders are almost never repre-

---

[19] The evolution of Klaus's politics from neoliberal ideologue to a "programmatic pragmatist" is described in detail in Stark and Bruszt (1998, ch. 7). That account focuses not on the personality of the Czech Prime Minister but on the institutional constraints that moderated and pragmatized his policies.

[20] PlanEcon Inc., "Results of Czechoslovak Voucher Privatization," PlanEcon Report, vol. VIII, December 1992, pp. 8–9.

sented (and the smaller IPFs are underrepresented) on the boards of directors of the "privatized enterprises," where board seats are typically distributed to the largest blockholders.[21]

In this Czech finance capitalism, voucher privatization did not sever ties between state and economic institutions, it reorganized them. The investment companies are not unambiguously private: the founders of six of the nine largest funds are predominantly state-owned financial institutions (banks and insurance companies).[22] For example, four of the five largest investment companies were founded by the largest banks—institutions in which the National Property Fund holds the controlling interest (44 percent of Komercni Banka, 45% of Vseobecn Uverova Banka, 45 percent of Investicni Bank, and 40 percent of Ceska Sporitelna). The same Fund, moreover, still owns about 20 percent of the book value of the "privatized" companies and directly holds seats on the boards of many enterprises. Meanwhile, the Ministry of Finance controls the Konsolidacni Banka, which is the major creditor of 80 percent of all medium and large firms in the Czech Republic.

Most importantly, as we see in figure 3.5, banks and investment funds are cross-owned and the investment companies are interlocked in networks of related holdings. That is, investment companies, founded by the major banks, in turn acquired shares of the banks through the voucher privatization. As John Coffee (1996) documents, sizeable stakes in the major commercial, investment, and savings banks were acquired by investment funds established by the major financial institutions.[23] In the typical case, a large investment fund holds shares in its sponsoring financial institution[24] as well as in one or more of the other major banks. In addition to their ties through their co-ownership of the banks, Czech investment funds are also linked to each other through their enterprise holdings. Regulations of the voucher-auction prohibiting an investment fund from acquiring more than 20 percent of a given enterprise virtually insured that the typical firm becomes a node at which investment funds intersect. Thus, one of the most important outcomes of voucher "privatization" is that the largest investment funds and the largest banks are crisscrossed by ties of interorganizational ownership.

[21] Brom and Orenstein (1994) estimate that the thirteen largest investment companies hold about seventy-five percent of the board seats won in the first wave of voucher privatization.

[22] Of the remaining three, two were founded by foreign (German and Austrian) banks. The third is the largest "independent" investment company, Harvard Capital and Consulting.

[23] Coffee (1996) also presents a thorough and lucid discussion of the major issues of corporate governance in the Czech investment funds.

[24] By creating subsidiary funds, investment companies easily circumvented the loose regulations that technically prohibited an investment fund from acquiring shares in the bank that founded it.

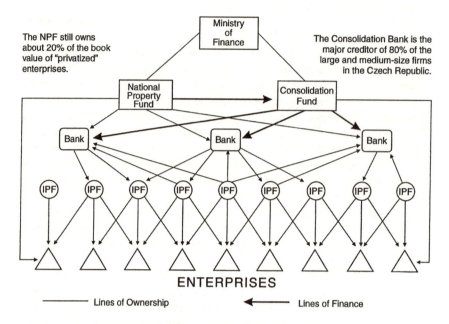

The NPF still owns about 20% of the book value of "privatized" enterprises.

The Consolidation Bank is the major creditor of 80% of the large and medium-size firms in the Czech Republic.

ENTERPRISES

———— Lines of Ownership   ◀——— Lines of Finance

Figure 3.5. Networks of ownership and finance in the Czech Republic.

INTERORGANIZATIONAL NETWORKS COMPARED

Are the Hungarian inter-enterprise ownership networks the East European counterparts of Taiwanese "related enterprises"? Are the cross-owning banks/investment companies Czech versions of the Korean *chaebol*? These questions suggest a comparative study of corporate groupings in modern economies. The more proximate question for this investigation of the postsocialist firm is to ask: How do the network properties of the Hungarian and Czech cases differ?

In both economies we find dense and extensive networks of interorganizational ownership. But the shape and patterns of these networks are distinctive in each economy, and consequently, the structure of corporate groupings are likely to differ. My analysis indicates that Hungarian networks are formed predominantly through enterprise-to-enterprise links, sometimes involving banks yet lacking ties between banks and intermediate-level institutions such as investment companies. The Czech case is the mirrored opposite. There, ownership networks are formed predominantly through ties at the meso-level among banks and investment funds, but direct ownership connections among enterprises themselves are rare. Restated in the language of network analysis; whereas Hungarian networks are tightly coupled at the level of enterprises but loosely coupled at the meso-level, Czech networks are loosely coupled at the level of enterprises and tightly coupled at the meso-level.

The distinctive patterns of the Czech and Hungarian ownership networks bear the marks of their respective societies prior to 1989 and of their differing pathways from state socialism. Each configuration has been directly shaped by different policies of property transformation (Stark and Bruszt 1998, ch. 3). But these economic strategies were not dictated or imposed upon the blank features of a postsocialist institutional vacuum. Instead, they interacted with the strategies of actors within each economy who possessed distinctive organizational resources and who were well practiced in different repertoires of action, themselves shaped by the distinctive character of the actors' preexisting network ties.

Through partial economic reforms in Hungary during the 1970s and '80s, enterprises were already gaining considerable autonomy, enjoying greater flexibility in choosing other enterprises as supply partners, and constructing networks of small-scale proto-entrepreneurial producers at (and even within) the boundaries of the firm. Moreover, legislation facilitating property transformation was already in place before the system change of 1989 and the installation of the first democratically elected government in May 1990. As a consequence, Hungarian firms already had direct enterprise-to-enterprise contacts and a legal framework in which these horizontal ties could be transformed into the inter-enterprise ownership networks of the present.

Czech enterprises, of course, had not enjoyed such autonomy under state socialism. But they were not without their own network resources in their ongoing conflicts with the industrial ministries of the old regime. The difference, compared to Hungary, was that these networks operated not through direct enterprise-to-enterprise ties but at a meso-level through "Industrial Associations" organized within industrial branches (e.g., metallurgy, chemicals, machining) or along regional lines. So resilient were these meso-level associations that they survived or resurfaced after several attempts at their elimination by the communist authorities (McDermott 1997). It is at this similarly meso-level, as opposed to direct enterprise-to-enterprise ties, that the networks of cross-ownership are most dense in the contemporary Czech economy.

In both cases, property relations are being transformed—but *within structures whose network features exhibit continuity even as their ownership content is altered.* In neither case is property transformation a simple transition from public to private. In both, it results in the blurring of the properties of public and private. And in both, we find strategies of recombinant property in which actors diversify their portfolios of heterogeneous assets and trespass organizational boundaries in attempts to maneuver through situations where organizational survival is fragile, not simply because of market uncertainties but also because the criteria of success, the measures of worth, and the selection mechanisms are themselves uncertain.

ACCOUNTS

In the highly uncertain organizational environment that is the postsocialist economy, relatively few actors (apart from institutional designers such as IMF advisors or local policymakers in Finance Ministries) set out with the aim to create a market economy. Many, indeed would welcome such an outcome, but their immediate goals have been more pragmatic: at best to thrive, at least to survive. And so they strive to use whatever resources are available. As they do so, they maneuver not only through an ecology of organizations but also through a complex ecology of ordering principles.

To analyze this process, I exploit a notion of accounts. Etymologically rich, the term simultaneously connotes bookkeeping and narration. Both dimensions entail evaluative judgments, and each implies the other: Accountants prepare story lines according to established formulae, and in the accountings of a good storyteller we know what counts. In everyday life, we are all bookkeepers and storytellers. We keep accounts and we give accounts, and most importantly, we can be called to account for our actions. It is always within accounts that we "size up the situation," for not every form of worth[25] can be made to apply and not every asset is in a form appropriate for a given situation. We evaluate the situation by maneuvering to use scales that measure some types of worth and not others, thereby acting to validate some accounts and discredit others (Boltanski and Thévenot 1991).

The multiple accounts voiced in Hungarian heterarchies respond to and exploit the fundamental, though diffused, uncertainty about the organizational environment. In transforming economies, firms have to worry not simply about whether there is demand for their products, or about the rate of return on their investment, or about the level of profitability, but also about the very principle of selection itself. Thus, the question is not only "Will I survive the market test?" but also, under what conditions is proof of worth on market principles neither sufficient nor necessary to survive?

---

[25] Issues of worth and justification raise important questions for the new economic sociology. Recall that the maturation of sociology was struck in an institutionalized bargain with economics separating their disciplinary objects of study (Camic 1989). The bargain can best be paraphrased as follows: "You, the economists, study value; we sociologists will study values. Acknowledging your jurisdiction in the analysis of the economy, we study the social relations in which economies are embedded." But economic sociologists are no longer bound by that bargain. Rejecting that division of labor opens the possibilities for a sociology of worth. See Stark (1990; 2000).

Because there are multiply operative, mutually coexistent principles of justification according to which you may be called on to give accounts of your actions, you cannot be sure what counts. By what proof and according to which principles of justification are you worthy to steward a given set of resources? Because of this uncertainty, actors will seek to diversify their assets: to hold resources in multiple accounts.

This ability to glide among principles and to produce multiple accountings is an organizational hedging. It differs, however, from the kind of hedging to minimize risk exposure that we would find within a purely market logic as, for example, when the shopkeeper who sells swimwear and sun lotion also devotes some floor space to umbrellas. Instead of acting within a single regime of evaluation, this is organizational hedging that crosses and combines disparate evaluative principles. Recombinant property is a particular kind of portfolio management. It is an attempt to have a resource that can be justified or assessed by more than one standard of measure (as, for example, the rabbit breeder whose roadside stand advertises "Pets and Meat" in the documentary film, *Roger and Me*). In managing one's portfolio of justifications, one starts from the axiom: diversify your accounts.

The adroit recombinant agent in the transforming economies of East Central Europe diversifies holdings in response to fundamental uncertainties about what can constitute a resource. Under conditions not simply of market uncertainty but of organizational uncertainty, there can be multiple (and intertwined) strategies for survival, based in some cases on profitability but in others on eligibility. Your success is judged—and your access to resources determined—sometimes by your market share and sometimes by the number of workers you employ in a region, sometimes by your price-earnings ratio and sometimes by your "strategic importance." And, when even the absolute size of your losses can be transformed into an asset yielding an income stream, you might be wise to diversify your portfolio, to be able to shift your accounts, to be equally skilled in applying for loans as in applying for job creation subsidies, to have a multilingual command of the grammar of credit-worthiness and the syntax of debt forgiveness. To hold recombinant property is to have such a diversified portfolio.

To gain room for maneuver, actors court and even create ambiguity. They measure in multiple units, they speak in many tongues. In so doing, they produce the heterarchical discourse of worth that is postsocialism. We can hear that polyphonic chorus in the diverse ways that Hungarian firms have justified their claims for participation in a debt-relief program established by the government after its earlier programs had precipitated a near-collapse of the financial system.[26] The following litany of justifications are

[26] Those policies are described in Stark (1996). The following chorus is drawn from the same article.

stylized versions of claims encountered in discussions with bankers, property agency officials, and enterprise directors:

- Our firm should be included in the debt-relief program because we will forgive our debtors.[27]
- Our firm should be included in the debt-relief program because we are truly creditworthy.[28]
- Because we employ thousands.
- Because our suppliers depend on us for a market.
- Because we are in your election district.
- Because our customers depend on our product inputs.
- Because we can then be privatized.
- Because we can never be privatized.
- Because we took big risks.
- Because we were prudent and did not take risks.
- Because we were subject to planning in the past.
- Because we have a plan for the future.
- Because we export to the West.
- Because we export to the East.
- Because our product has been awarded an International Standards Quality Control Certificate.
- Because our product is part of the Hungarian national heritage.
- Because we are an employee buy-out.
- Because we are a management buy-in.
- Because we are partly state-owned.
- Because we are partly privately held.
- Because our creditors drove us into bankruptcy when they loaned to us at higher-than-market rates to artificially raise bank profits in order to pay dividends into a state treasury whose coffers had dwindled when corporations like ourselves effectively stopped paying taxes.

And so we must ask, into whose account and by which account will debt forgiveness flow? Or, in such a situation, is anyone accountable?

Accountability

When they attempt to hold resources that can be justified by more than one legitimating principle, actors within heterarchies make assets of ambiguity. It is this ambiguity, together with the network properties that underlie it, that forms the basis for the kind of strategic play that Padgett and

---

[27] I.e., our firm occupies a strategic place in a network of inter-enterprise debt.

[28] I.e., if our liabilities are separated from our assets, we will again be eligible for more bank financing. Similar translations could be provided for each of the following justifications.

Ansell (1993) label "robust action." At the core of robust action is the fact "that single actions can be interpreted coherently from multiple perspectives simultaneously, the fact that single actions can be moves in many games at once, and the fact that public and private motivations cannot be parsed" (p. 1263).[29] The outcome is flexible opportunism, that is, maintaining discretionary options across unforeseeable futures in the face of hostile attempts by others to narrow those options.[30] Actors within heterarchies are doubly bound: bound in their associative ties, and bound to speak in multiple tongues. But this peculiar "double bind" produces not an organizational schizophrenia but an organizational flexibility.[31]

Is this acute flexibility an unmixed blessing? I think not. In this I depart from the now-standard formula in which the economic sociologist enumerates the problems created by markets, recounts the problems created by hierarchy, and then delineates the problems resolved by the new organizational forms (hybrids, networks, flexible specializations, etc.). But as the best practitioners are already recognizing, the new organizational forms also create new problems. The same opportunistic blurring of boundaries that leads to a recombination of assets and a decomposition and reintegration of organizations also bears a social cost: it erodes (or, in the postsocialist case, retards) accountability. The problem with the peculiarly diversified portfolios of the new heterarchies is that actors can all too often easily and almost imperceptibly switch among the various positions they hold simultaneously in the coexisting moral economies. To be accountable according to many different principles becomes a means to be accountable to none.

Heterarchies (hybrids, networks) pose a new set of conceptual problems for legal theory. Whereas organizational analysis (from different disciplinary and theoretical perspectives) now recognizes a new type of economic

[29] Teubner (1996, 62–3) adopts different language to the same effect: "What networks gain through double attribution is a drastic improvement of their environmental situation. One and the same configuration can appear in one environment as a multitude of individual actors connected by contracts and in a different environment as one collective actor, an autonomous player in a different game. This chameleon-like quality of networks gives them access to new environments which would not be accessible to them if they were either a mere nexus or a mere collective actor. . . . Indeed, in their hybrid character, networks seem to be tailored to the bridging of different contradictory rationalities."

[30] Crucial for maintaining discretion is not to pursue any specific goals: "For in nasty strategic games . . . positional play is the maneuvering of opponents into the forced clarification of their (but not your) tactical lines of action" (Padgett and Ansell 1993, 1265). Victory, hence, means locking in others, but not yourself, to goal-oriented sequences of strategic play that thereby become predictable.

[31] "Under certain conditions, hybrid arrangements can provide for an institutional environment where paradoxical communication is not repressed, not only tolerated, but invited, institutionally facilitated and turned productive" (Teubner 1996, 59).

agent, legal theory (with its construct of the legal personality limited to the individual and the corporation) does not yet recognize the new economic actor as a new moral agent.[32] Unless we are willing to posit "flexibility" as an overriding value and a meta-legitimating principle, we cannot escape the challenge that postsocialism poses, not uniquely but acutely, for our epoch: if heterarchies are viable economic agents of permanently ongoing restructuring, how can we make them accountable?

CONCLUSION

Several years after I bought the tin can described at the beginning of this chapter, a friend in Budapest told me about a board game he had played as a child during the socialist period. Prior to World War II, Hungarians had played Monopoly, known there as *Kapitaly*. But the competitive game of capitalism was banned by communist authorities, who substituted another board game, *Gazdálkodj Okosan!*, or "Economize Wisely!" In this goulash communist version of political correctness, the goal was to get a job, open a savings account, and acquire and furnish an apartment. My friend was too young to have a *Kapitaly* board, but his older cousins from another part of the country knew the banned game and taught him the basic rules. You did not need to be a nine-year-old dissident to see that Monopoly was the more exciting game. And so they turned over the socialist board game, drew out the *Kapitaly* playing field from Start to Boardwalk on the reverse side, and began to play Monopoly—using the cards and pieces from Economize Wisely. But with the details of the rules unclear and with the memories of the older cousins fading, the bricolage game developed its own dynamics, stimulated by the cards and pieces from the "other side." Why, for example, be satisfied with simple houses and hotels when you could have furniture as well? And under what configurations of play would a Prize of Socialist Labor be grounds for releasing you from or sending you to Jail?[33]

The notion of playing capitalism with communist pieces strikes me as an apt metaphor for the postsocialist condition.[34] The political upheavals

[32] On the conceptual problems for legal theory of recognizing networks as new moral actors, see the insightful work of Teubner (1991), Hutter and Teubner (1993), and Buxbaum (1993).

[33] The story itself was related while we watched my children playing their own hybrid version: having left the houses and hotels of their Monopoly set at a friend's house, they had started to use Lego building blocks (much preferred to the Monopoly pieces even after returned) to construct ever-more elaborate structures in a game whose rules evolved away from bankrupting one's opponents and toward attracting customers to the plastic skyscrapers that towered over the Monopoly plain.

[34] In East Central Europe (and especially Hungary), proximity to West European markets, more familiarity with democratic institutions, prior experience with market culture (a subtext

of 1989 in Eastern Europe and 1991 in Russia turned the world upside down. Misled by an *apparent tabula* rasa, the IMF and Western advisors issued instructions for the new "rules of the game," but it was played with the institutional remnants of the past that, by limiting some moves and facilitating other strategies, gave rise to multiple systems of accounting. Firms responded to these uncertainties by exploiting the uncertainties. The results are, as we saw, the networks linking statist institutions and "privatized" firms in the Czech Republic and the multiple legitimating claims in the polyphonic chorus of Hungarian debt forgiveness.

But, if our Hungarian chorus sounds strange and exotic, it should be so only upon first encounter. For, although that litany expresses multiple accounting principles in an especially acute form, the notion of coexisting evaluative frameworks is far from foreign in the highly uncertain environments of advanced sectors in the West. If the successful Hungarian manager must be as skilled in the language of debt forgiveness as in the language of negotiating with a prospective multinational partner, the CEO of a startup firm in biotechnology might well survive only if she is as adept in writing grant proposals to federal agencies as she is in making the pitch to prospective venture capitalists. We need not travel to Eastern Europe to encounter difficulties in assessing the value of firms, when stories of the difficulties of evaluating Internet stocks fill the front pages of our newspapers. We are not strangers to the problems of parsing public and private, for we need look no further than the complex proprietary arrangements between private firms and public universities in the fields of computer science, biotechnology, new media, and engineering. And the search for a mutually comprehensible language across the cultures of science, politics, and business in the human genome project offers no less acute problems of public and private accountability.

To write of "problems" is not to denounce the creative organizational solutions that are evolving in all of the areas mentioned above. On the contrary, it calls attention to the fact that the most sophisticated, dynamic, and path-breaking sectors are likely to be arenas where public and private are closely intertwined.

Complexity, in the field of organizations, is the interweaving of diverse evaluative principles. These principles can be those of public and private accountings, but they can also be the diverse worldviews of different professional identities, each with its own distinctive ways of measuring value

---

of my friend's story), and much higher levels of direct foreign investment have operated to channel the recombinant strategies along recognizably capitalist, though distinctively East European, lines. More challenging, politically and analytically, are developments in the former Soviet Union, where some of the pieces from the communist past are the firearms of the now criminalized parts of these economies, which are very far from child's play.

and selecting what counts. The assets of the firm are adaptively increased when there are multiple measures of what constitutes an asset. Value is amplified precisely because values are not shared. The heterarchical organization of diversity is sometimes discordant. But to still that noisy clash by the ascendancy of only one accounting would be to destroy the diversity of organizing principles that is the basis of adaptability.

CHAPTER 4

Japanese Enterprise Faces the Twenty-First Century

D. Eleanor Westney

IF THIS CHAPTER had been written in 1990, the temptation to portray the Japanese industrial enterprise as the firm of the twenty-first century would have been overwhelming. Management consultants, the popular press, and even a number of organizational sociologists looked at the Japanese manufacturing firm and saw the lean, flat, flexible, high-commitment, networked firm of the future. Japan's distinctive model had been further legitimated by its successful weathering of a series of external shocks (the two oil crises of the 1970s, the dramatic increase in the value of the yen in the mid-1980s, growing import restrictions in its major markets) that many critics of "Japanese-style management," domestic as well as foreign, had confidently asserted would shake the system to its foundations. Instead, it seemed to emerge stronger from each crisis. The discomfiture of the critics was reinforced by the fact that Japanese auto firms—exemplars of Japanese-style management—were convincingly demonstrating throughout the 1980s that key elements of the Japanese production system could be transferred to plants in North America and Europe. By the late 1980s, there was a note of triumphalism in much of the writing of Japanese management experts, many of whom believed that the Japanese business system had emerged as the prototype for the next stage in advanced industrial societies. Indeed, in the entire postwar period, Japan provided the only model of the business enterprise to offer a sustained challenge to the normative power of U.S. models of the firm.

But in the early 1990s, Japan's economy plunged into a recession that persisted for the rest of the decade and shows signs of continuing well into the twenty-first century. Just as the sustained Japanese economic growth of the 1980s had validated its distinctive business system, so the apparently intractable Japanese recession of the 1990s (a time when the U.S. economy was rebounding vigorously) eroded the legitimacy of the Japanese enterprise as the primary challenger to American shareholder capitalism. But another factor was the widespread perception that many of the most effective elements of its management systems had already been adopted and adapted by leading U.S. firms, in the restructuring of American industrial enterprise in the late 1980s and 1990s. In other words, the model of the

Japanese enterprise had already set its mark on the emerging model of the twenty-first century, less in its own right than through the influence it had already exerted on firms in the United States.

The Japanese enterprise model fell out of favor as abruptly in Japan in the 1990s as it did in the United States. In Japanese bookstores, the volumes extolling the triumphs of leading Japanese companies gave way by the mid-1990s to books on U.S. modes of reengineering, restructuring, and entrepreneurship, and on the crises faced by various Japanese companies (Matsuura 1994; Sakaguchi 1994). The belief at the beginning of the decade that Japanese companies were already the firms of the twenty-first century quickly shifted to a widespread conviction that they were not even up to coping with the challenges of the 1990s, let alone the future. Ironically, the most powerful model for Japanese enterprises today is the resurgent American firm, as Japan's managers are being urged by consultants, the business press, and many academics (particularly economists) to seize on some of the features of United States business most strongly attacked by the advocates of Japanese-style management in the 1980s: a focus on profits, returns on investment, and shareholder interests; increasing differentiation of rewards across employees, with stock options for managers; and aggressive shedding of workers, middle-managers, and even entire lines of business.

What features of Japan's business system made its firms appear, however briefly, to be harbingers of the future? What explains its fall from challenger to United States models of the firm back to pupil? And what, if anything, does the Japanese firm tell us about the evolution of the firm of the future?

Constructing Models of Japanese Enterprise

There has been, of course, no single model of the Japanese firm. In the four decades since the appearance of the first major study of the distinctive features of Japan's business enterprises (Abegglen 1958), Japan's companies have been the focus of more continuous and more extensive academic analysis than those of any single nation beyond the United States. Over the course of these years, the portrayals of the Japanese firm have shifted ground, as social science paradigms have risen and fallen and as the Japanese business system has itself changed. One of the principal tools of inquiry has been consistent over the years, however: the construction of ideal types, in the Weberian sense of models that capture the key features of a phenomenon or set of phenomena. There are two distinct variants of these ideal types. One focuses on identifying what makes the Japanese phenomenon distinctive, and is usually developed in the context of anti-convergence arguments in the social sciences (until the 1970s, largely in terms of modernization theory, and from the 1980s on, in terms of comparative capitalism). The other focuses on what has made Japan competitively successful and on what can be learned from Japan, and tends to have been developed primarily in the context of business and management. The first begins with the question, "What makes Japan different?" and often builds on the implicit assumption that what makes Japan different is inimitable as well as distinctive. The second asks the question, "What makes Japan successful?" and usually assumes that the answers have normative implications for business enterprises in any environment, particularly in environments where Japanese firms are significant competitors.

Both questions have been asked at three levels of analysis: the Japanese factory, the Japanese enterprise, and the larger system of interorganizational networks that link enterprises with each other and with organizations in other institutional sectors, particularly the state. Each has contributed significantly to the prevailing models of "Japanese-style management". At the level of the factory, one model—the Japanese employment system—has been primarily descriptive, and another—the Japanese production system—has been strongly normative. At the level of the enterprise, the model of Japanese corporate governance has been portrayed as a distinctively Japanese approach to corporate control, but another model—the vertical *keiretsu*—has been widely held up for emulation, especially in the United States. At the level of the system as a whole, the horizontal networks of Japan's six multi-industry business groups have been seen in the United States as somewhat anomalous products of Japan's economic history, although they have provoked interest from business leaders and policymakers in countries as diverse as Korea and France, as a possible model for the evolution of diversified business groups (like the *chaebol*) and of state-owned enterprises. On the other hand, the cooperative networks linking competing firms in Japan and connecting business and the state have been the subject of intense debate, both over the content of the model and over its normative implications for other societies. This chapter discusses each of these models in turn, and then considers the implications for the firm of the future.

LEVEL ONE: THE FACTORY

Japan's distinctiveness as the first non-Western society to develop an industrial base and achieve high levels of economic growth has drawn scholars, Western and Japanese alike, to investigate how the organization of work and of the economy in Japan resembles or differs from that in the first-comers to industrialization and in the other early followers, such as Germany (Landes 1965; Bendix 1967), and to ponder the likely trajectory of change (convergence with first-comer patterns or continuing distinctiveness). In modernization theory, which dominated comparative social science research in the 1950s and 1960s, the factory was seen as both a crucially important locus of modernization and a major vehicle for social change (Levy 1966; Inkeles and Smith 1974). Not surprisingly, therefore, the Japanese factory provided the first venue for developing a "Japanese model" for serious consideration by Western social scientists and managers.

The Japanese Employment System

The distinctive features of the social organization of Japanese factories were first brought to the attention of Western and Japanese social scientists in 1958, with the publication of James Abegglen's now classic study, *The Japanese Factory*. Abegglen explicitly challenged the then-dominant "convergence" assumption of modernization theory, which stated that the processes of industrialization would have much the same social effects in all societies (Abegglen 1958, 1–10). His study of 53 Japanese factories (19 large and 34 small establishments) identified the employment system as the core feature of Japanese industrial organization. In Abegglen's own words,

> [In the comparison of] the social organization of the factory in Japan and the United States, one difference is immediately noted and continues to dominate and represent much of the total difference between the two systems. At whatever level of organization in the Japanese factory, the worker commits himself on entrance to the company for the remainder of his working career. The company will not discharge him even temporarily except in the most extreme conditions. . . . The permanent relationship between employee and firm imposes obligations and responsibilities on both the factory and the worker of a different order than that on which personnel practices and worker-company relationships in the United States are built. (p. 11)

Abegglen's identification of the employment system as the key distinguishing feature of the social organization of Japanese factories shaped the analysis of industrial organization in Japan for over two decades. Subsequent studies elaborated considerably the model of the Japanese employment system as it developed in the high-growth era (1952–73), most notably Ronald Dore's 1973 *British Factory Japanese Factory*, whose rich and systematic comparative study of two Japanese and two British factories remains the touchstone for analysis to this day.[1] This book was also one of the very few

---

[1] See, for example, Shinji Sugayama's, "Work Rules, Wages, and Single Status: The Shaping of the 'Japanese Employment System' " (1995), which begins by invoking Dore ("Ronald Dore's study *British Factory Japanese Factory* [1973] remains a suggestive starting point for considering the evolution of employment relations in Japan"), and ends a historical analysis of the evolution of the employment system at Hitachi with the observation that by 1954, the employment system observed by Dore in the late 1960s was in place.

works on Japan to appear widely on social science reading lists before the 1980s (Abegglen's being another).

The model of the Japanese employment system, as defined by the mid-1970s, included the following key features:

- an employment system that recruited managerial, white-collar, and blue-collar workers directly upon school graduation, after careful screening, and provided all three categories of employees with an implicit assurance of employment security;
- the minimization of differences across blue-and white-collar workers, embodied in seniority-based reward structures, extensive training both on and off the job, and bonuses based on company performance for all categories of permanent employees;
- a cooperative and densely interactive industrial relations system characterized by the system of enterprise-based unions and annual wage negotiations;
- managerial ideologies that defined the enterprise as a community and accepted the employees' stake in the company, a stance that entailed a commitment to maintaining employment and acknowledged, at least in rhetoric, the enterprise's obligations to the larger society as well as to its employees.

It is worth emphasizing that the analysis of the Japanese employment system has focused on blue-collar workers. After all, in most large U.S. enterprises of the era, managerial employees enjoyed a de facto presumption of permanent employment. What was distinctive about the large Japanese enterprise was that the systems largely reserved in the West for managerial employees—employment security, a regular salary structure, training and advancement opportunities, etc.—were extended to production workers in the large companies (Lazonick 1991).

Over the years, both Western and Japanese scholars have argued about whether "the Japanese employment system" is an appropriate label, given that the system covered only male workers in large industrial firms and in the public sector (most estimates put this at between 20 and 30 percent of the total labor force). But it became increasingly clear that whether or not it provided an accurate empirical portrait of the organization of Japan's labor force as a whole, it was a powerful normative model in the Japanese business system, one toward which enterprises moved as they grew in scale (Clark 1979).

The fiercest debates, however, were waged over its origins. For Abegglen, the employment system was, in his words, "a consistent and logical outgrowth of the kinds of relations existing in Japan prior to its industrialization" (1958, 130). But although this was a plausible explanation, and one clearly believed and repeated by Abegglen's informants in the mid-1950s, labor historians found that the Japanese employment system was largely a postwar development, not a legacy from the early stages of industrialization when preindustrial patterns were most strongly entrenched. Most labor historians emphasized the role of labor unions and activists in demanding both employment security and the elimination of symbolic and real differentiation between white collar and blue collar workers as the price of stable industrial relations (Gordon 1985, 1993, 1998; Sugayama 1995). Economists, in contrast, tended to attribute the system's emergence and consolidation to "rational adaptation" to emergent conditions of high growth and scarce skills, which gave employers an incentive to train and try to retain skilled workers at all levels of the company: take, for example, the assertion of Imai and Komiya (1994, 23):

> The fundamental reason for the organizational success of Japanese firms may be considered to be that, at least in the postwar economic and social environment, the systems of lifetime employment and seniority payment and advancement have a greater economic rationality than alternative organizational and employment mechanisms.

Institutionalists from various disciplines argued that Abegglen's original attribution of the system to continuities from the past deserved serious consideration, on the grounds that "as industrialization progressed, preindustrial forms of cooperative social exchange were gradually revived in the economic sphere as effective means of solving problems arising from the instability of market outcomes" (Murakami and Rohlen 1992). And Ronald Dore (1973) put forward the premise that it was a result of "late development"—a complex interplay of factors in which learning from the mistakes of the first-comers to industrialization and the invocation of traditional values to underpin new institutions were both crucial elements.

This was—and is—more than an academic debate. From Abegglen onward, those studying the Japanese employment system have speculated on the sustainability over time of a system in which the core practices seemed so different from those prevailing in Western societies. Abegglen himself hedged his bets, seeing both the apparent stability and embeddedness of the system (1958, 137) and what he saw as the sacrifice of productivity entailed by permanent employment (ch. 7). As productivity levels in Japanese industry grew exponentially in the ensuing decade, the economic rationalists grew more assertive about the fit between the Japanese employment system and high rates of economic growth. The obvious but unstated corollary of their argument was that if growth were to slow substantially and the labor shortage were to give way to unemployment or underemployment, the system would "rationally" change, just as it had rationally developed. The institutionalists (and at least some of Abegglen's own arguments belong in this category) tended to believe that change would occur as the economic environment changed, but that it would occur much more slowly than the economic rationalists believed, and that it would very likely follow its own distinctive trajectory. Writing in the early 1970s, before the economic dislocations of the 1970s and 1980s, Dore stated (with remarkable prescience, as it turned out) that he was willing to "hazard a guess that in 1980, and even in 1990, Japanese workers will still be hired and promoted and paid and trained and socialized in a distinctively Japanese way" (1973, 337). He prudently did not take his prediction into the next century.

The Japanese Production System

The peak of the early stream of empirical research into the employment system and social organization of the Japanese factory occurred in the late 1960s and early 1970s (Whitehill and Takezawa 1968; Cole 1971; Marsh and Mannari 1971; Abegglen 1973; Dore 1973). During these years, as we now know, major changes were underway in the production system in Japanese factories, changes whose significance was not clearly recognized by researchers focused on the employment and industrial relations systems. So skilled a fieldworker as Ronald Dore observed some signs of these developments: his vivid contrast between the beginning of the workday in a British factory and a Japanese facotory rings far more portentously in our ears today than it did in 1973. He contrasted the beginning of the workday at Hitachi's plant—workers in position at their machines by the time the recorded music signaled the start of morning calisthenics, followed by a team meeting at which the team leader reminded the workers of the "tips for the day" (reminders of how to avoid production problems) and allocated work to the team members—with the somewhat haphazard patterns at the British plant, where the last stragglers arrived half an hour after the official starting time and extensive and unanticipated absenteeism led to production problems. Dore noted the quality problems in particular. He provides a vivid anecdote of a foreman instructing a last-minute replacement worker while "washing-machines go on past him as legless as ever. They will provide a job for the snaggers—the all-purpose defect-correctors at the end of the line" (Dore 1973, 26). But Dore's primary focus, like that of most studies on the Japanese factory before the 1980s, remained on the employment and industrial relations systems, rather than on the issues of the organization of production that surface in this description and that subsequently came to dominate the research on the Japanese factory.

During the early 1980s, the focus began to shift away from the employment system to a narrower set of management systems and production techniques that enabled the factory to move beyond the rigidities of traditional "Fordist" mass production to production that was characterized by high quality, flexibility, and continuous improvement. Sociologists can take pride in the fact that the first detailed description of quality control systems in Japanese factories was presented by a colleague: Robert E. Cole described the production system at Toyota Auto Body in his 1979 book *Work, Mobility, and Participation*. But much of the succeeding research on the social organization of the Japanese factory in the 1980s was carried out by management experts rather than Japan specialists or sociologists, and was primarily oriented toward developing a normative model of "best practice" for emulation and adaptation by Western (primarily U.S.) managers.[2]

Like the social scientists who had studied the Japanese employment system, these writers saw social structures and processes as central to understanding the Japanese production system, but they focused on a very different set of patterns, and linked them to different outcomes (quality, flexibility, and efficiency rather than harmonious industrial relations and cross-system divergence). A listing of key features of the Japanese production system would include the following:

- flexible, team-based work organization: individuals are assigned not to clearly defined jobs but to "activity clusters"—groups or teams, with considerable rotation across activities within each group—and line workers are assigned responsibility for tasks that are often performed by cadres of specialists in traditional Fordist organization, such as quality control and equipment maintenance;
- systems for tapping the knowledge of all employees: Employees are encouraged to make and implement suggestions for improving quality and productivity, drawing on their intimate knowledge of the production process (a knowledge that is broader than that of their Western counterparts because of their lack of specialization);
- dense networks with suppliers, embodied in "just-in-time" logistics and the elimination (or drastic reduction) of inventory for final assembly, so that parts and subsystems are "pulled" onto the production line as needed, and suppliers are fully integrated into production planning and product design;
- dense networks among the "output-set" of the firm, with production tied to demand from customers, through close links to distributors and retailers, to ensure that the output matches the needs of the market, and with the production system organized flexibly to accommodate rapid model changes according to demand;
- close integration of the factory and product development and design, with development laboratories often co-located with key factories and the movement of people from product development into manufacturing.

The model of the Japanese production system emphasized the key role of networks: internal networks in the team-based work organization, and the

---

[2] See, for example, the early work by the Harvard Business School Productions and Operations Management group, beginning with Hayes (1981) and Wheelwright (1981), and the work of the Future of the Automobile Project at MIT (Womack et al., 1990).

dense cross-functional linkages and external networks with suppliers and customers.

The portrayals of this model were far less deeply anchored in the Japanese institutional context than was the earlier model of the Japanese employment system. Several researchers did indeed trace the roots of the system to Japan-specific factors: the legacy of wartime production (Wada 1995), the relatively small market in Japan and the necessity of adapting mass-production techniques to small-lot production (Cusumano 1985), and even to the effect of the Japanese employment system, whose emergence pre-dated the development of most features of the Japanese production system (Cole 1989). But these conditions for its emergence were not necessarily seen as conditions for its continued operation even in Japan, let alone for its emulation in other countries. The years of the most assiduous "learning from Japan" in terms of production systems in U.S. companies were years in which many of those same companies reconfigured their employment system in ways that took them even farther from that of Japan. The changes included downsizing on an unprecedented scale even in profitable firms, the use of contingent workers and the radical reduction of employment security, and growing gaps between the take-home pay of workers and the enormous reward packages for top managers.

The Japanese production system challenged two basic and related tenets of Fordist production: increased specialization as the key to efficiency and productivity, and the buffering of core technical activities from other activities within the company and from the environment. The Japanese system, in contrast, relied on generalists at all levels of the company, from the blue-collar workers who maintained their own machines and cleaned their own work areas to the engineers with graduate technical degrees who moved, over the course of their careers, from the central laboratories through the factory-linked development facilities to line management in the factory. And instead of buffering core technical functions with boundary-spanning units or other modes of insulation, the different functions within the company were closely linked, even overlapping (Nonaka 1990); suppliers delivered direct to the production line; and customer orders passed directly to the factory (Fruin 1997).

For some scholars, these differences are sufficient to make the Japanese production system a new and more advanced model of production (Kenney and Florida 1993; Womack, Jones and Roos 1990; Fruin 1997). In their view, the recognition that production workers are not just factory hands but factory brains, the systematic engagement of these workers in continuous improvement, and the acceptance by managers of employees as key stakeholders in the firm are fundamental transformations in the industrial workplace. These scholars also highlight as a departure from classic Fordism the role of the factory as a key center for innovation in the company—

incremental rather than fundamental innovation, to be sure, and within the bounds of performance and productivity set by the company's management, but indisputably innovation (Fruin 1997).

For others, however, the Japanese production system is simply the next stage of Taylorist, Fordist manufacturing (Ledford 1993; Tomaney 1994; Kumazawa 1996; Price 1997). The fundamental basis for disagreement is whether Fordism is defined primarily as a set of production techniques premised on mass production, specialization, and the de-skilling of labor (as is tends to be for those who regard the Japanese production system (JPS) as a major innovation because of its departure from these features), or as a system of power in the workplace, where managerially established business objectives take precedence over worker welfare and empowerment. In Tomaney's view, for example, the criterion of whether the Japanese production system provides a genuinely post-Fordist system hinges on "whether the changes amount to a fundamental reorganization of the labor process as well as guaranteeing a new and better deal for labor" (1994, 157). He maintains that a "fundamental reorganization" involves not a different allocation of tasks but a shift of power from managers to workers (p. 183). From this perspective, the "empowerment" of Japanese workers to make improvements in the work process involves simply putting Taylorist tools in the hands of the workers, and making them the agents of their own exploitation. In the words of another, like minded critic, Kumazawa Makoto, "Today Japanese workers and unions, struggling to justify their existence, are upholding a Japanese style of management premised on near-complete managerial authority over the working lives of employees" (1996, 11). For the critics of the "JPS as post-Fordist" paradigm, however, the ultimate test is whether the system challenges the paradigm of managerial control that undergirds Western, and particularly U.S., industrial production. In the words of one such critic, "Japanese management embodies a more rational version of the traditional, control-oriented management model that dominates U.S. management thinking" (Ledford 1993, 147). William Tsutsui (1998) has suggested that one reason for this fit with the basic assumptions of U.S. management lies in the shared heritage of Taylorism as a primary influence on the techniques and ideology of production management. But an additional reason may well lie in the models constructed in the 1980s by Western and Western-trained management scholars, whose primary goal in identifying the key features of Japanese "best practice" was to encourage Western managers to learn from those models, and to translate them into concepts and frameworks acceptable to the most fundamental assumptions of those managers.

By the 1990s, much of the debate over the embeddedness of the Japanese model and the extent to which it was built on fundamentally different institutions and premises had migrated from the analysis of the Japanese factory to the analysis of the Japanese firm. The networked model of production management—with dense internal networks of teams on the production floor, close cross-functional networks linking production and technology development, and interorganizational networks linking suppliers with the production floor—had implications beyond the factory, extending to the model of enterprise itself. And here the fundamental assumptions of U.S. and Japanese managers differed far more dramatically.

Level Two: The Enterprise

The recognition that business enterprise in Japan did not fit easily into Western models of the firm was slower in coming than the awareness of the distinctive features of its factories. The 1980s saw a growing number of accounts of the differences between the behaviors and strategies of Japanese companies and those of U.S. firms (Kono 1984; Kagono et al. 1985; Abegglen and Stalk 1985). By the late 1980s, comparative research had established differences in the following areas:

- the priorities accorded to growth versus profitability, with Japanese companies favoring the former and U.S. firms the latter;
- patterns of vertical integration, with Japanese manufacturing firms typically being less vertically integrated than their U.S. counterparts, and yet at the same time having a smaller number of external suppliers;
- patterns of business diversification, with Japanese firms much more likely to favor strategies of diversification through internal growth into closely related arenas, and U.S. firms more prone to pursue strategies of acquisition and of unrelated diversification;
- patterns of geographic diversification, with Japanese firms more likely to favor export strategies, gradual incremental establishment of offshore production, and the establishment of functionally specialized subsidiaries closely tied to the parent company in Japan rather than the development of the strong, integrated country subsidiaries that characterized the classic American multinational corporation.

In the early and mid-1980s, relatively few of the academic studies of Japanese behavior and strategy linked these various aspects of the strategic behavior of Japanese firm. However, by the late 1980s, a number of academics, both economists and sociologists, were arguing that these patterns could best be explained not by life-cycle effects (Japanese firms as less "mature" than their U.S. counterparts) but by the recognition that the Japanese enterprise constituted a different organizational form with a distinctive governance system (Aoki 1988; Hamilton and Biggart 1988).

The Organizational Form of Enterprise: The Vertical Keiretsu

In the 1980s, the apparent anomalies in the organizational form of the Japanese firm were becoming increasingly evident to American managers, as they grew more interested in the supplier links that supported the Japanese production system and as they tried to engage in competitive benchmarking against their Japanese competitors. It quickly became evident to them that the Japanese enterprise was a distinctive organizational form that differed substantially from the North American multidivisional enterprise. The first element of its distinctive structure to receive widespread attention was the supplier network. Large numbers of the key suppliers for Japanese companies were owned, in whole or in part, by the final assemblers. Moreover, the term "parent company" was not a metaphor but a reality for many suppliers, which had originally been divisions or factories in the parent and had been spun off as separate companies. The relationships between these supplier firms and the parent company was neither that of conventional arm's-length contracting nor that of the hierarchical integration of business divisions in the multidivisional enterprise.

The competitive benchmarking that became widespread among United States enterprises in the mid-1980s made the apparent anomalies in the structure of the Japanese firm even more evident. When leading United States companies started trying to benchmark their performance against their Japanese competitors, they found the results either horrifying or meaningless. In the late 1980s, for example, Xerox had 113,000 employees versus Canon's 15,000. GM had over 700,000 employees in the early 1990s when it announced that it was about to "downsize" in North America by shedding 90,000 employees; Toyota was listed at the time in the widely used *Japan Company Handbook* as having only 65,000 employees, fewer than GM was about to shed. Clearly the "company" whose data appeared in the Japanese company handbooks was not the same kind of entity as the American corporation whose data were recorded in the Fortune 500. Yet when companies like Xerox or GM tried to expand their benchmarking to the Canon group or the Toyota group, they ran into difficulties identifying boundaries comparable to their own. Efforts to improve comparability by bringing Japanese accounting standards into line with North American practice by increasing the use and publication of consolidated company data (i.e., that which included all subsidiaries in which the parent company owned a certain percentage of the shares) created the illusion of comparability rather than the reality, given that the ownership stake in many Japanese group companies was below the mandated level for consolidation in North America. Clearly the "group" rather than the individual incorporated company was the appropriate level of analysis for benchmarking exercises, for international stock analysts interested in assessing investments, and probably for comparative organizational analysis. Drawing boundaries that were comparable to those of the Western firm proved extremely difficult. The boundaries of the firm are defined by law; the boundaries of the vertical business group are not.

The large vertical *keiretsu*, as the industrial group's organized under the aegis of a single final assembler are known in Japan, constitute a distinctive organizational form, comprised of several hundred companies. The prevalence and importance of these groups is demonstrated by the large number of handbooks and guides published each year, from the detailed listings published by Toyo Keizai that sell for several hundred dollars to the popular graphic guides to the groups published by most leading presses. According to one of the most detailed listings (*Japan's Enterprise Groups*, published annually by Toyo Keizai), Hitachi's extended group, included in 1995 more than 1,000 separately incorporated companies, Bridgestone (the tire company) had nearly 700 in its extended group, and Toyota over 300. The vertical *keiretsu* was solidly established as an organizational form in virtually every industry, services as well as manufacturing industries. Taisei Construction, for example, had 100 companies in its group in the early 1990s, Kirin Beer had over 80, and Toray Industries, a synthetic fibers and chemicals company, had over 180 (Toyo Keizai Shimposha 1995). It has been, however, the auto and electrical equipment industries, Japan's most successful in international markets, that have been the most studied and have provided the primary foundation for building the model of the *keiretsu* most familiar in the United States.

The vertical group, for most companies, is composed of two types of subsidiaries: *kogaisha*, which are companies created by the lead firm, usually by spinning off a division, department, or factory from its own organization, and *kanren-gaisha* (usually translated as "affiliate"), which is a formerly independent company that has developed a long-standing relationship, usually as a supplier, with the lead firm, and has been brought into the group. Either type of group firm can belong to another category: the consolidated subsidiary, in which the lead firm owns a set proportion of the equity. This is a category created by internationally accepted accounting standards, in which the performance data from such subsidiaries must be "consolidated" with the data from the owning company in the formal reports required of publicly listed companies. Companies differ in the extent to which the lead firm owns what Western management texts customarily call a "controlling share" of their group firms. Some, like Hitachi, Sony, and Suzuki, own actuarially significant stakes in over four-fifths of the companies in their groups; for others, like Toshiba, Sanyo, or Toyota, fewer than one-fifth of their group companies are consolidated.[3]

The lead firm of the vertical *keiretsu* itself contains both a corporate headquarters and a range of business divisions. The parent company of the Toyota group, for example, produces most of the company's models of autos and trucks; Matsushita Electric contains over forty business divisions producing a wide range of products, from office equipment to home appliances. The lead company in the group concentrates on high-value-added manufacturing (usually but not exclusively final assembly) and research and development for the core businesses of the group. The group companies engage in one of three types of activities: the manufacture of components and subassemblies (or in some cases lower-value-added final products); sales and distribution; and quasi-related businesses.

The manufacturing subsidiaries are those most frequently associated with the model of the vertical *keiretsu* in Western business publications. They produce components and subassemblies, and in turn each has a set of subcontracting affiliates that produce simpler components, in a production value chain that stretches across multiple formal company boundaries. Most of these companies also supply other enterprises outside the group, and the lead firm rarely relies completely on group companies for components, although group firms are preferred suppliers. In the auto industry, the prevailing practice is *parallel sourcing*, in which a final assembler such as Toyota or Nissan may use a single supplier for a part on one model, but turns to other suppliers for very similar parts for other models (Richardson 1993). In electronics, the prevailing practice is often to use both an internal and an external supplier for components. The participation in the open market disciplines pricing on both sides and allows the lead firm and the subsidiary both to maintain flexibility in their operations; it also allows supplier firms to build larger scale economies than would be possible for a captive supplier (Dore 1983; Nishiguchi 1994). A key point is that not all suppliers are members of the group.

Unlike most of the manufacturing group companies, the second type of vertical *keiretsu* subsidiary, the sales and distribution companies, are completely dependent on the parent firm: they are dedicated to handling the group's products. The lead firms in most industries have put much of the sales and distribution function into separate companies, often on a geographical basis (Hokkaido, the Kanto region, etc., for domestic sales; and

---

[3] Recent changes in Japan's accounting regulations, scheduled to come into operation in 2001, promise to change this: firms must consolidate the accounts of all firms over which they exercise management control. How effectively this will be enforced is an open question, but it will certainly change the accounting practices and the "mapping" of the boundaries of the extended enterprise.

separately incorporated country sales companies for overseas operations). These firms concentrate on the activities involved in getting the final products produced by the parent firms to the customer.

The third kind of group firm has considerably more independence: the subsidiaries in quasi-related businesses. Japan's leading firms have been much less diversified than their American competitors (Kagono et al. 1985). However, one reason for this is the proclivity of those firms for putting new businesses into separate subsidiaries. The lead firm assiduously pursues new business opportunities that are closely related to its core capabilities, a quest for new business that is driven primarily by the need to maintain employment and to make the company attractive to new recruits because of its growth potential. But the lead company also has a high propensity to spin off businesses that are not directly related to its central technologies and markets. For example, both Toyota and Matsushita have a subsidiary in their group engaged in producing and marketing prefabricated housing. For Toyota, this business builds on its capabilities in structural engineering and production (the housing is steel-frame construction); for Matsushita, housing provides a "container" for its consumer electronics products, and its subsidiary National Home has been particularly active in the marketing of the "intelligent house." But the development, production, and selling of prefab houses is sufficiently removed from each company's core capabilities that the activity has been spun off into a separate "child company". The vertical *keiretsu* structure gives this "intrapreneurship" a range of organizational strategies for developing new businesses, and helps explain why new industries in Japan have so often been fostered by existing companies.

During the last decade, companies have been particularly active in spinning off quasi-related businesses into separate firms in the network. In the "bubble" years, many of the large industrial firms set up financial services and real estate subsidiaries to take advantage of the profit potential in those sectors. In the recession years of the 1990s, companies often resorted to setting up such subsidiaries to provide employment for workers and managers who are made redundant in the core businesses. This mode of employment-driven business diversification is certainly not unique to Japan, but it has been uniquely widespread there.

Membership in the vertical group is symbolized by the lead firm's ownership of some shares in the group companies, either directly or indirectly (through its subsidiaries' ownership of shares in their suppliers). But as the variations in the level of parent company shareholding in group companies suggest, ownership is not the only or even the primary means of coordination and control in the vertical *keiretsu*. It is one of five mechanisms, the others being the interconnections of the value chains (that is, the flow of "things" across the formal boundaries of the member companies); the flows of financial resources in forms other than equity (both direct loans and the support of the parent company for affiliates seeking bank loans); the flows of information and technology; and, most importantly, the flows of people.

People move from the lead firm to the suppliers and from the suppliers to the lead firm. The latter type of transfer, however, differs from the first in being overwhelmingly and unambiguously temporary: people are transferred to work on specific projects or to learn specific skills that they take back to their "home" firms. The lead firm, in contrast, transfers its people to its subsidiaries on permanent as well as on temporary assignments, at all levels of the organization. This outflow serves several purposes: it maintains strong communications links across the network; it eases the transfer of technology and know-how from the lead firm to its subsidiaries; it enables the lead firm to stay "lean" and to select only the high-commitment and high-performance employees from its labor pool; and it provides senior management positions for those of its managers who have "plateaued" in the lead firm. The ability of lead firms to relegate lower-performing employees to subsidiaries helps to explain the Japanese employees' continuing commitment to work and performance that so bemused Western analysts of Japanese firms in the 1970s and early 1980s and has been so critically important an element of the Japanese employment system. Commitment is sustained in a regime of "permanent employment" and the seniority wage system in part because of the ever-present prospect of transfer into the lower-prestige and lower-reward subsidiaries. And yet a transfer into a subsidiary does not necessarily lower the motivation of the transferee: it provides the prospect of rising to high-prestige management positions, even company president or director for hundreds of managers who did not have such an opportunity in the lead firm. There is only one president of Hitachi; there are over eight hundred presidents in the Hitachi group. The ability of the lead firm to send employees into subsidiaries, often in positions higher, at least in terms of titles, than those to which they could have aspired in the parent firm has constituted an important incentive system in a status-oriented incentive system.

It has only been recently that analysts of Japanese business have realized the extent to which the Japanese employment system relied on the distinctive vertical *keiretsu* organizational form. The large firm's implicit contract with employees to ensure their employment up to retirement age meant employment within the vertical group, not necessarily employment within the lead firm. How extensive is cross-company mobility within the vertical *keiretsu*? Aoki (1988, 66) cites data from Japan's Central Labor Commission showing that in 1985, 8.2 percent of the total employees in manufacturing firms with over one thousand employees were on assignment in group companies. We have little information on how transfer patterns have changed over time, except the anecdotal information that transfers accelerate when the business of the parent company is under pressure. Mari Sako (1997, 8–11) has suggested that in the recession of the 1990s, lead firms have increasingly resorted to the transfer of employees into the subsidiaries within their networks in order to adjust the size of their own labor force to the slower pace of growth. In other words, the vertical *keiretsu* in Japan is an *employment network* as well as a business network: there is extensive cross-enterprise mobility within each extended enterprise network, and very little mobility across networks.

The dominance of the vertical group as a corporate form across industries in Japan suggests that there is a country-level explanation for its development, and indeed not surprisingly, country-level explanations have dominated discussions of the phenomenon. One factor that looms large in explanations of the development of the vertical *keiretsu* is the postwar labor settlement and the Japanese employment system. Under the JES as it emerged during the 1950s, as we saw earlier, company management conceded that all members of the enterprise union (which included all employees, including college graduates up to their first promotion into management) would receive wages calculated on a set of factors that were essentially homogeneous across all categories of employees, in which education and seniority were the factors most heavily weighted. In consequence, it was extremely difficult for management to differentiate across jobs or departments depending on the value added by their activities. Wages and salaries were pulled to the highest common denominator. This constituted a powerful incentive for management to put lower-value-adding activities into separate subsidiaries, in which wages were internally homogeneous but differentiated from those in the parent firm.

Another set of explanations looks at strategic adaptations to the postwar business environment. In this approach, the use of subsidiaries for horizontal diversification by the lead firm in the group is a risk-shifting strategy: that is, in new business areas, where the firm is stretching its capabilities, a separate enterprise avoids putting the name and the resources of the parent firm at risk. This is seen as particularly important in the Japanese business context, where the lifetime employment system imposes serious barriers to exit from unsuccessful business and where reputation is seen as a more important business asset than in the United States (Aoki 1988).

Still another set of factors has been invoked to explain the resort to smaller, more focused companies through the vertical network: the limitations on the face-to-face, relational kinds of coordination and control systems favored in Japanese companies. Itami Hiroyuki (1984) has established that Japanese firms encounter diminishing returns to scale more quickly than their U.S. counterparts, and has suggested that this may be due to the fact that, given the enormous complexities of the Japanese written language, Japan never really experienced the first office revolution introduced by the typewriter. Whatever the technological basis, it is clear that the coordination and control systems of Japanese firms today do rely heavily on face-to-face interactions, and that these clearly function less effectively in very large, vertically integrated firms than do more impersonal, less information-intensive systems.

All these explanations portray the emergence of the vertical de-integration of the firm as a response to problems and constraints, both those imposed on the firm from the business environment (labor cost explanation, risk shifting) and those rooted in the limitations of the firm's own coordination and control systems. It is difficult to assess the validity of these historical explanations, however plausible they may seem, in the absence of detailed case studies of the evolution of some of the vertical groups over time. But once the system developed, it was clear that it conferred a set of advantages on those firms who were able to use it effectively. Those advantages have sometimes been invoked to explain why the vertical group developed, but these functionalist explanations are better viewed as reasons why the group has persisted and the prospects for its serving as a model for other business systems, rather than as explanations for its original development. These advantages include the following:

- The disaggregation of activities along the value chain made costs more transparent and therefore controllable.
- The lead firm focused on core activities, which were primarily the high-value-adding activities of technology development and high-value-added manufacturing. This focus on technology-intensive activities made technology a more salient element of corporate strategy and contributed to the technological dynamism of the firm.
- Even large firms stayed relatively small: in 1990, only eleven Japanese manufacturing companies employed more than 40,000 people. This smaller size also contributed to the flexibility and dynamism of the firm, helping it to move quickly into new related technologies and product markets.
- The lead firm was able to achieve a greater efficiency in wages, keeping only high-value-adding activities on its employment roster and rewarding its high-commitment, high-value-adding employees appropriately.
- The "relational contracting" characteristic of the supplier networks of the *keiretsu*—management by "contact, not contract" (Mishina and Flaherty 1997)—reduced coordination costs, fostered the expansion of supplier capabilities and "co-specialized assets," and lowered production costs.

Kenichi Imai (1988) has also pointed to an advantage of the vertical network for the business system as a whole: the rapid diffusion of technology and know-how through the industrial system. The fact that relatively few of the firms in the value chain produce exclusively for their lead firm means that innovations in product and process tend to diffuse fairly rapidly through the system. While this may be a short-term disadvantage for any single innovative lead firm, even that firm benefits in the long run from the greater dynamism and efficiency of the system as a whole.

Another consequence of the vertical network is that because one of the key management skills is managing the linkages across companies in the network, managerial capabilities are less transferable across *keiretsu* than in industrial forms that depend more heavily on analytical skills and impersonal coordination and control systems. The lower interfirm mobility in Japan may therefore be as much a function of the pervasiveness of the vertical network as it is of any cultural preferences for loyalty and stability of employment.

The advantages of the vertical *keiretsu* structure, especially in terms of supplier links, have been sufficiently widely recognized that over the last decade, many large U.S. firms have radically reconfigured their supply networks in the direction of the Japanese model. But research has found that the control structures of the U.S. networks differ substantially from the multidimensional coordination mechanisms of the Japanese vertical *keiretsu*, especially in the absence of the extensive personnel transfers and much less frequent interactions (Dyer 1996b; Dyer and Ouchi 1993). The looser coupling of the American-style supplier group provides greater flexibility than the Japanese *keiretsu*, but also less of its strong support for the production system (see, for example, the account of the rapid response of Toyota's suppliers to the destruction by fire of a key factory in the Toyota network, in a 1997 paper by Nishiguchi and Beaudet). As with the Japanese production system, a generalized model developed on the basis of the Japanese experience provided a spur to change in the United States, but the resulting patterns constitute not a clone of the original system, but a distinctive organizational form shaped by a very different social and economic context (Adler et al. 1999).

The Organizational Form of Enterprise: The Governance System

Corporate governance has become an increasingly contentious issue in most business systems today, and Japan is no exception. The key question in corporate governance systems can be framed as, "In whose interests does the firm (or its top management) act, and how do those interests make their influence felt?" Adolph Berle and Gardiner Means (1932) identified the separation of ownership and control as the hallmark of a major transformation of capitalism that had occurred in the first three decades of the twentieth century. In the 1968 edition of their classic study, both authors asserted that the developments they had analyzed over the previous thirty years had intensified and were likely to continue to intensify. Means proclaimed that "the separation of ownership and control has released management from the overriding requirement that it serve stockholders." (Berle and Means 1968, xxxv).

This pronouncement has a strange ring at the dawn of the twenty-first century, when the United States has become the stronghold of "shareholder capitalism." In contemporary America, managers of large companies are widely viewed as the agents of shareholders, disciplined by those shareholders through the board of directors, and given incentives to serve shareholder interests through stock options that have tied their personal rewards to the share price. This has severely eroded the separation of ownership and management control identified by Berle and Means, as has the practice in entrepreneurial high-tech firms of attracting technical and managerial talent by providing equity in the firm in lieu of high salaries (a practice that has increasingly made smaller high-tech firms attractive employers for current cohorts of MBA graduates). Japanese corporations, however, still exemplify the Berle and Means model of the separation of ownership and control, and are under growing critical fire from economists, analysts, and the business press for doing so.

In the Japanese corporation, most shareholders have not been individual or institutional investors seeking immediate returns, but companies with a business relationship or a historical tie to the corporation, who have focused on the continued viability rather than on their own financial returns. Consequently, Japan did not develop an active market for corporate control (to use the language of the financial economists). Companies in Japan were acquired by other companies only by mutual consent, and so mergers and acquisitions have been relatively rare events. The board of directors is not composed of external representatives of shareholders but of the company's own executives and former executives. If there is an external person on the board, it is usually a representative of the lead bank.

The "lead bank" role in the Japanese business system has been the subject of extensive research and even more extensive speculation. Before the "bursting" of the "bubble" economy in the early 1990s, the lead bank was widely regarded as the functional equivalent of the shareholders in terms of corporate governance, acting as a brake on managerial actions that might endanger the viability of the firm. The financial crunch caused by the crash of the Japanese stock and real estate markets has seriously reduced the ability of banks to sustain this role, and has raised serious questions about how competently they played it even in the 1980s. Mark Scher (1998), for example, has pointed out that the lead bank had two roles that were potentially at odds once the economy encountered difficulties. As a creditor, the lead bank had a concern with the long-term viability of the company; as a lender, however, it had its own interests in expanding its business with the company by encouraging it to borrow money and to turn to the bank for sophisticated financial products to fund expansion. In the context of the "bubble" economy, this tended to feed rather than restrain managerial enthusiasm for large and sometimes ill-advised investments in new plant and business expansion.

While analysts agree on the empirical features of Japanese corporate governance, they disagree on their implications. Some writers, like Itami (1994, 75), see the Japanese enterprise system as characterized by "employee sovereignty," in which "the firm belongs to the people who have committed themselves to it and worked in it for long periods." Others, like Aoki (1988, 150–203), see the governance system as one in which managers balance the claims of a set of stakeholders, among whom employees are prominent but share legitimacy as claimants with shareholders. Whatever the interpretation of the strength of various stakeholder voices, in the 1980s and early 1990s Japan's corporate governance system was widely portrayed as a source of competitive strength. Since the beginning of the recession, however, many contemporary analysts have seen the absence of an effective disciplining effect on managerial behavior—from the threat of takeovers or from activist board members—as a source of many of Japan's current problems. Clearly, it is closely connected with the unexpected strength of the firm's commitment to provide employment for its members. Employment-driven diversification (the expansion into unrelated fields with the aim of providing outplacements for employees), participation in cost-sharing arrangements with related companies who accept redundant workers, and reductions in dividends and in managerial salaries and bonuses have all been common strategies for coping with economic downturn in large Japanese firms, and have obviously placed the interests of employees ahead of those of shareholders.

But rarely have discussions of corporate governance moved beyond the framing derived from United States models of enterprise, which focus on the firm-level of analysis, particularly on large industrial firms. And yet as we have seen, the form of the Japanese enterprise, the vertical *keiretsu*, suggests that questions about governance could usefully be raised at the level of the extended enterprise rather than exclusively at the level of the individual firm.

Although a number of studies have analyzed how Japanese manufacturing companies manage their supplier networks (Smitka 1991; Nishiguchi 1994; Dyer and Ouchi 1993; Fruin and Nishiguchi 1993), remarkably little systematic research has been done on how the lead firm in the vertical *keiretsu* manages the group as a whole. The discussion of the vertical *keiretsu* above indicated that the dense flows of things, information and technology, financial capital, and people have been as important, if not more important, than ownership in the coordination and control of the system. Data on the boards of directors and top management teams of subordinate firms in the network provide some fodder for discussions of corporate governance within the network. The Toyo Keizai yearbook of 1994, for example, provided some interesting data on the transfer of personnel at the top management levels in auto and electronics groups, although it covers only a limited number of publicly listed top-tier subsidiaries. As of 1993, the proportion of company officers in these subsidiaries (including the chairman, president, vice-presidents, directors, and auditor) coming from the parent company was substantial: well over a third in six out of seven electronics firms, and from nearly a quarter to a third in the three auto firms for which data were compiled. The industry effect here is demonstrable: the electronics firms show a remarkable similarity across companies, and the proportion of "dispatched" senior managers is higher than in the auto industry. This suggests that the various modes of coordination and control have complex interrelationships. In the auto industry, where the flow of "things" makes the group companies more dependent on the parent, the flow of officers is a less important mechanism than in the electronics industry, where subsidiaries sell more of their products on the open market. That the one exception in the electronics industry is Matsushita provides some support for this hypothesis: Matsushita's justifiably famous tight control of financial flows may serve to lower the importance of the flow of company officers as a control mechanism. Clearly the parent firm in these networks has multiple levers for exerting control over the group, but empirically tracing these links is extraordinarily difficult, given that so many of the companies in the vertical *keiretsu* are not publicly listed firms.

If the coordination and control systems of the vertical networks have been under-studied, those of a very different kind of business network, the horizontal group, have been extensively analyzed. Whereas the vertical group can be considered the functional equivalent of an enterprise, with a clearly identifiable central or parent organization and systems for coordinating key activities of the constituent units, the horizontal *keiretsu* is indisputably a network of separate companies, and is best analyzed in terms of inter-organizational networks.

LEVEL THREE: INTERORGANIZATIONAL NETWORKS

The image of Japan's enterprise system as the epitome of networked capitalism is reinforced by two phenomena at the interorganizational level. One is the longevity of a type of enterprise group that is, confusingly, often given the same Japanese term as the vertical *keiretsu*—that is, the horizontal *keiretsu* or *kigyo shudan*. The second involves the multiple networks linking competing or potentially competing firms in a variety of associations, councils, and consortia. Of the two, the former has been widely seen as a distinctively Japanese pattern; the latter as a normative model for the densely networked "enterprise society" of the twenty-first century.

The Horizontal Keiretsu

The horizontal *keiretsu* is a fundamentally different type of enterprise group from the vertical *keiretsu* previously described. Such groups bear some of the most famous names in Japanese industry—Mitsui, Mitsubishi, Sumitomo—and differ from the vertical *keiretsu* in scope, number, and structure.

SCOPE

Where the vertical *keiretsu* operates within an industry, broadly defined, the horizontal *keiretsu* consists of firms from virtually every major industry in the economy, with especially strong representation in the key industries of the high-growth period that was the era of its greatest strength (heavy industry, petrochemicals, materials processing, and of course banking and trading).

NUMBER

While virtually every large Japanese firm heads a vertical *keiretsu*, there are only six horizontal *keiretsu*, which were formed in the 1950s. Three are direct descendants of the prewar *zaibatsu* (Mitsui, Mitsubishi, and Sumitomo), and three were formed at the initiative of banks and also have their roots, less directly, in the prewar *zaibatsu*.

STRUCTURE

The horizontal *keiretsu* are much less tightly coordinated than the vertical *keiretsu*. There is no single dominant firm in the horizontal *keiretsu*, and no hierarchical control structure. Whereas the vertical *keiretsu* has a cascading structure of shareholding and of personnel transfers (from lead firm to first-tier suppliers, from first-tier to second tier, and so on), the horizontal *keiretsu* is characterized by cross-shareholding among the various member companies, and personnel movements are much more limited, concentrated at the level of the board of directors. The flows of goods are also more limited: according to Japan's Fair Trade Commission, the average horizontal *keiretsu* firm relies on other members of its group for approximately 13 percent of purchases (a much lower level than in the vertical *keiretsu*) and 15 percent of sales (*The Economist* 1 May 1991). The principal coordination mechanism is the "president's club," a regular meeting of the top managers of the group companies. It is mirrored by sets of parallel (and less frequent) meetings of functional managers (finance, personnel, R&D). No publicly available information on the content of these discussions exists, but information exchange is presumed to be their primary function (Gerlach 1992).

The prewar business groups (*zaibatsu*) are crucial to an understanding of the postwar horizontal *keiretsu*. The former had far greater structural similarities than do the postwar horizontal *keiretsu* to the intermarket business groups that have developed in most economies outside the Anglo-Saxon societies, especially, but by no means exclusively, in Asia (Granovetter 1993): they were family-controlled conglomerates with a formal coordination mechanism, the holding company, which was largely family-owned. It held significant blocks of shares in the most important companies in the group, appointed the top executives of the top-tier member enterprises, and allocated resources for new industrial enterprises within the group. And like the industrial groups in many countries, their formation was linked to and encouraged by government policy. The "old" *zaibatsu* (including Mitsui, Mitsubishi, and Sumitomo) spread their reach across industries in the sell-off of state-owned enterprises in the 1880s; the so-called "new" zaibatsu of the 1920s and 1930s were heavily involved in the expansionist policies of the government in Taiwan, Korea, Manchuria, and China (Morikawa 1992; Lynn and Rao 1995).

The close links of the *zaibatsu* to the military state and their dominant role in the wartime economy led the American Occupation authorities to target the *zaibatsu* for dissolution as agents of Japanese militarism and imperialism (Hadley 1970). One mechanism for attacking the *zaibatsu* was the purge of top managers, which affected virtually all companies in the Japanese economy (opening up the top ranks of Japan's largest companies to a new generation of managers); another was the confiscation of shares held by the designated *zaibatsu* families. Another, specifically targeted at the *zaibatsu*, was the prohibition of the use of the famous *zaibatsu* company names (for several years Mitsui and Mitsubishi, for example, were banned from the mastheads of Japanese companies) and the forced break-up of key companies. Mitsubishi Heavy Industries, for example, was divided into three separate regional companies; the Mitsui trading company was broken into over a hundred separate entities. But another mechanism, more lasting in its effect, was legislation that outlawed holding companies, which in one blow eliminated the key element of the vertical control structure of the groups. This prohibition lasted until the late 1990s, when the Diet finally passed legislation to make holding companies legal, thus reversing, after half a century, this legacy of America's "trust-busting."

To the astonishment of the architects of these "trust-busting" policies, however, the groups reemerged during the 1950s: the old names reappeared once the Occupation ended, the dismembered companies merged again, and a formal group identity was created through the presidents' clubs. The coordination structure was, however, of necessity very different from the prewar pattern. The family ownership of the prewar era had been thoroughly eradicated, but even in the 1920s and 1930s professional managers had been developed to occupy key administrative positions. More dramatic a change was the "associational" character of the group, by which was meant an apparently stable grouping without any hierarchical control system.

Economic analyses of the development of the horizontal *keiretsu* have stressed the advantages of group membership in the environment of the 1950s and 1960s. The group bank played a key role, not only in providing loans directly but also in mobilizing other financial institutions to make financing available to the group companies. The trading company was also a key player, particularly in the 1950s, when foreign exchange controls were stringent and knowledge of international markets was scarce within the management ranks of the member companies, especially after years of autarky, war, and occupation.

In succeeding decades, the group provided a kind of "mutual insurance system" (Tezuka 1997), in which the interlocking shareholding protected member companies both from any threat of takeover by foreign companies trying to enter the Japanese market by acquisition and from pressure from equity markets. In times of crisis, group firms could be counted on to step up and help: when Mazda was on the brink of bankruptcy in the mid-1970s, for example, not only did its group bank, Sumitomo, intervene to provide a new CEO and financial guidance for the company's turnaround, but Sumitomo group-company employees were urged to place orders for Mazda vehicles, with substantial financial inducements to do so (Rohlen 1983). The shielding of member companies from shareholder pressures is reflected in a study by Nakatani comparing matched pairs of group-member companies and independent companies in the 1980s: he found that group companies had lower growth rates and lower profitability, but greater returns to employees and greater stability in performance across the fluctuations of the business cycle (Nakatani 1984). These explanations for the persistence of the horizonal groups, which are grounded on attributions of economic rationality, can be augmented by institutional explanations that emphasize the importance of the historical legacy of interpersonal networks and shared identity within the *zaibatsu* groups. Only the groups in which these features were strongly entrenched made the transition to the postwar model. Imai has estimated that by the end of World War II, there were about eighty *zaibatsu* in Japan (Lynn and Rao 1995, 57); despite all the advantages postulated by the economic analyses, there are only six horizontal *keiretsu* in postwar Japan, and their number has not changed since the 1950s.

On the other hand, it is possible to argue that the horizontal *keiretsu* had an effect on the Japanese business system well beyond the confines of their own groups, in the form of the role of the "lead bank." The role played by the *zaibatsu* banks of the prewar years evolved in the postwar *keiretsu* into a central role in mobilizing loans from other financial institutions and, as noted above, holding the legally permitted maximum of 5 percent of shares outstanding and acting as a "watchdog" on the performance of management. Other banks who were not involved in the horizontal *keiretsu* emulated the key elements of this role in acting as "lead bank" for their largest and most important customers.

Even more unambiguously than the models of the Japanese employment system and the Japanese enterprise governance system, the horizontal *keiretsu* has been seen by American analysts as a distinctively Japanese form, a product of a specific institutional environment and a demonstration of the varieties of capitalism, rather than a normative model for other societies. But for countries where family-controlled intermarket business groups are significant players in the national economy, the Japanese horizontal *keiretsu* provides an interesting normative model of the "mature" enterprise group. The looser and less exclusive coordination mechanisms of the horizontal *keiretsu* provided many of the advantages of the diversified business group of the prewar years while addressing some of its most acute disadvantages (the enriching of certain dominant families, the dangers of arbitrary control by owners, imposed constraints on managerial discretion, and imposed intragroup exclusivity). Variants of some of the key Occupation antitrust measures—particularly restrictions of holding companies—could provide some possible models for government policies for dealing with the Korean *chaebol* or the southeast Asian business groups (or even, in the future, the emerging East European business groups). What the horizontal *keiretsu* do not and cannot provide is a model of the natural evolution of the family-owned intermarket group: the trajectory of development of the *zaibatsu* was radically altered by external force in the form of the American Occupation.[4]

Associational Networks

Any modern capitalist society is characterized by associational networks linking competing and potentially competing firms in a variety of collective activities (Aldrich and Marsden 1988) . In Japan, however, the number and variety of these networks seem to be particularly large, a pattern that has contributed to the image of Japan as a network-based business system (Imai 1988). Political scientists and political sociologists have focused on the networks coordinated by the government, with an eye to their role in indus-

---

[4] The horizontal *Keiretsu* may, however, provide a model of the evolution of bank-centered enterprise groups if the banks face a combination of the deregulation of financial markets and extended financial problems. Japan's long financial crisis and the heavy debt load of the main banks, combined with the liberalization of financial markets, have led in the past few years to unprecedented bank mergers, including some mergers across the horizontal groups. The effect on the six horizontal groups is still far from clear, but the groups most likely to survive remain those with a long history of cross-enterprise cooperation.

trial policy and competitiveness: R&D consortia, recession cartels in depressed industries, *shingikai* (the ministerial advisory councils),[5] and a variety of informal linkages—ranging from the extensive informal consultations between bureaucrats and managers known as "window guidance" to the "descent" of elite bureaucrats into financial and industrial firms upon their relatively early retirement from government service. Less studied have been the even more numerous private sector associations. Japan in the 1990s had 14,000 business associations, slightly more than the United States, which had, of course, twice the population, giving Japan almost twice the density level (Pempel 1998). These included both cross-industry associations—from the "peak" national associations such as Keidanren and Nikkeiren to the local Chambers of Commerce (dating from the nineteenth century)—and industry associations, which have been extremely active in managerial and technological change as well as in efforts to influence government policy (Lynn and McKeown 1988). In addition, there are a number of important cross-industry associations that have been very active in identifying and disseminating "management best practice." Among the most active and best-known abroad are JUSE (Japan Union of Scientists and Engineers), which played a leading role in the development and dissemination of quality techniques in Japanese industry (Cole 1989); the Japan Management Association, the heir of the prewar Japan Efficiency Association; and the Japan Productivity Center, founded in 1955 to "act as a conduit for introducing advanced management methods into Japan, stimulating interest in new techniques, educating managers in modern approaches, and coordinating programs of research and reform" (Tsutsui 1998, 136).

Both the roots and the effects of the number and range of associational networks among Japanese firms deserve more extensive discussion than the brief treatment possible here. A historical legacy of collective organization, from the guilds of preindustrial Japan (Hauser 1974) through the wartime top-down organization of the economy, played a role in shaping the density of associational networks. So did the pressures of technology followership, which provided strong inducements for firms to cooperate in identifying and acquiring foreign technology and managerial know-how. Some analysts have also noted that the physical proximity of government and corporate headquarters and industrial operations in the national capital (and the

---

[5] The *shingikai* are councils put together by various government ministries to assess and advise on policies. For example, in the late 1980s, both the Ministry of Construction and the Ministry of Posts and Telecommunications appointed their own *shingikai* on the subject of intelligent buildings, involving representatives from the major construction firms and telecommunications equipment providers, the major national newspapers, and distinguished academics in the field. Each committee produced a report with assessments of the developing market for intelligent buildings and recommendations for policy and strategy.

relative proximity of the second major industrial center, Osaka, which is three hours by bullet train from Tokyo[6]) makes dense communications and associational networks across companies and between companies, politicians, and bureaucrats quite easy (especially compared to the United States, with its continental spread of industry and the concentration in Washington, D.C., of government functions).

The consequences of these dense associational networks are more controversial. The most widely debated issue is the relative power of bureaucrats, businessmen, and politicians in Japan's industrial and economic policymaking. Chalmers Johnson's widely cited 1982 study of MITI (the Ministry of International Trade and Industry) postulated a central role for the professional government bureaucracy, and triggered a decade and a half of case studies of policymaking. It would be inaccurate to suggest that these analyses have produced a new orthodoxy, but there is agreement on several key points. First, there has been significant variation over time in the locus of power in business-government networks, with the bureaucracy enjoying its greatest dominance in the high-growth era of the 1950s and 1960s, when its control of foreign exchange and technology licensing approvals and its strong controls over financial services gave it a powerful (if temporary) set of policy tools. Second, even in the early decades, the bureaucracy's dominance varied across sectors: government policy was more easily formulated and seemed more effective when the dominant players in the industry agreed within their own networks on a desirable policy and when potential mavericks could be brought into line by pressure from other firms and from the government. Third, the dense associational networks that pervaded the economy, and that were encouraged but not controlled by the government, were crucial to whatever degree of policy coordination and implementation was observed (Samuels 1987; Okimoto 1989; Noble 1998). It is worth noting that even in the mid-1960s, when the bureaucracy's powers were greatest, William Lockwood (1965, 503), an economist and Japan specialist, characterized the networks that linked government and business in Japan as "a web with no spider." In other words, the dense connections and linkages—the networks—had a structure but no single architect and no controlling center.

Unquestionably, one of the most-noted effects of the many-faceted linkages between government and business is their contribution to frequent consultation and coordination between the two sectors. In the late 1980s, several Western commentators suggested that the United States would do well to follow Japan's example, if not in terms of an industrial policy then at least in a more cooperative relationship between business and govern-

---

[6] The high-speed Hikari Shinkansen, which reduced traveling time between Tokyo and Osaka to three hours, began service in 1964.

ment, in the interests of competing more effectively with Japan and Western Europe. A less widely noted effect of the dense associational business networks in Japan has been powerful isomorphic pressures within and across organizational fields. These have had both positive effects, in the dissemination of technology and new management practices, and negative effects, in the pressures to constrain "deviant" behavior that might have led to significant change in the existing structure of competition.

Summary: Cross-level Interdependencies

If the firm of the future is indeed network based, then it is obvious why, in the late 1980s, Japan seemed to exemplify the enterprise system of the future. Networked internally in a production system based on teams and cross-functional flows of people and information, networked as an organizational form in the extended enterprise of the vertical *keiretsu*, and networked externally in webs of collaborations and alliances, associations, and policy networks, the large Japanese firms exemplified the network enterprise.

And yet these aspects of the Japanese firm, held up as normative models by consultants, academics, and managers in the late 1980s and early 1990s, were closely linked to other aspects of the Japanese system that were regarded as much more idiosyncratic. The employment system in particular, the first model to be clearly articulated (and the earliest to be institutionalized), stretches across all the others: the years have validated Abegglen's insight about its centrality in the Japanese company (1958). It was an important factor in the emergence of the Japanese production system, even though the analyses of the 1980s assumed that once developed, the production system was sustainable in the absence of many features of the key institutional underpinnings of the employment system, at least in the context of its adoption and adaptation in other societies (Adler et al. 1999). Japan's distinctive corporate governance system has an even more complex relationship with the employment system. Employees have no formal representation on the board of directors, as they do in several European countries, nor are they represented among the leading shareholders, nor is the right to secure employment formally guaranteed in law. Yet as we have seen, employees have been recognized as privileged stakeholders in the company. Throughout the ups and downs of the business cycle, even in the recession of 1990s, large companies in Japan have taken extraordinary steps to maintain the employment system, steps that in North America and even perhaps in Western Europe would be regarded as impossible or even irrational: setting up spin-off enterprises to provide employment, eliminating management bonuses, slashing recruitment of new employees, reducing overtime, freezing wages (with the agreement of the enterprise union), and even reducing top management salaries (Mroczkowski and Hanaoka 1997).

The relationship between the Japanese employment system and the vertical *keiretsu* is also complex. The vertical *keiretsu* is not only a business network: it is an employment network in which the skills of coordination and management are highly network-specific and are most useful and valued within a given network (Westney 1996; Higuchi 1997). As an organizational form, the vertical *keiretsu* has both supported the employment system, by maintaining the employment security of lead-firm employees through transfers into group companies, and has relied heavily on it. Those transfers have helped to maintain the social contract to provide employment; equally important, the firm's ability to transfer its employees across the formal boundaries of its network has constituted a key element of the coordination system. And in the 1980s, as the growth rate slowed for many companies, large firms accelerated their spin-off of "child firms" in order to provide employment for those whose jobs with the parent were eliminated in the widespread downsizing undertaken by most manufacturing firms. Employment-driven diversification, especially into quasi-related or even unrelated enterprise, expanded the size and range of the vertical *keiretsu*.

The relationship between the horizontal *keiretsu* and the employment system is less apparent, but is indicated in Nakatani's (1984) finding that companies in the six groups show higher returns to employees than do independent companies. The horizontal *keiretsu* seem to exemplify most clearly the employee-as-key-stakeholder model, and have drawn much of their legitimacy and cohesiveness from this. And finally, the links across firms and the networks between government and business have been supported by the *parallel hierarchies* of the employment system: employees advance in their respective companies at similar rates, maintaining relationships with colleagues (and former classmates) at other companies or agencies—relationships that begin at junior levels and continue through the parallel ladders of firm and government ministry (Yoshino and Lifson 1986). The predictability of career ladders and the stability of employment mean that positional and personal links are mutually reinforcing.

The normative models of the Japanese production system and the vertical *keiretsu* that were so influential in the restructuring of American manufacturing enterprise in the 1980s proved useful outside Japan to an extent that often surprised the Japanese. Those models were, as we have seen, often constructed so as to reduce the salience of "embedded" elements that depended on their specific institutional context, especially the tight coupling with the employment system that has seemed so salient in Japan itself. One of the questions that confronts Japanese enterprises as they approach the next century is how institutionally embedded and how flexible are the various elements of Japanese enterprise. (A question too seldom asked is how institutionally embedded is the proposed U.S. model in the distinctive society of the United States.)

JAPAN'S ENTERPRISE SYSTEM FACES THE TWENTY-FIRST CENTURY

By the late 1990s, a growing chorus of voices both within Japan and abroad were calling for major changes in Japan's enterprise system. The chairman of a MITI committee on industry structure voiced a widely held opinion when he declared, "The patterns of Japanese management—the company *keiretsu*, [reciprocal] shareholding, the main bank system, lifetime employment, the seniority reward system, and so on—constitute a system that is best called an artifact of catch-up style industrial policy. However, the rationale for its existence has passed" (quoted in Dore and Ushio 1999, 84, translated by the author).[7] The view that Japan's enterprise system was developed in (and was suited to) an environment that was substantially different from that facing companies today has been asserted by Japanese economists (Nakatani 1997), top company managers (Ushio Jiro, in Dore and Ushio 1999), and foreign critics (Katz 1998). One recent popular Japanese book on restructuring listed twenty-one changes in the economic and industrial environment of the Japanese firm, ranging from the unprecedentedly long domestic recession to the emergence of sexual harassment lawsuits (Murata 1998, 17). The premise that major changes in the business environment necessitate changes in an enterprise system that was superbly adapted to the environment of an earlier period is rapidly becoming conventional wisdom within Japan. This framing simultaneously pays tribute to the virtues of the established system *for its time*, and provides a rationale for change.

It is a view that should have considerable resonance for organizational sociologists. For the last two decades, organizational sociology has witnessed the development of paradigms focusing on the interactions between environment and organizational forms, with much of the focus on the effects of the environment on organizational populations or fields. Japan today provides a fertile ground for using these paradigms to explore and explain organizational change. Yet the various paradigms highlight different aspects of environments. Population ecology sees the environment as a resource pool; institutional theory, as a set of structuring agencies shaping perceptions of legitimate and successful patterns. Both paradigms have been criticized for neglecting a third aspect of environment, the political— the power and interests of different organizations and socioeconomic groups, which can both exert disproportionate influence on the generation

---

[7] The chairman went on to say that the catch-up era had ended with the rise of the yen in 1985.

and allocation of resources and shape the rhetoric of legitimation. All three aspects of the environment have been invoked in the discussions of Japan's changing business environment.

The dominating feature of the Japanese business landscape in the 1990s was the continuing recession. The effects of the stagnation and even shrinking of the domestic market on the resources available to Japanese firms have been amplified by the extreme volatility of the yen, which has oscillated between 80 and 145 yen to the dollar over the last eight years. This has accelerated the move of production for export to offshore plants. Whereas in the 1980s the slowing of growth within Japan (to 3–4 percent per year) was offset in several industries by an expansion of production for export, in the 1990s those same industries (autos, consumer electronics, even steel) have seen Japanese companies resorting to offshore production for their foreign markets. This means that production levels in Japan have fallen both because of the domestic recession and because fewer foreign markets rely on Japanese plants. The contraction of the resource base in Japan has been further intensified by the banking crisis, which abruptly ended the ready availablity of investment capital that marked the "bubble" years of the late 1980s.

The shift to a zero-growth or even negative growth environment has put enormous pressure on the employment system, especially on the seniority-based reward system. As many analyses have pointed out (Aoki 1988), the Japanese employment system was exceptionally well adapted to an economy in which continuous growth was the norm, but currently faces great problems under persisting conditions of zero or negative growth. Another dimension of the changing resource pool that has attracted extensive attention and clearly affects the employment system has been the "graying" of the Japanese population. Japan is undergoing a rapid demographic shift, from having one of the youngest populations among the OECD countries to having, by 2010, one of the oldest. Managers worry about the shrinking number of young workers and customers, especially given the need to adopt new information technologies in the office and expand electronic commerce in the marketplace, developments which come more easily to young people.[8]

The challenge to the employment system has been exacerbated by an intra-organizational demographic crisis that faces virtually all of Japan's large firms. The "bubble" economy (1987–1991) was characterized by the annual hiring of very large cohorts of new graduates (these were the years

[8] These concerns were recently articulated by Sony's President Nobuyuki Idei, in an interview published in *Ekonomisuto* in April 1998, in which he expresses the worry that Japan is ten years behind the United States. in moving to knowledge industries, and that one of the challenges Japan faces in the shift is its aging population (Idei and Tanaka, 1998).

when Japanese managers and policymakers were bemoaning the labor shortage in Japan, especially the shortage of engineers). When the recession hit, most firms responded by drastically reducing (and in many cases eliminating) recruitment, a common response to the short downturns in growth that Japan had experienced in the past. But as the recession stretched on, and recruitment continued to lag, the demography of Japanese firms increasingly threatened the continuation of seniority-based employment system, with the huge cohorts of the "bubble bulge" advancing in the organization with very small or negligible succeeding cohorts.

These demographics have also set up major conflicts of interest across cohorts within large companies. Older employees who have "paid their dues" within the established system are much less receptive to changes in the employment system than younger workers who see their paths blocked by the large cohorts of senior workers (and who therefore strongly favor merit-based evaluation and promotion systems and the shedding of expensive older workers). Adaptive changes in the employment system risk alienating both groups, older employees because the changes violate the "psychological contract" of the old system, younger employees because they are not radical enough to open up opportunities for them. The tension is greater within the managerial ranks than on the shop floor: younger managers and potential managers often feel that top management in the late 1980s and throughout the 1990s failed to recognize the scale of the problems facing the firm, and has followed for too long the recipes of incremental change that worked so well in the earlier era.

The seemingly endless recession has not only changed the resource environment of Japanese firms; it has undermined the legitimacy of a business system that in the 1980s was widely validated by the success of the Japanese economy. When a business system is proclaimed the key to the success of an economy, then surely it cannot escape indictment for economic failure (a lesson United States pundits might do well to remember). The perceived shortcomings of the Japanese enterprise and the Japanese business system are linked to the fact that Japan's greatest successes are perceived to be in the industries of the twentieth century, not the twenty-first: in autos, consumer electronics, and hardware, not in bio-technology, software, financial services, or electronic commerce. The Internet was an American development, not Japanese. Despite massive industry spending on R&D in the "bubble" years, Japanese firms have not succeeded in leaping into new technological terrain, offering families of dazzling new products and technologies. Individual Japanese firms continue to be profitable and widely regarded as exemplars (Toyota being perhaps the most notable), but the list of such firms is much shorter than anyone would have believed in 1990. As we approach the millennium, the Japanese firm looks more like the apotheosis of the of the firm of the twentieth century, not the harbinger of the next.

Moreover, although in the 1980s Japan's vertical *keiretsu* provided a model of a "networked organization" that seemed innovative and flexible, by the end of the twentieth century it had a somewhat dated look. Information technology is often presented as an important driver of the move to the "network organization" in North America (Upton and McAfee 1996). But the "network organizations" of the Japanese vertical *keiretsu* and horizontal *keiretsu* predate by several decades the emergence of the new information technologies of the late twentieth century, and to this day Japan lags significantly behind the United States in IT applications in business. Its network organizations have been linked not so much by advanced communications technologies as by personal contact, and the very success of the personal networks may well have lessened the perceived need for advanced computer networks.

The legitimacy of the Japanese business system also suffers from the erosion of the credibility of other elements of the Japanese business environment, most notably the nation's political institutions. The fracturing of the long-dominant Liberal-Democratic Party and the squabbles among the factions and the fractions of the LDP (elements of which broke off to form new parties, often with little to distinguish them except for their leaders), a series of scandals indicating astonishing levels of incompetence (the slow and often obstructive response to the Kobe earthquake, for example) and even corruption in the hitherto sacrosanct bureaucracy, and the failure of the Ministry of Finance to respond effectively to the recession and the banking crisis all contributed to a widespread disillusionment with Japan's institutions overall.[9] It seems plausible that the delegitimation of the Japanese political system, which has been so closely identified with the business system and with Japan's past economic success, would have a contagious effect on the business system itself.

The changes in the contours of Japan's power structure went beyond the weakening of the government and the steady erosion of the policy tools available to the bureaucracy to protect and foster industry (due to the strengthening of international pressures, GATT, and its successor the WTO). The transformation of Japan's political landscape in the 1990s involved the politicization of industrial and economic policy, as the fracturing of the LDP intensified the political parties' search for electoral support (Pempel 1998). The decade saw widespread and intensifying complaints within and outside Japan about the apparent policy paralysis in the face of the continuing recession and the banking crisis. A major contributing fac-

[9] For an excellent discussion of these phenomena, see T.J. Pempel's recent book, *Regime Shift* (1998).

tor has been growing conflicts of interest within the business community, and the consequent lack of consistent pressure on bureaucrats and politicians in support of a policy program. Just as the firm itself is increasingly divided between managers favoring radical change and those preferring adaptive change, so the business community is divided by tensions between companies and industrial sectors that favor deregulation and those that oppose it, those that favor modified market solutions for financially distressed industries and those that favor strong government intervention and support, and those that are interested in adopting and adapting the current crop of fashionable "solutions" (from reengineering to stock options for managers) and those that oppose them.

This last point is significant: the growing consensus that change is necessary does not mean that there is consensus on the direction and extent of change. Pempel (1998) has noted that although Japan is clearly undergoing what he calls a "regime shift," the outcome of the shift is still highly uncertain. The same is true for the business system. In contrast to the political system, however, Japan's business system is faced with one coherent and systematic model for change: the move to United States-style shareholder capitalism. The increasingly global business press, the international consulting firms, the business schools, and the leading international financial services firms and investment banks all share a general model of the business system of the future: based in highly flexible labor markets with high interfirm mobility; characterized by the rapid creation and failure of entrepreneurial enterprises; with flexible rather than highly structured interfirm networks; with managers who are agents of shareholders and responsive to their demands (and who are themselves shareholders in their own firms); with high-performing individuals rewarded handsomely for their contributions—but only as long as they are performing at an exceptional level; with individuals responsible for their own careers and their own welfare. It is a model that makes many Japanese, and many Americans, uneasy (Capelli et al. 1997).

The aspect that generates the greatest uneasiness is the employment system, simultaneously the most vulnerable aspect and the most central to the other dimensions of Japan's enterprise system. Much of the distrust of American shareholder capitalism is its apparent disregard for the welfare and claims of employees. Although much of the commentary from the Western business press has focused on the employment security aspect of the employment system as the element most in need of change, it still has strong support in Japan, as a recent analysis of Japanese labor and management indicates: (Sugeno and Suwa 1997, 56)

> Both labor and management maintain a deep attachment to the long-term employment system with its merits in stable employment and efficient human re-

source development. The system will therefore remain intact for quite a while with its strong inertia although it is likely to undergo significant modification.

The main area of modification promises to be a shift from a seniority-based to a merit-based system. . In a network-based system, such as the Japanese vertical *keiretsu*, experience is a critically important factor in merit, because knowledge of the multilayered networks of the enterprise comes through experience. It is, however, no longer seen as sufficient. Much of the strain created by the "bubble bulge" can be addressed by adjusting promotion and reward systems and by episodic adjustments of the workforce, rather than a frontal attack on the social contract of employment security that would generate serious conflict with the enterprise unions. Many Japanese managers also fear that ending employment security would erode employee willingness to accept unquestioningly the assignments and transfers that underpin their person-dependent coordination systems.

Such adaptive changes are likely to continue well into this century. Japan has a long tradition of learning from abroad, in organizational as well as material technologies. But if we compare previous experience with that of today, we see two very great differences. One is the degree to which Japan's own business system was established when it faced the challenge of new systems from abroad; the other is the level on which those systems operated. In the Meiji period, in a classic industrial revolution mode, new organizational forms were adopted in new industries that rapidly took over the organizational landscape. Subsequently, most of the acquired organizational technologies (such as mass production, scientific management, quality control) were focused on the work process rather than the form of enterprise, and could easily be adapted into business enterprises whose basic form, even through decades of change, differed considerably from that of the originating organizations. The current orthodoxy of American shareholder capitalism (even—perhaps especially—in the new, entrepreneurial network version of it) centers on the form of the firm itself, making adaptation into existing enterprises considerably more difficult.

One way to portray the current situation in Japan is to see two paths of change stretching before the Japanese business system. One involves sorting out specific elements of the American model to distinguish elements of work process from organizational form and from interorganizational networks, and then adapting the former to an evolving but still very different enterprise structure (a process we have seen intensifying in the last few years). The other involves creating new organizations to populate the emerging twenty-first century industries, organizations that may have a form rather like that described in Powell's chapter of this volume, with distinctive Japanese twists. Of the two, the first is likely to dominate, at least in the early years of the twenty-first century. Japan's large firms have long exhibited a strong proclivity for moving quickly into new industries, in contrast to the dominant United States pattern of new firms emerging to lead new industries. Some will do so by internal diversification, some by setting up new "child companies" in the *keiretsu*. Whichever pattern dominates, it will mean that many of the existing patterns of the Japanese enterprise system will be carried over into the new.

What we are seeing in Japan today, at the beginning of the twenty-first century, can be seen as a de-institutionalization of the hitherto strongly institutionalized patterns that have held sway over large Japanese firms for nearly half a century. Those patterns are still very strongly entrenched, but they are increasingly challenged, both cognitively and normatively (to use W. Richard Scott's [1992] distinction). In an era when the business press, consultants, and academics are vociferously pushing the inevitability of "global standards" of enterprise and when Japanese corporate leaders like Sony's President Nobuyuki Idei names Bill Gates, Andy Grove, and Jack Welch as role models (Idei and Tanaka 1998), few Japanese can be unaware of alternative ways of doing things and be firmly convinced of the normative superiority of Japanese management. Japan's companies are searching for ways to retain many of the advantages of the old ways with innovations that overcome their disadvantages. The changes are likely to occur in different ways and at different rates in different industries and even in different companies. The strong pressures from the triumphant "American shareholder capitalism" model are likely to be stronger in financial services, for example, than in manufacturing. The difference across sectors in the pace and direction of change is not the only factor making predictions about the firm of the twenty-first century in Japan a perilous activity. Throughout the postwar era, the models of Japanese enterprise have been articulated well after the emergence of the developments they describe. Changes are likely to occur through experiment and emergent change, rather than through planned change and the articulation of models like those so popular in America (e.g., the "virtual company," the "virtual factory"). The process is made all the more difficult by the brief but heady experience in the 1980s of believing that they were in fact the models for others. The sudden fall from preeminence in the eyes of the world is a very significant factor in the de-institutionalization of the Japanese enterprise system.

IMPLICATIONS FOR THE FIRM IN THE TWENTY-FIRST CENTURY

The case of Japan raises many points of interest for the evolution of twenty-first century firms, but three stand out. One is the key role of interorganizational networks; the second is the importance of the employment system; the third is the complex interplay between the pressures for cross-border convergence that are one element of the phenomenon called "globalization."

It is becoming increasingly clear that between the two levels of analysis that have long dominated organizational sociology, the organization and the environment, there is an intermediate level: the organizational network, which is itself shaped by the external environment and in turn shapes the organization. The growing importance of this network seems to be one of the key elements of the future evolution of business firms. One consequence of the growing salience of business networks concerns the nature of work. Japanese enterprises have much longer experience of the individual and social costs of a "network-based" business system that within companies relies on teamwork and shared responsibilities, and within interorganizational relationships depends on relational contracting with suppliers and relationship marketing with customers. The long work hours, the demand for the unstinting application of the creative energies of employees to solve problems, and the measurement of employee quality by visible effort (especially by the amount of time the employee spends at work) have been recognized as problems in Japanese companies for nearly two decades. Often they have been portrayed as distinctively Japanese pathologies. In fact, they seem inseparable from the diffuse obligations of the networked organization. The phenomenon of *karoshi* (death from overwork) is only the most extreme manifestation of a much more widespread problem, one that American managers and workers are now struggling with, even if they have yet to develop a word for death from the stresses of overwork.

The growing importance of the network or the "extended enterprise" model has two additional challenges for comparative organizational sociology, beyond the effect on the nature of work. One is the need to extend research on coordination and control and governance systems beyond the firm to the level of the network. The Japanese vertical and horizontal *keiretsu* illustrate how complex network governance can be, and how seemingly different patterns can coexist within the same society. A second challenge is to understand the extent to which business networks function as employment networks. In Japan, the extensive intranetwork mobility is complemented by very low levels of mobility across competing networks. In the United States, it seems likely that the links between business networks and employment networks differ in structure but not in importance.

This point leads to the second theme: the importance of the employment system in the evolution of new organizational forms. The employment system (by which we mean the established patterns through which people are recruited into and move within and across firms, and the various obligations incurred by the firm when it takes on different categories of employees) can have a powerful effect on the formation of new organizations and on the patterns of diversification of existing firms (as we have clearly seen in the case of Japan). The extent to which the existing employment system carries over into new organizational forms, versus the extent to which new forms are made possible by a weakening of the established employment system, is an issue raised by both the Japanese and the American cases.

Finally, the Japanese case reinforces the theme of David Stark's chapter in this book: that although "network organizations" are likely to emerge as dominant organizational forms in most major business systems, the form and the governance systems of those networks will differ significantly across national business systems, much as the form and governance systems of firms have differed throughout this century. The trajectory of change in the patterns and forms of business enterprises will be profoundly influenced by supranational isomorphic pressures from an increasingly global "organizational field" composed of the business press, the international consulting firms, the investment banks, and business schools. However, those pressures will influence but not determine the development of business systems in various countries, as these pressures will inevitably interact with local institutional pressures (such as employment systems) to produce distinctive patterns in each society. What seem to be pressures for the reduction of variety across systems, as David Stark's chapter indicates, in fact become sources of innovative combinations of previously institutionalized patterns and new models. They even increase intrasystem variety as different populations or fields adopt and adapt new patterns at different rates or of different types. In short, we can expect to see Japan in the next century produce not a clone of American network capitalism, but the next generation of the Japanese capitalist firm.

PART TWO

Commentaries

CHAPTER 5

The Durability of the Corporate Form

Reinier Kraakman

THE COMPANY, the corporation, the enterprise—the firm by any name structures modern market societies almost as pervasively as the family or the nation-state. It is therefore important news that the firm is evolving in novel ways on the margins of these societies, as two of the principal contributors to this volume suggest. In his provocative essay on the firm in the twenty-first century, Walter Powell argues that hierarchical firms in the knowledge-based industries (at least) are dissolving into fluid "network[s] of treaties," networks in which project-based collaborations and joint ventures diffuse firm boundaries and may even supplant them entirely. Similarly, David Stark argues that the real economic actors in the privatizing economies of Hungary and the Czech Republic are not firms but networks of firms organized in corporate groups with extensive cross-ownership ties. Of the principal contributors to this volume, only Eleanor Westney strikes a note of caution about the dissolution of corporate boundaries. In her discussion of Japanese firms, she observes that the vertical *keiretsu*, once held out as a "network-based" alternative to the freestanding American corporation, no longer seriously challenges the dominant Anglo-American model of competition among freestanding firms.

NETWORKS AND FIRMS

Insofar as they address the future of the firm, then, all three commentators focus on the extent to which the firm's boundaries, as a legal and organizational entity, have been (or will be) displaced by crosscutting networks of individuals and firms. But what does it mean for firms to be displaced by networks? On my reading of the principal contributors, three meanings are possible.

First, the claim that network's displace firms as economic actors might be an observation about the declining importance of a legal form—specifically, the corporate form—in environments in which network structures have become institutionalized. This would be a claim about the economic value of the legal attributes associated with the corporate form, including the value of its explicit allocation of risk, return, and ownership rights among participants in the firm, and of its capacity to facilitate transparent contracting among these participants.

Second, the claim that networks displace firms might be an observation about how existing firms become less significant as they are absorbed into larger networks that dominate their policies or coordinate their outputs. This claim can be understood as an extension of Ronald Coase's (1937) distinction between the coordination of production across markets or within firms. Network structures presumably fall on a continuum between hierarchically organized firms and spot markets in which buyers and sellers fully negotiate the terms of their transactions. Thus, as firms affiliate with larger networks, network ties coordinate relations between firms that were once transactional (if they existed at all). The affiliated firms are partly integrated: they are no longer governed entirely by market transactions, but neither are they fully integrated into a single large firm.

Third, the claim that networks displace firms can also mean the converse of the integration of firms into larger networks: namely, the disintegration of firms into networks of smaller firms or individuals. Once again, such networks represent a middle ground between full integration under the auspices of a single firm and complete dissolution into the medium of the market. The third form of displacement, then, is similar to but opposite in direction from the second. The integration of firms into networks is a half step *away* from market coordination of production; the dissolution of firms into networks is a half step *toward* market coordination, with a concomitant increase in flexibility and transaction costs.

The scholar of corporate law can view the integration of firms into larger groups or their dissolution into smaller networks with equanimity. Networks pose a real threat of embarrassment only if they can somehow displace the corporate form as a device for organizing economic activity. To explore this possibility, I next review the core legal elements of the corporate form. The remainder of this overview argues that the organizational analyses offered by the principal contributors to this volume tend to affirm rather than undermine the economic import of the corporate form. I then make this point for the examples of foreign firms integrated into network structures offered by Stark and Westney. Finally, I provide a parallel argument for the examples of high-tech networks offered by Powell.

The Corporate Form

From the legal perspective, a firm is above all a judicially recognized entity possessing key attributes of legal personality, such as the legal power to contract and to own property. Although there are many legal forms that can confer these powers on an enterprise, one form—the corporate form (or the "company" form in British parlance)—dominates the organization of large-scale business enterprise in every jurisdiction, from Delaware to Japan. This fact is itself a noteworthy regularity of modern economic life that underscores the value of the core attributes of the corporate form. Five such attributes are well recognized in the legal literature. A moment's reflection will suggest why each of them has useful economic properties.

First, corporations have legal personality, which, as mentioned earlier, permits them to contract with third parties, own property, pay taxes, and sue or be sued as free-standing entities. Legal personality can be viewed as a device for economizing on transaction costs. It is the corporation's fictional personality that permits it to serve, quite literally, as a "nexus of contracts," in the happy phrase of Jensen and Meckling (1976). The multiple participants in the firm can vastly simplify the coordination of their activities by contracting with the corporation rather than forming bilateral relationships with one another. The absence of centralized management makes the internal coordination of informal networks difficult. Moreover, because networks lack the legal capacity to transact as entities, they cannot coordinate relationships with outsiders except when—as in the case of the family company—they organize collectively in the corporate form.

To be sure, the legal personality of a flesh-and-blood individual can substitute for the corporate entity when firms are small. But large firms that must pool the capital of many contributors require separate entity status and separate accounts to protect the providers of capital against expropriation. In theory, providers of capital could transfer ownership rights to a manager for exclusive investment in business activities in exchange for the manager's contractual undertaking to pay out the net proceeds of the business after debiting a management fee. In practice, however, such a scheme would be vulnerable to a significant risk of managerial theft or poor performance (Hansmann and Kraakman 2000b).

A second key feature of the corporate form is that corporations are investor-owned in the sense that shareholders—the contributors of capital—have control rights and a legal claim to the profit or residual economic return from the enterprise after other participants receive their contractual due. Again, firms do not have to be investor-owned. Other legal forms of enterprise vest ownership rights in other factors of production: the cooperative form permits worker, supplier, or customer ownership; the nonprofit form eliminates ownership entirely. Nevertheless, it is the investor-owned corporate form that dominates business everywhere. A strong case can be made that the homogeneous interest of shareholders in increasing corporate value lowers the governance and decision-making costs of the firm, and thereby favors investor ownership over other patterns of ownership (Hansmann 1996). By contrast, complex network structures among heterogeneous firms blur ownership rights in the joint outputs of these networks, which leads to what Stark (this volume) terms "asset ambiguity." It follows that these networks face formidable obstacles in taking joint decisions or engaging in self-governance. In particular, it is unclear how they can divide commonly produced value among their heterogeneous members—unless, of course, they are organized by a detailed multiparty contract or possess a strong internal hierarchy.

The third universal feature of the corporate form is the delegation of decision-making power to a single authority within the firm. Any company with multiple owners must have a mechanism to ensure that it is managed in its owners' interests. The more widespread ownership is, the more important delegated management becomes for coordinated decision-making, and the more acute the agency problem becomes of ensuring that the firm is managed in its owners' interests. The corporate form typically solves the agency problem by vesting ultimate management authority in a board of directors or similar committee organ. Centralizing authority serves importantly to reduce the costs of informing and polling the firm's owners— its shareholders—about any but the most fundamental corporate decisions. Moreover, vesting ultimate decision-making authority in a board of directors that is formally separate from the operational managers of the company has other functions as well. It serves as a check on delegated decision-making (Fama and Jensen 1983), and it makes the board a convenient focus for control mechanisms based on legal duties such as shareholder suits (Hansmann and Kraakman 2000a).

By contrast, unincorporated networks naturally lack the centralized management and decision-making advantages of the board structure unless they follow the direction of a corporate leader. This lacuna severely limits their ability to coordinate production, unless there is a strong hierarchy among firms, and compounds the governance problems that arise from ambiguous ownership rights.

The fourth universal feature of the corporate form is limited liability. The corporate form creates a default term in contracts between firms and their creditors that limits the claims of creditors to assets that are the property of the firm itself, and excludes further claims against the firm's shareholders, managers, or other participants such as employees and suppliers.

Historically, limited liability was not always associated with the corporate form. Until relatively recently, some important jurisdictions still made unlimited shareholder liability for company debts the governing rule (Blumberg 1987). Nevertheless, limited liability is now a universal feature of the company form, which strongly indicates its value as a contracting tool and financing device.

To begin with, limited liability is a low-cost device for partitioning assets into distinct pools that can be separately pledged to the particular creditors who are best able to evaluate and monitor them. As a consequence of limited liability, a shareholder's personal assets are automatically pledged as security to his or her personal creditors, who are well-situated to monitor the shareholder's personal credit, while company assets are pledged to corporate creditors, who are better able to monitor business assets. In addition, limited liability allows companies to employ corporate subsidiaries to pledge different pools of assets to different creditors according to their comparative advantages in monitoring—thus enhancing the collateral value of company assets (Hansmann and Kraakman 2000b). Finally, limited liability permits flexibility in the allocation of risk and return between shareholders and company creditors, reduces the transaction costs of collection in the case of insolvency, and simplifies the pricing of stock in an active trading market (Easterbrook and Fischel 1985)—a point that I return to later.

To be sure, networks also enjoy limited liability of a sort. Since they are not legal entities, they cannot be liable for the contracts or torts of their members. But without the corporate form, such homemade limited liability is also of limited value. It cannot protect the personal assets of investors from business risk except when the members of the network are themselves corporations. In addition, without ready access to the corporate form, networks—even networks of firms—cannot easily invest jointly in the equity of common projects without placing all of their assets at risk.

The transferability of shares is the fifth and last of the core attributes of the corporate form. Corporate law everywhere provides that the legal personality of the firm is distinct from that of its owners, who—absent agreement to the contrary—may transfer their ownership rights (shares) without disrupting the continuity of the company's operations. Transferability in this sense has obvious value. It provides shareholders with liquidity and with the ability to construct and maintain diversified investment portfolios; it underwrites the formation of active trading markets; and it permits firms to conduct business uninterruptedly as the identity of their owners changes. Needless to add, these financing opportunities are not open to unincorporated networks—although, again, they may be open to the individual members of corporate networks.

In sum, the legal features of the corporate form arise from the economic exigencies associated with raising capital, controlling agency costs, facilitating decision-making, and allocating risk among the participants in the firm. The corporate form is now universal; its features are unlikely to change. Instead, corporate governance is likely to converge under the pressure of international capital markets, global business culture, and the now-dominant view that corporations should be managed in the interests of shareholders (Hansmann and Kraakman forthcoming).[1] The corporation as we know it is simply too useful to disappear or radically change.

---

[1] At least three alternative models of corporate governance have come and gone over the past fifty years: (1) a trusteeship model, in which independent directors manage firms on

NETWORKS OF FIRMS

But if the corporate form, like the wheel, is likely to persist, the next question is, So what? Apart from creating legal personality, legal forms are ultimately just standard-form contracts for use by the participants in enterprises. If network structures are the economic actors that matter, they will presumably adapt the corporate form to their own ends. Indeed, most examples of firm networks that behave as economic agents in their own right—the Hungarian enterprise networks and Japanese *keiretsu*, discussed in this volume by Stark and Westney respectively. Korean *chaebol*; and the many corporate groups of Western Europe—are stitched together internally by the ties of interlocking share ownership. Moreover, these ties assume many forms, ranging from pyramids and strong parent-subsidiary groups to the weak cross-ownership links within Japanese horizontal *keiretsu*. What light does the corporate form shed on these structures?

Groups and the Corporate Form

The short answer is that all of these corporate groups coexist easily with the corporate form. The corporate form facilitates group structures by permitting a shareholder (which may be a second corporation) to purchase a controlling interest in a firm, appoint its own directors to the board, and exercise managerial power as it wishes, consistent with observing the rights of minority investors. When one corporation controls another, the corporate group that results is not only a de facto entity but also a de jure entity for most purposes, since it is likely to be dominated by the board of the controlling firm. In the extreme case where the acquired firm becomes a wholly owned subsidiary, its separate legal personality is merely a convenient device for allocating business risks to creditors and protecting the contract rights of the acquired company for the benefit of the parent.

In circumstances in which corporate groups maintain control over their members by holding on to control rights in these firms while relinquishing economic rights, the architecture of corporate groups can, however, come

---

behalf of all corporate constituencies; (2) an employee representation model, in which labor representatives share board seats with stockholders following the example of German code-termination; and (3) a statist model, in which the government intervenes in corporate governance to safeguard the interest of society. All three of these alternatives have lost credibility. The conglomerate wave of the 1960s has persuaded most observers that managers, if given the chance, are likely to favor their own interests over those of anyone else. German-style codetermination, once highly popular in Europe, is now recognized as a dead end, in part because of its large governance costs. And finally, statist intervention is in bad repute everywhere after a generally poor track record, the widespread success of economic privatization, and the worldwide collapse of socialism (Hansmann and Kraakman forthcoming)

into conflict with the economics of the corporate form. Several legal devices can force such a separation of cash flow rights and control rights.

One of these devices is the formation of pyramid ownership structures, which are common in Israel, Sweden, South Africa, and Canada (Bebchuk et al. forthcoming). In a pyramid structure, a controlling shareholder holds a control block in a holding company, which in turn controls an operating company (two-tier pyramid), or in a second holding company that controls an operating company (three-tier pyramid). With each successive holding company, the controlling shareholder retains control rights in the underlying operating company while selling off additional claims to the residual cash flows of the operating company. The controller of a three-level pyramid needs to hold the equivalent of only 12.5 percent of operating company stock to maintain an unshakable lock on control; the controller of a four-tier pyramid needs only 6.25 percent

A second device for separating control from ownership rights is to attach differential voting rights to corporate shares. In the extreme, the company can recapitalize with a large class of nonvoting common stock held by public investors and a small class of voting stock held by company insiders. As with pyramid structures, the economic stakes of the controller under a dual-class stock regime can be set arbitrarily low without jeopardizing his or her voting control unless corporate law limits the use of this device (as it does in a few jurisdictions). Dual-class equity structures are common in Canada and throughout Europe. In France, for example, forty-six of the top two hundred firms have dual-class equity structures (*The Economist* 8 August 1998: 58).

Finally, control rights can be separated from ownership rights through cross-holdings among companies that buttress the grip of a lead firm or controlling shareholder. Once again, controllers can use cross-ownership to exercise absolute authority over operating companies with arbitrarily small economic stakes (Bebchuk et al. forthcoming). Stark (this volume) has documented the pervasive cross-ownership ties among large Hungarian companies. Ethnic Chinese families based in Thailand and Indonesia frequently employ cross-holdings as well as pyramids to secure control of their business groups. As compared to pyramids, cross-holdings have the advantage from the controller's perspective of obscuring the locus of control, which may account for their relative popularity in Asia (Weidenbaum 1996).

Severing the relationship between control rights and economic rights—whether through pyramids, dual class equity, or cross holdings—dilutes the corporate form by shifting control to parties who are not full residual claimants. On the plausible assumption that these controllers can extract private benefits unavailable to other shareholders by virtue of possessing control, the result is to distort the incentives of these "minority" controllers relative to those of a 100 percent owner whose sole objective is to increase corporate value. More particularly, controllers with small economic stakes have powerful incentives to select investment projects that maximize their own private benefits (rather than corporate value) and to overinvest in the firm relative to an efficient scale of investment (Bebchuk et al. forthcoming). Of course, a perfect market for control would rapidly eliminate such inefficient ownership structures by buying out minority controllers and restoring the traditional correspondence between cash-flow rights and control rights. But whether real markets control can do the same is less clear. It depends, among other things, on whether controllers are willing to sell control, and on whether the prevailing legal regime permits them to keep—rather than share—enough of the value of resulting efficiency gains to offset their loss of control benefits (Bebchuk and Roe 1999).

Vertical Keiretsu, Horizontal Keiretsu and Cross-Ownership Networks

The model of a corporate group in which a parent company or controlling shareholder employs voting rights to dominate the management of multiple firms describes many Asian and European corporate networks as well as parent-subsidiary relations among U.S. firms. But as we have seen, this model actually illustrates the key role of the corporate form in cementing corporate groups. In effect, it demonstrates how corporate planners can force the partial integration of firms through the simple expediency of purchasing large blocks of voting stock. Control stakes translate automatically into authority over the firm's assets and employees; after all, that is the meaning of centralized management.

Yet one structure described in this volume deviates from the usual model of multiple companies stitched together principally by a shared ownership structure of cross-shareholdings. This exception is Westney's "vertical" keiretsu (this volume). To be sure, these keiretsu resemble conventional groups in some ways. They are hierarchical, since they are designed to permit a lead company (like Toyota) to focus principally on the final assembly of products while coordinating earlier stages in the manufacturing process through a network of dependent suppliers. In addition, they are said to perform at least two economic functions. First, they allow lead firms and their suppliers to contract without fear of opportunistic hold-ups, since they each hold large stakes in one another (Gilson and Roe 1993; Ramseyer forthcoming). Second, as Westney notes in this volume, they provide an internal labor market that allows employees to be moved among firms within the network in the interest of providing the lead firm with hiring flexibility and encouraging good relationships within the group.

What distinguishes vertical keiretsu, however, is that their principal "glue" is not necessarily a common ownership structure. Lead firms may or may not hold controlling stakes in their suppliers; but when they do not, other kinds of ties—including the personal ties of employees and the institutional ties of established supplier-customer relationships—suffice to bind affiliated companies and lead firms. As Westney indicates, these close, multiplex relationships have no precise analogue elsewhere. For this reason, the vertical *keiretsu* is indeed a form of "network entity" that is partially independent of the corporate form. But precisely because it is uniquely Japanese, it is unlikely to be replicated outside of Japan unless it can be reconstructed with ownership ties—the usual cement of corporate groups.

In contrast to vertical *keiretsu*, the horizontal *keiretsu* described by Westney (in her chapter) appear to be something less than full-fledged corporate groups. These *keiretsu* feature numerous unrelated firms linked to one another by reciprocal cross-shareholdings and loosely arrayed around a main bank. The function of the cross-shareholdings in these structures presents a puzzle. They are usually too small to give significant influence over corporate policy to their holders, and they do not ordinarily track trading relationships. One traditional explanation—that the *keiretsu's* aggregate cross-shareholdings assist main banks in monitoring the managements of affiliated companies—no longer seems plausible after the banking crisis of the late 1980s. A more promising explanation presented in chapter 4 is that *keiretsu* cross-shareholdings were originally established to protect managers from hostile takeovers. Despite the traditionally managerialist cast of Japanese corporations, Japan's corporate law is—paradoxically—unusually protective of shareholder rights and adverse to anti-takeover defenses (Shishido 1997). Thus, the cross-ownership of shares may be one of the few effective anti-takeover defenses open to Japanese managers.[2] If so, it would seem to follow that horizontal *keiretsu* are not true corporate groups at all—at least not in the sense of parent-subsidiary structures, Korean family-dominated *chaebols*, or vertical *keiretsu*. Rather, they are defensive confederations of unrelated firms assembled principally to protect the interests of top managers.

An interesting question raised by the distinction between horizontal and vertical *keiretsu* in Japan is whether a similar distinction can be drawn for the corporate networks of formally socialist countries. For example, Stark's observation (this volume) that extensive cross-ownership ties among Hungary's top two hundred firms function as a buffer against economic uncer-

---

[2] Other explanations for cross-holdings in horizontal *keiretsu* range from the assertion that these relatively small cross-holdings are purely symbolic—an expression of affiliation rather than a means of policing it—to Mark Ramseyer's claim that main bank holdings permit banks to profit from trading on nonpublic information (Ramseyer forthcoming). Whatever the explanation, however, there is evidence that cross-shareholdings in horizontal *keiretsu* are beginning to unwind as a result of bank mergers and competitive pressure to seek higher returns on capital (Abrahams and Tett 1999).

tainty bears a passing resemblance to the anti-takeover rationale for horizontal *keiretsu*. Alternatively, it is worth asking whether vertical ties among Hungarian firms might serve to control opportunistic contracting between suppliers and end user, much as they do within Japan's vertical *keiretsu*.

The Future of Groups

Stepping back from particular network structures, it is apparent that the corporate form defines the boundaries of corporate groups no less than it structures the identity and management of individual firms. Most groups are bound together by stock ownership or, more precisely, by the control rights that stock confers. Whether a public holding company or a tight-knit family exercises the decisive votes, the right to select and discharge the managers of affiliated companies is the power to set the policies of these firms as well as those of the group as a whole.

Even if corporate groups build on the corporate form rather than displace it, however, the question remains whether such groups are likely to play a dominant role in the world economy of the twenty-first century, as they do now in Hungary and the Czech Republic (Stark, this volume), and in much of the rest of the world as well (La Porta et al. 1999).

Although no one can answer with any confidence, my best guess is that corporate groups will decline rather than increase in importance. The worldwide trend is toward simplifying group structures, dismantling cross-shareholdings, and releasing freestanding firms to pursue the interests of their shareholders. The closest American analogue is the "deconglomeration" wave of the 1980s, which undid the ungainly conglomerates built up in previous decades. Westney (this volume) rightly observes that the world today has "only one systematic and coherent model" of a healthy economy: a market-based model of flexible labor markets, flexible intercorporate relationships, and corporate managers who pursue shareholder interests. This vision of fluid markets and focused firms—the only plausible vision today—necessarily accepts individual firms (with their managers and shareholders) as the private sector's paramount economic actors and, correlatively, tends to delegitimate groups, especially when these larger structures separate corporate ownership from control or serve to insulate managers from shareholder demands.

Economic crisis and the worldwide currency of the market model have already initiated a process of "deinstitutionalization" of the Japanese economy, in Westney's apt phrase (this volume), and they threaten to do likewise in the rest of Asia. Outside of Asia, corporate governance reform spearheaded by an increasingly active shareholders rights movement is also having an effect. Indeed, one of the most important global developments over the past decade may be the rise of a self-conscious constituency of public shareholders, not only in the United States but in Europe and even Japan. For example, partly in response to shareholder pressure, France's forty largest firms have begun to dismantle their elaborate cross-ownership stakes (*The Economist* 8 August 1998: 59). Similarly, suits by minority shareholders against management that were once unheard of in Japan have now become common (Shishido 1997, 161).

In addition, legal developments are contributing indirectly to the dismantling of corporate groups. One key reform is the reduction of intercorporate capital gains taxes. For example, a recent proposal to lower these taxes is expected to significantly reduce the shareholdings of Germany's financial firms in its industrial firms (Simonian 1999).[3] A less obvious reform with similar consequences is the growing protection of minority shareholder rights worldwide, and particularly in the European Community. There is a strong global correlation between the appearance of freestanding, widely held firms and strong legal protection for minority shareholder rights (LaPorta et al.1998). It follows that the global trend toward improved financial accounting, increased transparency, tougher duties for corporate managers, and improved securities regulations should reduce the attractions of corporate groups and increase the viability of stand-alone firms.

SMALL-FIRM COLLABORATION AND JOINT VENTURES

The preceding discussion has focused on the aggregation of firms into larger group structures, primarily through ties of share ownership. As Powell's contribution to this volume reminds us, however, not all corporate networks integrate business activity. Networks may also reflect the *dis*-integration of corporate activity, as when networks or joint ventures undertake projects that would otherwise be pursued by fully integrated firms. It is these collaborative structures—in Coasian terms, half steps from the firm to the market—that Powell's essays in this volume and elsewhere (Powell 1996) depict as the organizational hallmarks of a "new economy" in high-tech America.

On the important dimensions of durability, substance, and legal character, the new high-tech, information-based networks could hardly be more different from traditional corporate groups. The new networks arise in highly competitive markets, often for sophisticated technological products.

---

[3] The American literature of the 1980s celebrating the role of German universal banks in monitoring German managers failed to note that financial institutions were deterred from selling their shareholdings by extremely high (up to 60 percent) capital gains taxes. Elimination of these taxes is expected to greatly reduce German cross-holding structures over time (Simonian 1999).

They arise between autonomous firms and individuals who cooperate together in individual projects, and they are groomed by venture capitalists and management consultants who prescribe flat hierarchies, relational contracting, and performance-based compensation (Powell, this volume). Far from colliding with the market model, the inhabitants of the new networks celebrate it with stock options. Nevertheless, relationships within the new networks are not ordinarily based on the cross-ownership of shares; these relationships are too transitory. The watchwords are flexibility, trust, and relational contracting. Firms pursue multiple projects; shifting networks of companies coalesce around emerging opportunities; and success belongs to the network of players who arrive first with the opportunity, the capital, and the requisite expertise.

As in the case of traditional groups, however, the corporate form is an indispensable foundation for this brave new world. It is the high-powered incentives of share ownership and stock options that drive entrepreneurs to found startup firms and venture capitalists to fund them. In addition, corporations are essential as hitching posts in larger networks of supply contracts and joint ventures. As the "nexus of contracts" metaphor suggests, one of the most important functions of the corporation is precisely to provide a durable point of legal attachment for the wider network of participants behind every firm (Hansmann and Kraakman 2000b). Far from being displaced by networks, then, corporations anchor networks and clarify the rights of their core participants. To see this point, consider the archetypal life cycle of the Silicon Valley investment opportunity. The idea first appears within an informal network of engineers, perhaps employees of an already established firm. As the idea matures, its entrepreneurial authors will launch a startup company and pursue their contacts in the venture capital community (another network) in search of financing. If their efforts succeed, they will strike a deal with one or more particular VC firms. Next, the company, once it begins operations, will itself spawn a new network of contractual relationships among investors, suppliers, employees, customers, creditors, and technical specialists. This company network may even extend further—to regulators, stock analysts, and public investors—after an initial public stock offering. At each step, then, the evolution of firms and networks moves in tandem.

Of course, Powell could rightly observe that there is another sense in which this Silicon Valley story might be said to reflect a displacement of firms by networks. It might be that in the past the entire cycle of conceiving, financing, and developing the idea would have occurred under the legal umbrella of a single, established firm, while today it may move through several environments before coming to rest in a new firm nurtured by outside networks. In this case, collaborative networks of small firms might be said to displace *portions* of much larger companies. The principal case in point is the symbiotic relationship between smaller biotech firms and much larger pharmaceutical companies, which is well documented by Powell (1996; see also Hansmann 1996). Where drugs were once developed largely in-house by the pharmaceutical companies, these companies now finance and ultimately acquire new drugs that are developed outside by creative networks of smaller biotech firms. The story is not unlike a manufacturer's decision to contract out an important step in the production process, although the decision was presumably less voluntary in the case of the pharmaceutical companies.

Conclusion

Is the network displacing the firm, then? Not surprisingly, the answer turns on what it means to displace the firm. On the level of legal forms, there is no evidence that the firm—the corporate form—is in any danger of being displaced. Indeed, the network structures explored by the principal contributors to this volume overwhelmingly depend on the legal attributes of the corporate form. The Hungarian networks described by Stark turn on cross-ownership stakes for Hungary's largest firms and vertical ownership ties for its group structures. In both cases, partial integration across firms rests on the control rights that accompany share ownership under the corporate form. Moreover, similar cross-ownership and group structures are common in virtually all economies that lack a well-developed stock market (and even in some countries that have such a market, such as Sweden and Canada).

By contrast, ownership rights structured by the corporate form do not undergird the loose collaborative networks that Powell identifies as the organizational innovation of America's knowledge-based industries. Joint ventures generally assume a corporate form with the co-venturers sharing stock ownership in their common company. Parent companies often retain equity stakes in firms that, for financing or incentive reasons, are spun off as separate corporations. But collaborative networks in which a lead firm relies on other firms to undertake key tasks in a common project are built upon relational contracting, trust, and reputation (Powell, this volume). These networks are too project-specific and rapidly evolving to assume a rigid structure based on cross-ownership ties. Nevertheless, the corporate form is critically important for these networks in other ways. Even relational contracts require contracting parties with legal personality, assets, and reputation. The firm—the corporation—is the repository of all three. In addition, the high-powered incentives created by common stock and stock options—and the financing possibilities created by preferred stock and convertible debt—are the economic foundations of the startup firms that dominate the knowledge-based industries.

Regardless of the size of firms and the extent of network integration, then, the corporate form is likely to provide the only compelling legal structure for enterprises in the future. All of the principal commentators in this volume caution against the expectation that the organization of enterprises will converge across major economies. With respect to the legal form of the firm, however, convergence is already largely a *fait accompli*. The core legal attributes of the corporate form have already converged; the fine structure of corporate and securities law, as well as accounting systems, are likely to converge in the future, as the emerging consensus about the function of the corporate form and the value of developed capital markets gathers momentum.

Given that the corporate form remains a stable backdrop, we may find it hard to make out the case for either an increase or a decrease in the integration of economic activity within firms or across networks and markets. Stark has documented the extensive formation of corporate groups in the unstable economic circumstances of Eastern Europe, but group structures are weakening in Western Europe, and Westney speaks of the deinstitutionalization of network structures in Japan. Similarly, the balance between large firms and networks of smaller firms is uncertain even within the American knowledge-based industries. Powell describes a world of collaborative networks and high-tech niche firms that collectively undertake projects that would be more costly—and perhaps impossible—for any single large firm to develop on its own. But while small firms collaborate in networks, large firms continue to merge to capture global market share and exploit economies of scale. Indeed, the pharmaceutical sector itself is a paradigmatic example of global consolidation. The forces favoring integration into single firms, or devolution into network structures, depend on many factors including technology, capital requirements, market structure, the protection of intellectual property, and the compensation of entrepreneurial innovators. It is simply unclear how these forces will affect the social structure of economic activity in the future. My only prediction is that the corporate form will remain central to this structure, whatever its characteristics in other respects.

CHAPTER 6

The Future of the Firm from an Evolutionary Perspective

David J. Bryce and Jitendra V. Singh

THE PURPOSE of our essay is to provide a commentary, from an evolutionary point of view, on the provocative and interesting chapters authored by Walter Powell, David Stark and Eleanor Westney that appear earlier in this volume. We believe that the central issues addressed by all three chapters can benefit significantly from the exploration of their points of contact with an evolutionary perspective on organizations. Such an approach can help push the themes raised by the three chapters to conclusions that may not otherwise be evident.

It is useful to begin with the broad features of our approach. We begin this chapter by focusing on the difficulties inherent in prognostication. Prognostication is not only perilous in general, but it is also all the more difficult in the context of organizations, given the complex nature of the units of study. Next, we outline briefly the key features of our evolutionary perspective. In the third section, the core of this commentary, we develop several themes that apply in common to the three chapters by Powell, Stark, and Westney. Our purpose is to develop specific implications from these themes by taking an evolutionary perspective. Finally, we summarize and close this essay with some of the questions that are not developed by the three chapters.

THE PERILS OF PROGNOSTICATION

As someone once said, "Prognostication is always very risky, but especially when it pertains to the future." However, the *ex post* human tendency to believe that "one knew all along how things would turn out" is strong. This "hindsight bias" (Nisbett and Ross 1980) is well documented in the psychological literature. The question of predictive difficulty applies in particular to firms because they are complex entities, both in their internal processes and in their interdependencies with elements in their external environments.

We humans have a tendency, while making predictive statements about the future, to extrapolate from present circumstances. While this may make sense under some conditions, it can clearly lead in the wrong direction under other conditions. It is especially inappropriate to extrapolate from the present when there exists some amount of residual true uncertainty, which is the case in most circumstances, and given the many cognitive limitations of human beings. In order to make this point more precisely, we invite you, the reader, to perform a thought experiment. Imagine we have a time machine in which we can ride to different points in time in U.S. history. Also assume that in so doing, our memory of the future from whence we came gets temporarily erased, or is otherwise inaccessible. Thus, any decisions we make during these time travels are based solely on contemporaneous knowledge and information from the immediate or near past.

Let us now take this time machine to about the year 1900 A.D. In this year, armed as we are with only the knowledge available at the time, let us say we prognosticate about the future of the firm. We look around to find the world populated with family-owned, functionally structured firms, many of which are narrowly focused, and guess that the dominant organizational form of the future will likely resemble such firms.

Still ensconced in our imagined time machine, let us now zoom forward to the 1940s, again in the United States. Here again we carry out our prognostication task. To our contemporary view, the organizational world now appears populated by multidivisional organizations. Extrapolating from the success of these multidivisional organizations, success being inferred from their numbers, we guess that the multidivisional form is likely to dominate in the future.

We can repeat the thought experiment with a journey forward into the 1960s. The time traveler might now conclude that the world will soon be dominated by conglomerate organizations. Finally, if we travel forward to the end of the twentieth century and repeat the exercise, it is more than likely that the new answer will focus on some variant of network forms of organization as the future form.

We hope the key argument is clear. The point of the thought experiment is the following: At every point in time, it is likely that prognosticators making predictions about the organizational forms of the future will be most influenced by the predominant form of that time. However, we know that being dominant at one point in time does not provide any guarantees about future dominance. This idea applies more broadly than just to the world of organizations; it holds also in the natural world. Taking a longer evolutionary sweep of time, we know from the fossil record that many life forms that were dominant at one point in time are now dead and gone, having been replaced by new life forms. (Studying the various ramifications of this question keeps several subfields of science well occupied). Yet these very forms were once abundant and prospered. The catch lies in how, over time, quite different demands for fitness were made of these life forms. This is a direct consequence of how the uncertainty was eventually resolved. In the organizational world, the more that new fitness requirements diverge from earlier capabilities, the more unlikely is the successful transition by extant organizational forms to the new regime, and the more vulnerable the extant forms are to replacement over time by new organizational forms.

To summarize, prognostication is fraught with peril precisely because the context in which organizations evolve contains a degree of true uncertainty, our cognitive capacities are rather limited, and we naturally put too much weight on currently dominant forms as we think about the future. We do not take into account seriously enough that the evolution of organizational forms is shaped by institutional, political, and economic arrangements that are subject to constant change. The specific ways in which some of these factors play out over time can fundamentally alter which forms will dominate future organizational landscapes.

Yet we do not believe that nothing can be said. Even if the possibility exists that they may be proved wrong, Powell, Stark, and Westney raise provocative questions respectively about the future of organizational forms, postsocialist organizational forms in Hungary and the Czech Republic, and the future of Japanese enterprise. While the specific focus for each author is different, we abstract four themes that apply in common to the three chapters: the concept of a network form, foundations of selection environments, the dynamics of nested entities, and global convergence or divergence of organizational forms. We address each of these four themes from an evolutionary point of view and draw implications that provide another point of comparison for the conclusions of the three chapters.

THE EMERGING EVOLUTIONARY SYNTHESIS

Evolutionary thinking about organizations has moved in the last twenty-five years into the mainstream of organizational thinking (Nelson and Winter 1982; Hannan and Freeman 1989; Baum and Singh 1994a; Aldrich 1999). However, it is still true that there is not widespread agreement on what an evolutionary perspective on organizations entails. Therefore, we will next lay down below some of the main features of such an evolutionary synthesis. The following overview builds upon ideas developed elsewhere (Baum and Singh 1994a; Rao and Singh 1998, 1999.) References to an evolutionary perspective in subsequent sections of this essay will be based on a concept of organizational evolution as a process that has the following features:

- it involves dynamic change over time;
- the evolving entities are subject to selection pressures in inverse proportion to their fitness to the selection environment;
- the evolutionary trajectory is history or path dependent, i.e., future steps depend on previous states attained;
- selection processes involve the interplay of ecological and genealogical entities (Baum and Singh 1994b);
- selection processes involves multiple, nested levels of analysis such that different nested entities are simultaneously subject to selective influence.

We suggest that although questions of organizational evolution have drawn more attention in recent years with the relative fecundity of research in organizational ecology, the scope of questions in organizational evolution is considerably broader. Organizational evolution is a central question in the study of organizations more generally. Indeed, various leading theories of organization—contingency theory, resource dependence theory, institutional theory, organizational ecology, organizational learning, evolutionary economics, and punctuated equilibria—may all be reframed as specifying the detailed processes by which organizational evolution takes place.

The emergent evolutionary synthesis involves several key shifts in the research literature. While it is likely that there may not be universal agreement on these shifts, we believe some of them include the following:

- a shift from strong to weak selection: whereas the earliest theoretical formulations stated that selection was the predominant mode of change, the burden of empirical evidence from numerous studies better supports a view in which selection plays an important role, but occurs together with adaptive change in organizations. Thus, adaptation and selection are not only unopposing forces, but they also act in complementary ways;
- a shift from a focus primarily on Darwinian mechanisms to a focus on Lamarckian mechanisms, such that organizational learning can be transmitted within and between organizations over time. Whereas it is clear that Darwinian selection does operate, it is increasingly evident that Lamarckian selection is often a better descriptor of intraorganizational and higher order change;
- a shift from organizational populations as the primary level of analysis to the study of selection at multiple levels of analysis, in particular their nested (one level contained within the next higher level), hierarchical nature;
- a shift from an examination of entities in their respective ecological contexts to a simultaneous interest in their genealogical lines of descent;
- a shift from viewing environmental context as exogenous to seeing it as endogenous, leading to a coevolutionary perspective;

- a shift from focusing primarily on macrostructure (vital rates affecting the population and higher levels, as a whole) of organizational populations to a simultaneous focus on macro- and microstructure (primarily at the lower of the nested, hierarchical levels), involving the simultaneous study of nested levels of analysis;
- a shift from viewing institutional and selection perspectives as antithetical, to the view that institutional contexts—whether the state and its actions or changing social beliefs and values—often provide the selection context, highlighting the complementarity of the two views.

It is to this backdrop of an evolutionary framework that we will next connect themes from the chapters by Powell, Stark, and Westney.

Four Themes from the Powell, Stark, and Westney Chapters

Powell, Stark, and Westney provide a sweeping look at organizational trends and changes occurring in the United States, Eastern Europe, and Japan. In the discussion that follows, we first examine more closely key differences in the network forms identified by the authors, discuss why these differences matter, and conclude that such differences imply variation in fitness for network forms. Next, we highlight the underlying differences in selection environments for organizations across the regions and, using evolutionary reasoning, briefly explore how shifts in these underlying features could lead to developmental trajectories for organizations that are at variance with those suggested by some of the authors. Third, we discuss the nested hierarchical feature of network forms and the selection pressures that occur at different levels within this hierarchy. Using this reasoning, we suggest that interactions among nested hierarchical entities may abate or promote the development of some types of network forms. Lastly, we briefly construct evolutionary arguments for and against global convergence of organizational forms, and suggest that the forces for divergence are stronger than those for convergence; implying global convergence of form types may still be a temporally distant phenomenon.

Differences in Concepts of Network Forms

Powell, Stark, and Westney each introduce notions of network forms in their chapters: Powell describes alliance networks, Stark discusses "heterarchies," a label he applies to Hungarian and Czech networks, and Westney discusses the vertical and horizontal *keiretsu*. However, their network forms differ in important ways, a quality obscured if we apply one shared label.

In order to compare the key similarities and differences in how they refer to network forms, we need to focus on the concept of organizational form.[1]

Although there are many approaches to classifying organizations, we rely on the work of Rao and Singh (1999) who, following Richard Scott (1995), suggest distinguishing between core and peripheral properties of organizations and using the former to distinguish organizational forms (1999, p. 4):

> Core features include goals, authority relations, technologies, and markets (Hannan and Freeman 1984; Scott 1995), and vary in the ease with which they can be changed. At one extreme, goals are at the innermost core feature of organizational forms and are the hardest to modify. At the other extreme, markets are relatively less deep in the core and are easier to change. Peripheral features refer to all other attributes.

One form differs from another primarily according to the core features of the form. These four core features comprise a four-dimensional space. Organizational forms may shift their position within this space by changing one or more of the form's core features. Not all points in the space are occupied, and empty spaces may represent viable or innovative organizational form alternatives, or impossible combinations. Similarities in core features can also link an organizational form with its ancestor forms. Organizational forms are strongly distinct when they differ on all four core features (referred to as strong speciation by Rao and Singh). Forms are weakly distinct when they differ on only one or two core features (referred to as weak speciation by Rao and Singh). Using this definition of organization form and, in particular, the four core features, we now draw comparisons among the network forms described by Powell, Stark, and Westney.

[1] Researchers have utilized various classification approaches for organizations (Rao and Singh 1999.) Contingency theorists, organizational economists, and ecologists have relied upon essentialist and sometimes nominalist approaches. Essentialist typologies rely upon a very few, unchanging taxonomic characters to make classifications. Nominalist approaches, on the other hand, alter the definition of forms to fit the research question. Numerical classification has also been used, wherein researchers attempt to group organizations on the basis of large numbers of measurable attributes (Haas et al. 1966; Pugh et al. 1968). Finally, evolutionist approaches to classification attempt to identify organizational species as a polyphyletic group of competence-sharing populations (McKelvey 1982). Each of these approaches holds limitations. Essentialist and nominalist approaches resolve the organizational-form definition issue in specific cases, but these approaches are seldom generalizable across populations of organizations, and offer little guidance to researchers examining altogether different populations. Numerical approaches may suffer from overspecification or misspecification and have the added challenge of supplying appropriate weights to various attributes so that meaningful clusters emerge. Evolutionary approaches face the challenge of identifying competencies, or "comps" (McKelvey 1982), or routines (Nelson and Winter 1982) within organizations and then successfully comparing and identifying similarities and differences in these across fields of organizations.

GOALS

Though the general goal of producing a profit is the same for each network (and most other commercial organizations we could name), additional primary goals are somewhat different.[2] Powell's networks are primarily oriented to gaining admission to high-speed learning races in markets characterized by intensive, knowledge-based competition. An important goal of Hungarian networks, however, is spreading risk through the development of extended webs of reciprocal assets and liabilities. Czech networks center around providers of capital, implying that access to such resources is an important goal. Westney identifies, in part, the roles of the lead firm and subsidiary firms in the vertical *keiretsu* with differentiated value-chain activities, especially in manufacturing, but also calls attention to the transfer of employees within the network. Jeffrey Dyer's work (1994, 1996a) suggests some reasons why such vertical value-chain relationships may be beneficial. He shows how the structure of relationships among organizations in the vertical automobile *keiretsu* work to lower transaction costs through asset-specific investment by the parties (see also Williamson 1975, 1985). By mutually committing to specialized assets, the parent firm structurally promotes cooperation between its subsidiary firms, mutually binds fates, and lowers or eliminates repeat learning costs, which leads to higher profitability. The vertical *keiretsu* as an employment network serves to indoctrinate and retain employees in the system, facilitating technology transfer and lowering recruitment, training, and retraining costs. For purposes of this discussion, we identify this pathway to the competitive outcome as the revealed goal of the vertical *keiretsu*.

Although some overlap exists in network goals, broad differences remain among the authors' networks. Since the goals of an organizational form lie deepest at the core of what makes organizational forms distinct (Rao and Singh 1999), differences in their goals strongly portend distinct organizational forms.

AUTHORITY RELATIONS

We construe authority relations broadly to include both structure and governance relationships (Rao and Singh 1999). We therefore briefly examine the mechanisms, linkages, and relationships that create a recognizable network entity in each of the three regional author's network forms.

---

[2] Some readers may object to our ascribing a single set of goals to the entire network, given that the goals of individual organizations, or even of human actors within organizations, may be widely divergent (see Gibbons's discussion of networks as multiparty extended games where different players have distinct objectives). At the broadest level, however, a network's collective action is at least partially observable and reveals the preferences, or goals, of the entity at large.

The vertical *keiretsu* are defined by full or partial ownership of subsidiaries by a common parent, where there may be a cascading structure of shareholding and personnel transfers. As Westney points out, the dense networks over which products, information and technology, financial capital, and people flow—and the contours of these network relationships—may be even more important than ownership in the coordination and control of the vertical *keiretsu*. Yet ownership relations clearly coexist with these more varied types of relations, and clearly shape the pathways along which multifaceted relations emerge. In Powell's networks, on the other hand, network entities are defined by collaborative and often transient relationships among firms. Ownership seems an exceptional case. Coordination takes place through relational contracting based on reputation, friendship, interdependence, and altruism (Macneil 1995). In addition, any individual firm may be part of multiple networks, which span the same or different markets. Networks are held together as long as relationships continue to be mutually beneficial. When benefits cease, relationships are dissolved or reconstituted. Hungarian networks materialize on the basis of significant firm-to-firm cross-ownership, which may extend across sectors. The state continues substantial involvement. Mutual ties to banks and investment funds define Czech networks. Cross-ownership ties are prevalent at this meso-level, where the state holds a controlling interest in a high proportion of the banks and funds, but less prevalent at the firm-to-firm level.

In sum, our brief review finds some similarities, but mostly differences in the binding relationships and mechanisms holding networks together and, thereby, in the authority relations within the networks.

TECHNOLOGY

Technologies utilized by the networks are as variable as the products and services they produce. One way to truncate the analysis is to move to second-order considerations; that is, to compare the degree to which technological heterogeneity is present within any one network.[3] Taking this approach, the rather sharp differences among network forms can readily be seen. Powell's networks are created in the interest of developing a specific technology or product and are thereby likely to be somewhat homogenous in the technologies utilized. On the other hand, the horizontal *keiretsu* and Stark's "heterarchies" are engaged rather decidedly in risk-sharing and risk-avoidance activities. These extended risk-based and co-ownership networks are not typically vertically connected by markets (though examples exist, such as the metallurgy company Heavy Metal and its corporate satellites), implying extensive technological heterogeneity across the network.

---

[3] We thank Paul DiMaggio for suggesting this approach.

The technologies within the vertical *keiretsu* are, not surprisingly, vertically related, suggesting perhaps a middle ground of technological heterogeneity. The lead or parent firm concentrates on high value-added manufacturing, though not always final assembly, and also on research and development for the core businesses of the group. The logic of the network follows the logic of the value chain, with group companies engaging in manufacturing of components or subassemblies, sales and distribution, or quasi-related businesses (Westney, this volume).

MARKETS

This dimension refers to both the markets pursued and the marketing strategy utilized. At the network level, marketing strategy either differs markedly or is nonexistent in the authors' network forms. In the case of the vertical *keiretsu*, the entire network is often the competing unit, not just the parent firm (Dyer 1996a; Gilson and Roe 1993). Powell's networks, however, neither compete as networks all of the time, nor are they consistently permanent in their membership. Additionally, one division or subunit of a firm may be temporarily tied into one network, while another subunit of the firm is tied into a different network. When these networks do compete as units, it is likely to be for a short duration in a race to develop technology or other new knowledge. The nature of high-speed learning races demands that relationships are both rapidly formed and easily broken as challenges and opportunities evolve. The nature of the game in these environments is one in which individual firms advance their own competitiveness through network ties. Even when alliances compete directly, they may be competing with other firms rather than with other networks. And since the network relationships are often transitory, it is possible to compete and partner with the same firm in different markets.

The Hungarian and Czech networks, and to these we add the horizontal *keiretsu*, do not appear, as a rule, to compete as networks. No uniform logic for organizing and segregating activities among firms in the network appears to be present. Cross-ownership ties may extend across sectors in the Hungarian case, as they do in the Japanese case, or have no obvious integrated business logic, as in the Czech case. An exception in Hungary is the corporate satellites. Heavy Metal holds 100 percent stakes in firms possessing related core technologies or value-chain capabilities and lower ownership shares in firms less related to the core business (Stark, this volume).

Given the differences outlined in all four of the core dimensions identifying organizational forms, we conclude that the network forms discussed by the authors are strongly distinctive. Each network form emerged on a foundation of dramatically different socioeconomic, political, and legal history, so we should not be surprised they differ. But why do the differences matter? They matter because if network forms are to be the organizational form of the future, as some observers have claimed, we should be able to clarify just what this network will form will look like. What will be its goals for existence? Will it compete as a unit? What will be its primary technologies, and how homogenous will these technologies be within the network? What will be the primary relationships and linkages that together define the network? How will the network be governed? We do not suggest that all networks will or should look alike. And yet the network character of the forms discussed in the three chapters is different enough to leave us rather perplexed about the future. For example, will the network forms discussed by each of the authors eventually cross regional lines? And if they do, won't the resulting recombination produce yet another distinctive form that bears little resemblance to extant forms? How do we predict the contours of such a "recombinet?"

In sum, we suggest caution in applying the "network form" label to all forms of interorganizational ties. The concept of a network form used by the three authors differs in important ways. Moreover, these differences in network forms are all the more significant because they are likely to lead to differential selection pressures. But at the very least, the differences hamper our ability to predict the future. Selection pressures, of course, will have ultimate bearing on what types of network forms, if any, will eventually persist.

We now explore more deeply the institutional selection environments across the three regions and consider their implications for network organizations.

Foundations of Selection Environments

Institutional selection plays an important role in the retention of new organizational forms. Indeed, for new organizational forms, the burden of selection pressures may lie more in the realm of institutional selection than in the realm of competitive selection (Rao and Singh 1999). How selection processes operate through competition between organizational forms is now well understood. But organizational forms are not only shaped by competitive forces alone. The institutional context also plays a crucial selecting role.[4] Whereas the selection pressures of the institutional context are clearest in the extreme case of legal proscription of organizational forms with certain features, the phenomenon has more generality. Thus, organizational forms can sometimes decline because of the erosion of the

---

[4] The concept of institutional selection is related to later discussions of deinstitutionalization, but is broader in that it includes both the facilitative and destructive influences of the institutional context.

institutional context or because of discontinuous legal changes. A global change in values over a period of time can also lead to delegitimization of a form. On the other hand, some organizational forms that do not fit the demands of the institutional context never come into existence. A comparison of the regional chapters reveals this important feature in that it helps us to see more clearly how political, legal, and some, but not all, economic structures are at the foundation of institutional selection environments for organizational forms.[5] When these underlying structures are stable, differences in organizational forms are determined largely by competitive selection forces. However, when these structures are in transition, the institutional environment will be turbulent indeed, leading to shifting regimes of legitimacy, and presenting an entirely different set of survival requirements to extant and emerging forms.

Consider the U.S. case on which Powell bases much of his discussion of the changing landscape for labor and the emergence of network forms. In the United States, political, legal, and economic foundations are stable and mature. The country has a two-century-long experience with democracy; the ownership of private property is protected by constitutional amendment; and the country has operated within the framework of a free-market system since its early beginnings. Discontinuities to the degree witnessed recently in Eastern Europe have not taken place since before the industrial revolution.[6] When the institutional selection environment is stable, the environment is taken for granted. It is the backdrop on which organizations emerge, but not the primary force by which they are selected. Competitive forces become much more salient, creating the conditions for the kinds of unencumbered, market-based transactions that characterize Powell's networks.

In Eastern Europe, the situation is dramatically different. Processes of democratization, privatization, and marketization—which pair up respectively with political, legal, and economic structures—are underway not only simultaneously, but also in the context of an already extensive economic infrastructure of producers. The uncertainty for extant producers is

---

[5] By including economic structures at the foundation of institutional selection environments, we mean to say that economic dynamics frequently result in policy decisions or collective expectations that shape institutional selection. One example is antitrust legislation, which arose fundamentally from an economically based dynamic. Another example is the emergent Internet companies. The early apparent success of the business model of these companies has led to rapidly rising market capitalization based on the promise of future earnings. As a result, Internet companies have been rapidly legitimized. If the market believes it, it would appear, so does society.

[6] In some U.S. sectors, bouts of institutional discontinuity-producing legislation have occurred—anti-trust, McFadden Act, Glass-Steagall, Prospective Payment System in health care, to name a few examples.

profound. The winnowing forces of selection come simultaneously from many different directions. Consider the discontinuity produced by privatization alone. In the transition from socialism, Hungarian firms established cross-ownership ties along the social pathways that emerged during the socialist years as individuals and firms operated within a centrally managed economic system. This fact suggests, ironically, that the new selection environment favors those firms that were the most vulnerable during the socialist regime, the firms that found it necessary to establish informal relationships with other firms in order to survive within the centrally planned system. Likewise, firms that required few or no informal mechanisms, which flourished upon central government policy, may have the most difficult time making the transition. As the selection environment readjusts, the fitness equation for organizations dramatically shifts, causing turmoil and outright extinction for many.

Stark outlines one result of the discontinuous institutional regime in Eastern Europe. Diverse network ties emerged in the crucible of the shifting environment as firms entertained multiple, simultaneous organizing "logics." And yet, such organizing logics in no way ensure survival. Because the political, legal, and economic structures underlying the institutional environment are still in transition, extant network forms in Eastern Europe are also in transition. The implications of this observation are rather important. "Heterarchies" may survive the transitional environment by trading off efficiency for flexibility, but when institutional context stabilizes, efficiency may be the preferred organizational characteristic. Those forms that are encumbered with multiple external relationships, tightly coupled, and woven into the institutional fabric may suddenly be at a decided disadvantage. What then becomes the organizational form of Eastern Europe's future?

This ability of a changing institutional environment to reverse its selection regime is not an unknown, or merely theoretical, phenomenon. The early automobile industry in the United States is a case in point. Around the turn of the twentieth century, the industry cycled quickly through different legitimacy regimes. Those organizations that could produce reliable cars won early support, independent of how fast the cars could travel. Later, automobile associations began valuing speed as an important feature of the automobile. This eventually led to a reversal in the selection regime from one that favored organizational forms that could produce reliable but slow cars to one that favored organizational forms that could produce fast cars, even if less reliable. Clearly, competition did occur among the different automobile producers, but the grounds upon which they competed were defined by the institutional context. Likewise, the U.S. biotechnology industry operated with capricious governmental policy stances in the early years, which stifled or delayed the establishment of research centers (Rao and Singh 2001). Now, however, such activities on the part of biotechs are not only legitimate, they are supported, if even indirectly through research grants, by the U.S. government.

Changing institutional regimes (again, in the United States) are deinstitutionalizing extant forms even at the writing of this chapter. Consider the health care case. During the 1980s and early 1990s, following the implementation of the MediCare Prospective Payment System (PPS), the logic of business and competition replaced the logic of a cost-plus, protected industry. Old organizational forms—the traditional hospitals—failed in large numbers. New forms emerged: Health Maintenance Organizations (HMOs) to capitalize on an opportunity to reduce resource expenditures, and health networks in order to access economies of scale in care delivery and to consolidate patient volume to provide clout with the insurers. By the mid-1990s, the majority of U.S. hospitals claimed to be part of a health system or network, and these networks were thought to be the future of health care organization and delivery. What is so remarkable about this example, however, is that at the close of the twentieth century, the future of health-care networks was in doubt. The logic of integrated care delivery did not seem to deliver on promised benefits. A number of health systems formed early on disbanded. Others chose to stop far short of truly integrated health-care delivery, opting instead to identify organizations with whom strategic relationships might be established, rather than with whom assets might be merged. Pressures for change continue to come from multiple quarters—government, payers, health-care consumers. Hence, integrated health-care delivery is disintegrating (Health-Care Advisory Board 1997). Likewise, the public and governmental backlash against HMO efforts to manage the costs of care has gained momentum. Institutional constraints on HMO methods are being rapidly created and imposed.[7]

---

[7] As an example, in 1995, when Kaiser Permanente of Southern California announced a pilot program of eight-hour hospital stays for some women following normal infant delivery (Olmos 1995), there was immediate and widespread opposition. "The Newborns' and Mothers' Protection Act of 1995" was introduced in Congress and by the end of 1997, 36 states had passed legislation requiring a minimum hospital stay of forty-eight hours for normal delivery (Rose 1997).

As another example, consider the life-or-death struggle of U.S. cigarette makers in the late 1990s. This struggle appeared to arise from the very nature of the product they bring to market, cigarettes. The research, production, and marketing processes of cigarette companies have faced trouble because they appear to run counter to changing "institutionalized beliefs" (Meyer and Rowan 1977) about the role of firms in society. Specifically, there are strong prohibitions against firms producing and marketing products that have potential for harmful effects. Although the legitimacy of tobacco firms has been contested since the Surgeon General's report in the 1960s, the pressure certainly increased with the discovery of documents allegedly revealing that cigarette manufacturers had been aware for some time about the addictive properties of nicotine, an active ingredient in cigarettes. For the first time, a jury

As in the United States, the foundational political, legal, and economic structures in Japan are relatively stable. Yet Westney's analysis indicates that the Japanese *keiretsu* may also be under deinstitutionalization pressures based on shifting labor demographics, a changing work ethic, and a sluggish economy in the 1990s. Japan is possibly the most prolific modern example of a networked economy, where an elite class of individuals are networked through personal relationships and where banks, government bodies, commercial firms, and capital markets are bound together in cascading chains of assets and liabilities. Webs of relationships transcend the *keiretsu*, extending across the economy in ways that tie the fates of the many to the fates of the few. The difficulty with such extensive relationships, however, is that the more tightly coupled the relationships and the more integrated the economy, the more vulnerable the members, should any one of them suffer hardship. Likewise, when the few are prosperous, the many benefit. This interdependence may help to explain why an economy that seemed capable of limitless growth and prosperity in one decade, finds itself on the brink of disaster in the next. In tightly coupled systems, extremes in performance are easy to reach, and—unfortunately for Japan in the 1990s—in the case of a downturn, difficult to recover from. Due to its own tightly linked interconnectedness, the *keiretsu* may simply be a microcosm of this larger, economy-wide phenomenon.

Although sometimes it is economic pressures that culminate in institutional change, the above examples illustrate the point that even in stable institutional environments, institutional events can occur that serve to delegitimize extant organizational forms and approaches. In the United States, the seeming invulnerability of late-twentieth-century network forms could rapidly dissipate through institutional pressure. Consider U.S. antitrust law. This body of law has historically been aimed at single firms, seeking to avoid or redress unfair competition brought on through asset merger, where the resulting merger consolidates market power in ways that stifle competition. In a very real sense, however, technology networks or strategic alliance networks may accomplish precisely the same thing—the conferral of significant market clout on a single network of a few firms. The U.S. Justice Department places little emphasis in this area now, but it could easily increase its vigilance in the future. Change in the foundational

---

found a tobacco firm guilty in the cancer-caused death of a long-time smoker (although the verdict was later thrown out by an appeals court since the case was not filed before the statute of limitations ran out). A massive class-action lawsuit was begun in Miami, Florida on behalf of half a million smokers. Though it may yet take some time, the demise of the tobacco industry, or at least its serious downsizing, seems imminent in the United States based on current indicators.

antitrust legal structure could overnight create an institutional environment where some types of network forms are illegal.[8]

Consider yet another major influence on environmental selection regimes: technological change. Changes in information and communications technologies—the emergenence of the Internet, the ever increasing speed of microprocessors, and other advances in telecommunications—are having and will continue to have major influences on organizations. Impacts will include the way organizations are structured, the markets they pursue, their modes of communication, the goals they achieve, or how they compete. Already these technologies are expanding the capacities of organizations both to communicate and to coordinate increasingly complex operations over vast distances, while connecting firms to their customers in unprecedented new ways.

A common characteristic of new technology is that with time and human experience, it is often eventually applied in ways that create systemic change.[9] Imagine, for a moment, a world where systemic effects of technology were to commoditize certain types of knowledge such that the extended webs of human relationships now required for knowledge access were no longer necessary. As just one example, artificial intelligence and expert systems are having growing impact. The day when they substitute for professional judgment within reasonable parameters is not far distant. Engineering or manufacturing expertise that is today accessed through webs of alliances may be readily obtainable in an electronic market transaction from a firm with a savvy system that can solve the purchasing firm's problem in real time. In such a world, strategic alliances are replaced by electronic linkages, where units of knowledge are facelessly traded by firms whose objectives are to solidify their own dominance, rather than to promote the competitive vitality of their network. Firms trade knowledge resources with many and varied entities, depending on the nature of the knowledge required. Business strategy consists of determining which external knowledge units are the most valuable and which internal units are the

[8] It is worth noting that governmental scrutiny of alliance networks is proceeding apace in some industries. A proposed alliance between American Airlines and British Airways was called off after governmental scrutiny of code sharing arrangements, schedule coordination, and other issues. The European Union had initially provided approval on the condition that the airlines give up a large number of flight slots between the United States and London's Heathrow Airport. Thus, the anti-competitive consequences of alliances are routinely scrutinized in the airline industry.

[9] Malone and Rockart (1991, 128) identify such systemic changes as third-order effects. Third-order effects of technology go beyond simple technology substitution or finding new uses. For example, now that enough U.S. households have home computers and the capability to be online, systemic changes are beginning to occur in patterns of purchasing due to electronic commerce and also patterns of work with the increase of telecommuting.

most tradable, similar to the ways in which firms today identify which labor resources are the most desirable, and which the most expendable. Under this scenario, systemic effects of technology make the firm more, not less, self-reliant and its boundary less, not more, permeable. In such an environment, current network forms are inadequate. They disappear as rapidly, and readily, as the m-form.

We have offered considerations for how changing selection environments can be hostile to some types of forms, placing emphasis on institutional selection. We turn now to a more specific focus on a discussion of network forms and their nested hierarchical nature.

Dynamics of Nested Entities

Baum and Singh (1994b) propose a dual hierarchy for organizational evolution that outlines successive nested entities along both genealogical and ecological lines. Genealogical entities are "formed by components of institutional memory engaged in the preservation and dissemination of production and organizing information" (p. 9). Ecological entities are the "result of the cumulative effect of variation and selection over time, and the structural and behavioral expressions of entities of the genealogical class" (p. 9). Successive ecological entities are nested; that is, the interactions of entities at one level hold the entities at the next level together. Baum and Singh's ecological hierarchy consists of jobs, work groups, organizations, populations, communities, and ecosystems. The genealogical hierarchy consists of routines (Nelson and Winter 1982) or comps (McKelvey 1982), organizations, species, and polyphyletic groupings. The elements of the two hierarchies interact, each regulating change within the other and thereby producing the patterns of organizational evolution. Successive hierarchical levels also interact, producing both upward and downward causation effects within the hierarchy. What occurs at one level of the hierarchy produces effects at all other levels, though the effects diminish at more distant levels. In this way, hierarchical levels both comprise and react to the entire hierarchy. Such systems are termed heterarchies (Hofstadter 1979).[10]

Baum and Singh's theoretical formulation makes clear that entities can neither operate independently of their adjacent levels nor expect that actions at other levels will not affect them in repeated waves of dynamic interaction. The heterarchy, therefore, is more than just a network-level entity; it consists of all of the nested entities both below and above the network. Each entity operates in its own sphere, subject to its relevant

---

[10] Although Stark makes use of the term "heterarchy," he uses it differently than an earlier literature following Hofstadter (1979). Our use of heterarchy is consistent with Hofstadter and with Baum and Singh (1994b).

selection pressures, yet affected by dynamics reverberating from both local and remote locations within the hierarchy. For an example of this mutual dependency up and down a hierarchy, consider a network that creates standards of membership that firms must continually meet in order to preserve their status in the network, as in the case of the Japanese *keiretsu*. As firms leave the network for noncompliance, the network itself changes character. Jack Welch is reported to have imposed such standards upon GE's operating divisions—to be ranked number one or number two in their respective markets, or suffer potential divestiture. Similarly, selection on networks also occurs as a result of community-level pressure. If networks are producing and otherwise supporting competing standards during a period of ferment in a technological community, eventually one standard may become the dominant design, leading to the collapse, or dissolution, of firms or networks offering competing designs (Rosenkopf and Tushman 1994). The Betamax-VHS race in videocassette recorders is by now a classic example of such competition and collapse.

In capitalist economies or competitive regimes, selection pressure on entities may be modified but usually cannot entirely be eliminated. The selection pressure may be diffused, as when endorsement by other external actors ameliorates selection pressures (Singh, Tucker, and House 1986), or when embeddedness in the institutional environment (Baum and Oliver 1992) reduces the force of selection. Selection pressures may also shift within the hierarchy. Entities naturally seek to ameliorate or even shift selection pressures, whenever such control or ability is present. However, the fact that different hierarchical levels are interdependent means, at the very least, that some residual selection pressure is likely to remain or even to return via some pathway in the nested hierarchy. When hierarchical levels are loosely coupled, the shifting of selection pressure by entities is more difficult, but more lasting. When the coupling between hierarchical levels is tighter, shifting entity-specific selection risks is easier, but less permanent.

With the foregoing theoretical discussion as background, we turn to application. Efforts by firms to achieve flexibility are a response to fast-moving environments and are thought by some, including firm managers, to enhance the survival chances of the firms that undertake them. Two flexibility-seeking moves by firms are addressed by Powell: the detachment of workers to firms, where workers become the "shock absorbers in the flexible economy" (Benner 1996); and the rise of firm-to-firm alliances and affiliations, resulting in competitive networks. These two mechanisms help to resolve different business challenges. Labor detachment strategies address the risk of over-extended labor costs in the event of a market about-face, while also providing access to specialized expertise where required. Alliance strategies address the need for access to new markets, know-how, and sources of revenue, and help to hedge against the risk that a firm will not be in possession of competitive capabilities when they are required.

The trouble is that Powell's "new logic of organizing" doesn't eliminate, but rather shifts, firm-level selection pressure to the entities that have come to absorb their uncertainty—primarily to networks of alliances and to labor. Managers happily sign up for alliances in order to mitigate firm-specific risk while unwittingly signing up for network-specific risk. It is therefore unclear whether "flexibly adapted" firms in the new selection regime are any more likely to survive, in the long run, than their inflexible counterparts in the old regime. We think the risks that come with network membership are understated, even poorly understood. In fact, at least some of what firms may have accomplished by joining interfirm networks is to cede their ability to adapt to firm-level selection pressure because it now takes place on a higher order entity, that is, the "network", which is remote from the corporate office. A firm that embeds itself in network relationships for sources of knowledge, resources, products, and customers may find disentanglement difficult, if not impossible, should the network proposition become less viable. Needless to say, the viability of the network is the crucial factor here from which other implications flow.

Some modern examples of network-level risk that is not readily reducible by firm managers bear mentioning. In 1978, Chrysler Corporation was entwined in more than 6000 Michigan-based supplier relationships representing $3.3 billion in annual Chrysler spending[11]—a sort of American *keiretsu* (Dyer 1996b). When the collapse of Chrysler became imminent, suppliers suddenly found themselves in possession of significant network-level risk with little or no control over the outcome, at least on an individual firm basis. Without a bailout by the federal government, many such firms might have failed. For these and other reasons, the federal government provided sizeable loan guarantees that saw Chrysler through this dark period. Likewise, Microsoft's antitrust battle with the U.S. Department of Justice was joined not only by executives from its own corporate suite, but also by executives from the suites of many other corporations whose software was coded Microsoft-compatible and whose destiny depended on continued Microsoft prosperity (Grimaldi 1998). Indeed, in testimony Bill Gates, the CEO of Microsoft, pointed to the overall negative economic consequences of the Department of Justice delaying the launch of their new operating system. For Microsoft, as with Chrysler, being deeply embedded in a network of relationships increased its relative ability to negotiate with the government, due largely to the strong dependence of numerous other firms upon its continued well-being.

[11] Report of the Subcommittee on Economic Stabilization of the Committee on Banking, Finance and Urban Affairs, U.S. House of Representatives, 1980.

In the dynamically evolving system of hierarchical interactions, entities do not lie still. As networks and labor absorb firm-level uncertainty, these entities in turn find ways to dissipate entity-level selection pressure. For the Japanese *keiretsu*, member firms may be forced to bear the brunt of network-level risk as the "shock-absorber" analogues of labor at the firm level. Westney describes vertical *keiretsu* parents' use of employee transfers to other *keiretsu* member firms. The goal is both to dispose of underperforming employees and to motivate higher performing individuals. During the Japanese recession of the 1990s, non-parent *keiretsu* firms increasingly had to absorb workers from the parent whose slower growth required trimming of the labor force (Sako 1997, 8–11). In this case, the network dissipates its own risk by passing it down to specific other-member firms in the network.

As labor absorbs higher levels of uncertainty arising from the new labor contract, individuals feel the heat of rising job insecurity. The natural result is for individuals to find ways to buffer themselves from risk. One way for this to occur is through labor organization—founding entities uniquely adapted to the flexible corporate environment described by Powell, and to the "knowledge economy" mentioned elsewhere.

Imagine for a moment that just such a contingency occurs—new labor organizations are founded as a reaction to labor detachment strategies. What might be the characteristics of such organizations? We suggest that they would be different than traditional unions or temporary employment agencies. Given the context that Powell describes, such organizations would be small, specialized, filled with individuals possessing advanced college degrees—engineers, scientists, project managers, and other specialists—and, depending on size, tied exclusively to individual firms for relatively short periods of time. The typical labor organization would possess an administrative apparatus responsible for marketing the services of the members of its organization. Size of the new labor organization could vary, but might be very small in some cases: two to five persons. For example, imagine a group of key engineers at a semiconductor firm who develop an important new chip design and upon project completion, disassociate from the firm to market their collective talents to other firms. Likewise, for some types of workers organizations might be very large. In either event, the organizations are designed to mitigate uncertainty for individual workers, and to hold out for contingent or temporary contracts with the firms willing to pay the most for their services.

As in the case of alliances, the shunting away of uncertainty by firms through the decoupling of the labor force may bring only a temporary hiatus from selection pressures for the firm. In fact, the specter of droves of chip designers leaving firms to market themselves to others should cause considerable apprehension for business managers. The new competitive regime is about knowledge acquisition, retention, and management. Decoupling of specialized talent could lead to considerable erosion of a firm's knowledge stock in the near term and to frustrating scarcity of knowledge resources in the longer term, as labor organizations sell out—temporarily at least—to the highest bidder. When a firm loses significant knowledge assets and must in turn seek to acquire the same in an external, more costly market, it will find it has acquired significant labor market risk. Once again, much of what firms accomplish by advocating the contingency of labor may be to cede significant aspects of firm-level adaptive control to entities remote from the corporate office, while still retaining the selection risk.

This playing out of the evolutionary implications of a contingent labor force suggests possible shortcomings of the contingent labor argument. The firm-level risk of having to obtain specialized knowledge on the spot market may place, *ex ante*, severe constraints on the degree to which specialized labor becomes contingent. If the labor force is to be made contingent, and trends would suggest that at least some aspects of it already are (Kalleberg, Reynolds, and Marsden 1999), we suspect that it will not be in highly specialized or scarce fields, but rather in fields characterized by commodity knowledge, where the spot market price for a unit of labor is at some competitive equilibrium. The specialized worker will mitigate her personal risk by selling out for semi-permanent attachment to the highest bidding firm. The commodity knowledge worker will cast his lot *de novo* with a labor organization that will seek to consolidate market power and provide the worker with some employment smoothing. Free-floating labor resources may thus never materialize to any significant degree, as many predict.

With nested entities dynamically jockeying for survival, prediction about which organization form will ultimately succeed becomes rather perilous. Firms are likely to find that certain types of network relationships present levels of risk sufficient enough that such network forms never come to dominate the landscape. Likewise, the risk of being unable to obtain key labor resources when required may keep labor semi-permanently attached to most firms indefinitely. These countervailing winds are likely to exert strong retention forces on existing firm boundaries.

Global Convergence or Divergence of Organizational Forms

In considering the question of whether a new form (e.g., networks) will emerge that will dominate across the world in the future, we suggest a cautious stance. Although social technology appears to be diffusing more rapidly across national borders, strong historical and institutional contexts continue to shape organizational forms in unique ways (Guillén 1999). Even where broad similarities can be seen, replicating forces are often absent. For example, family conglomerates in India (Palepu and Khanna

1996), the Korean *chaebol*, the Japanese horizontal *keiretsu*, or more precisely, the prewar *zaibatsu*, are similar in origin and in their ultimate, diversified forms. We wonder whether the continuing survival of most of these forms implies a foundational structure that is competitively better adapted than other possibilities. At the same time, additional forms of this type have not emerged in recent years, implying that whatever advantages exist are either not readily imitable or that the conditions that created the forms in the first place have been foreclosed. Further, in our day, foreign currency market perturbations or flight of foreign capital could create dramatic vulnerabilities for these or other global forms in short order. In fact, some see the 1990s collapse of multibillion-dollar Yamaichi Securities, which the Japanese government failed to rescue, as a microcosm of a broader meltdown of the much-touted Asian miracle. Book titles such as *"Asia Falling"* (Henderson 1998) capture the irony in a region billed as *"Asia Rising"* (Rohwer 1995) just a few years before. The implications of these events for the large, well-established enterprises of Asia remain presently somewhat unclear.

Earlier, we argued that political, legal, and economic structures are at the foundation of institutional selection environments. It follows that global convergence of forms, if it is to occur, must therefore be preceded by convergence in these underlying structures. Supranational isomorphic pressures (Westney, this volume) do exist and could wield growing influence on the global institutional environment. Organizations like the IMF, World Bank, and the United Nations exert standardizing isomorphic pressure on organizational forms. Firms respond to such pressures for isomorphism, whether they come from local (Rosenzweig and Singh 1991) or from global environments. Still, as currently construed, it is hard to imagine how such institutions could have both universal and penetrating influence on the types of forms that emerge in industries uniquely born of the comparative advantage or institutional context of particular nation-states.

Clearly, in order for global convergence of organizational forms to occur, the pressures for convergence must outstrip those for divergence. Here we outline briefly what we believe to be some of the primary forces for each. We address some of the pressures for convergence first.

DIFFUSION OF SOCIAL TECHNOLOGY

Weber ([1910] 1978) and later Stinchcombe (1965) argued that the organizational inventions that can be made at a particular time in history depend on the social technology available at the time. When social technology is universally available, common forms emerge and persist. Stinchcombe does not precisely define social technology, but our view is that the term is broadly encompassing and should include factors relevant to the shaping of organizational forms. Thus, we define social technology to include the technologies of microelectronics, information, telecommunications, manufacturing, and management. Of course, some of these technologies were not very advanced at the time of Stinchcombe's writing and were nonexistent at the time of Weber's. This fact itself is an illustration of the phenomenon that Stinchcombe describes. Social technology diffuses across borders, often by its own means, in a kind of virtuous cycle. Telecommunications technology, for example, makes the citizens of countries aware of other available technologies, stimulating demand and leading to a convergence in tastes (Levitt 1983). Efforts by firms to sell products across international borders is also a primary diffusion mechanism.

GOAL-SEEKING ADAPTATION

When an apparently successful form is identified, pressures for replication will be present. Westney's (1987) analysis of the adoption by the Japanese of Western business practices during the *Meiji* period is one example. The desired adoption by U.S. firms of Japanese practices in the 1980s is another (Westney, this volume). Campbell (1969) cautioned against the notion that purposeful, or goal-seeking, adaptation can be successful in the way organizational actors expect it to be. We suggest, however, as Campbell also did, that even though variation in the result of adaptive efforts exists, not all variations are equally probable. The reasons for this in social systems are different from the reasons in biological systems. In social systems, human actors, possessing individual cognitive intent, are active participants in variation-generating processes. This is not the case in biological mutation, though, of course, even here, not all mutations are equiprobable (Dawkins 1996). Human actors can deploy their will in directions that they believe will be productive a priori. In a community in which an observable, favorable new organizational innovation has emerged, human actors throughout the community are likely to attempt its adoption in their own organizations. Even though they cannot necessarily observe accurately nor implement correctly the innovation that makes others successful (Alchian 1950; Nelson and Winter 1982; Szulanski 1996; Romanelli 1999), we suggest that with high numbers of human agents pulling in similar directions, the variations that are produced are likely to center around the intended result in successive adaptive efforts. One end result is organizations that look much alike.

LAMARCKIAN TRANSMISSION

The Lamarckian view of evolution, as contrasted to the Darwinian, explicitly permitted learning in the mechanisms of genetic transmission. Above, we mentioned goal-seeking adaptation by organizations. Observation is one way to learn about another organization's traits. More often, however, some agent will transfer key information. International consulting firms, venture capitalists, foreign-educated students joining organizations in the homeland, or transferring personnel are all carriers of learning on management practice or new organizational forms. When deployed within a firm, such agents can shape its evolutionary development.

ASCENDANCY OF GLOBAL ECONOMIC ORGANIZATIONS AND TRANSACTIONS

Kobrin (1997a) has argued that nation-states are faced with a trade-off between efficiency gains from cross-border economic activity and loss of state autonomy. In strategic industries such as telecommunications, pharmaceuticals, semiconductors, and aerospace, where the scale of technology is large and markets are fused transnationally, states face a discrete decision: participate in the world economy or forgo technological development. Yet participation creates mutual dependence of nation-states and increasing reliance upon external economic organizations for continued improvements in state competitiveness. Thus, country borders become increasingly permeable, resulting in fewer limitations on the capacity of organizational forms to propagate across borders. Likewise, the rise of a digital economy in which transactions take place in cyberspace has the potential to render the borders of national markets virtually meaningless (Kobrin 1997b).

Whereas the above forces push toward global convergence, there are other pressures that push for divergence. We address these next.

PATH DEPENDENCY

New forms emerge in historical context. The configuration in the last period has a strong influence on the configuration in the current period. As we have seen, institutional history differs significantly among countries. Our comparison of the differences in network forms across the regions demonstrates the stark differences in forms that have emerged in the different regions.

INSTITUTIONAL DIFFERENCES

Related to the first point, and as we have discussed extensively, institutional contexts and selection pressures result in differing regimes of legitimacy across nation-states. For example, the types of heavily networked economic relationships that have developed in Japan could never have developed in the contemporary United States, due largely to antitrust laws and an orientation to arms-length transactions. We cannot think of any immediate shocks that would serve to homogenize institutional environments across nation-states, though supra-isomorphic pressures (Westney, this volume) and Kobrin's (1997b) observation about the effect of the Internet on international borders will have continuing influence. Resistance of unique institutional environments to homogenization is perhaps the

strongest deterrent among the above forces to global convergence of organizational forms (Guillén 1999).

Though the divergence list is shorter, we suggest that collectively the
forces for divergence operate sufficiently to hedge the forces for convergence so that global convergence of network forms is not likely to occur
in the near future.

Summary and Conclusions

Our goal in this commentary has not been to suggest that Powell, Stark,
and Westney are incorrect, or to suggest that we do not believe that network forms will have growing and continuing influence. Rather, our point
has been to demonstrate the complexity of evolutionary systems. Where
multiple nested hierarchical levels interact and selection forces operate at
many different levels simultaneously, particularly in light of the cognitive
limitations of human decision makers and of the residual true uncertainty
in environmental contexts, predictability is compromised. Yet we hope that
even if we cannot make predictions about the future of organizational
forms with a great degree of confidence, our commentary does suggest
which factors to take into account in thinking about the evolution of organizational forms and about the complex shaping influences of competitive
and institutional contexts.

Finally, we want to highlight a curious omission from all three chapters:
the dramatic evolution of information technology (including computing
and communication technologies) in recent years and how it has the potential to revolutionize the future of firms worldwide. The argument is quite
fundamental, in our view. A useful way to look at organizational forms is
that they are efficient in information transmission (Arrow 1974; Galbraith
1973). Indeed, Oliver Williamson's (1975) influential argument about the
conditions under which hierarchies (organizations) replace markets rested
upon this observation as a central premise. As information technology-
related developments have evolved rapidly in recent years—computing,
voice mail and e-mail, telecommunications, GroupWare, voice recognition
software, the World Wide Web, to give a few examples—it is becoming
clear that traditional hierarchical organizations are giving way to a ferment
of experimentation. As Clemons (1991) has pointed out, information technology can have the effect of reducing transaction costs in hierarchical
exchange, making contractual exchanges across firm boundaries much easier due to reduction of information asymmetries. We think this is a fundamental trend. Already, the effects of information technology have, among
other factors, led to the "death of distance" (Cairncross 1997). Although it
is too early to comment with a great deal of confidence on what organiza-

tional forms will finally dominate the landscape, it is more than likely that information technology will have a central role to play in such organizational forms of the future. As information technology continues its rapid evolution, with almost law-like improvements in information processing and communication speeds every year, it is not too far-fetched to imagine dramatic changes in organizational forms unfolding in future years.

CHAPTER 7

Firms (and Other Relationships)

Robert Gibbons

BY NOW, many noneconomists know the two key events in the birth and revitalization of the economic theory of the firm. First, in 1937, Ronald Coase argued that firms will exist only in environments in which firms perform better than markets could. To create space for firms, Coase suggested that some environments might be plagued by "transaction costs" that cause markets to perform poorly. Second, in 1975, Oliver Williamson significantly deepened the discussions of why markets might perform poorly and why firms might perform better than markets. Roughly, Williamson argued that markets rely on formal contracts (i.e., those enforceable by a court), but formal contracts are typically incomplete, whereas firms might use "relational contracts" (i.e., informal agreements not adjudicated by courts) to overcome some of the difficulties with formal contracts.

It seems underappreciated in economics that the second prong of Williamson's argument borrowed a central theme from four decades of organizational sociology. Williamson relied primarily on Barnard ([1938] 1975) and Simon (1951), but many others had also emphasized the importance of informal agreements in organizations, including Blau (1955), Dalton (1959), Gouldner (1954), and Selznick (1949) in the landmark case studies that signaled American sociology's departure from Weber's emphasis on formal organizational structures and processes. By 1962 it was uncontroversial (at least among sociologists) to say that "it is impossible to understand the nature of a formal organization without investigating the networks of informal relations and the unofficial norms as well as the formal hierarchy of authority and the official body of rules." (Blau and Scott 1962, 6).

But informal agreements can be crucial between firms as well as within. In sociology, Macaulay (1963) documented the importance of such "noncontractual relations" between businesses. In law, Macneil (1978) com-

This essay draws heavily upon my joint work with George Baker and Kevin J. Murphy, especially our recent paper "Relational Contracts and the Theory of the Firm." Any good ideas I offer here were codeveloped with them. I am also grateful for helpful advice on cross-disciplinary communication from Paul DiMaggio.

pared classical contracts (enforced to the letter by courts) and neoclassical contracts (interpreted and updated by arbitration) to relational contracts (interpreted and updated by the parties). And in organization theory, Dore (1983) was the first of many to describe Japanese supply relationships as relational contracts, and Powell (1990) emphasized that relational contracts exist horizontally as well as vertically, such as in the networks of firms in the fashion industry or the diamond trade.[1]

Given this emphasis in the sociological literature on relational contracts both within and between firms, it is not surprising that the main chapters in this volume—by Walter Powell, David Stark, and Eleanor Westney— all accord important roles to such relational contracts. As one example from within firms, Powell notes the importance of semi-autonomous project teams, but such a team's autonomy can be revoked at any moment by higher management, (that is, such autonomy is backed by promise and reputation, not law). And in discussing alliances, partnerships, and other collaborations among U.S. firms, Powell argues that "fixed contracts are ineffectual" and so are replaced by "relational contracts" supported by "reputation, friendship, interdependence, and altruism." Similarly, in describing "recombinant" organizations in postsocialist Hungary and the Czech Republic, Stark emphasizes the continuing importance of "informal and interfirm networks that 'got the job done' under socialism." Interestingly (for Stark's argument and for my purposes later), even such networks may not result in flawless coordination and control: in one Hungarian network, the central firm had to try repeatedly to "introduce stricter accounting procedures and tighter financial controls," apparently without full success. Finally, in characterizing large Japanese firms circa 1950–90, Westney notes not only the "implicit contract" within the firm concerning employment security and seniority-based pay but also important relational contracts between firms. In particular, supply relationships in vertical *keiretsu* were managed by "contact, not contract": coordination and control were often achieved not by ownership but by dense flows of information, technology, capital, and people across firm boundaries. And these flows, like a project team's autonomy, are backed in part by promise and reputation rather than entirely by court-enforced contracts.

In this brief essay, I begin by summarizing a recent economic model of relational contracts within and between firms (Baker, Gibbons, and Murphy 2001). This model uses the theory of repeated games to create a stick-

---

[1] For further examples of relational contracts between firms, see Nishiguchi and Brookfield (1997) on hand-in-glove supply relationships, Kogut (1989) on joint ventures, Gerlach (1992) and Gulati (1995) on alliances, Kogut, Shan, and Walker (1992) and Podolny and Page (1998) on networks, Granovetter (1995) and Dyer (1996a) on business groups, and Chesbrough and Teece (1996) on "virtual" firms.

figure rendition of relational contracts like those described by Powell, Stark, and Westney. The model's relevance to this volume is not in its caricature of real relationships, but rather in its reconceptualization of relational contracts and the boundary of the firm: in this model, the parties' relationship takes center stage; the integration decision is merely an instrument in the service of that relationship.[2] For example, in a supply relationship between an upstream supplier and a downstream user, the best feasible relational contract between the two parties can differ dramatically depending on whether the parties belong to one firm (vertical integration) or two (nonintegration). In this case, the vertical-integration decision is driven by whether integration or nonintegration facilitates the superior relational contract. Simply put, the old "make-or-buy" decision should instead be viewed as "make or cooperate" (Kogut, Shan, and Walker 1992), where *both* options involve important relational contracts.

Having articulated this new perspective on relational contracts and the boundary of the firm, I then return to the Powell, Stark, and Westney chapters. In particular, I use the model to consider three overarching themes: (1) contingency, such as Powell's contention that rapid technological change places a premium on relational forms of organization and Westney's observation that the Japanese employment system was premised on continuous growth; (2) efficiency, such as Stark's observation that even relational forms of organization have their problems, including "problems of accountability that accompany the relentless pursuit of flexibility" and (3) path dependence, such as Stark's and Westney's arguments that understanding which relational forms of organization come into existence and flourish depends on the history of prior relationships. For each theme, I find encouraging agreement and complementarity between the economic model and the sociological accounts.

A One-Shot Supply Transaction

Consider the following model of a one-shot supply transaction involving an upstream party (supplier), a downstream party (user), and an asset (production equipment). Suppose that the upstream party uses the asset to produce a good that can be used in the downstream party's production process. The value of this good to the downstream party is Q, but the good also has an alternative use with value P. Such a supply transaction is shown in figure 7.1.

---

[2] See Gibbons (1999) for other kinds of contributions that formal models can make to organization theory.

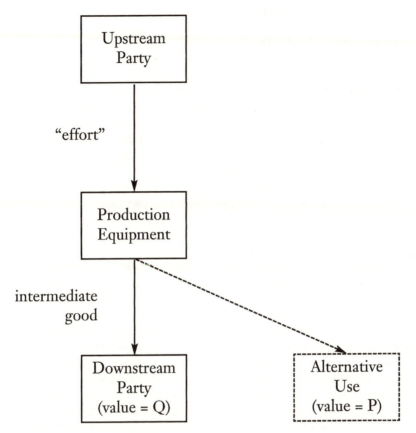

Figure 7.1. A one-shot supply relationship.

If the upstream party owns the asset, we will call him or her an *independent contractor* (i.e., someone who works with her own tools); if the downstream party owns the asset, we will call the upstream party an *employee* of the downstream organization (i.e., someone who works with the boss's tools). Alternatively, we can think of the upstream and downstream parties as firms rather than as individuals, in which case it is more natural to use terms such as "supplier" and "division" rather than "independent contractor" and "employee," respectively. Whether the parties are individuals or firms, if the upstream party owns the asset we will call the parties "nonintegrated," but if the downstream party owns the asset we will call the parties "integrated."[3]

[3] Grossman and Hart (1986) originated the idea that asset ownership patterns define who works for whom, and consequently whether a supply chain is integrated or not. As I describe

To be concrete, much of the discussion will be cast in terms of a famous business-school case: Crown Cork and Seal Company (Gordon, Reed, and Hamermesh 1977). The details of the case become important later in this discussion; for now, it suffices to say that in the 1950s and '60s, Crown made metal cans for the soft-drink industry. So suppose that Crown owns a can plant located near a Pepsi plant, but there is also a Coke plant two towns away. That is, Crown is the upstream party, Pepsi the downstream party, and Coke the alternative use. In actual fact, Crown was never integrated with Pepsi or Coke, but we will at times consider the hypothetical case in which Pepsi has purchased the can plant from Crown (in which case the can plant is a "division" of Pepsi).

Suppose that ownership of the asset conveys ownership of the good produced using the asset. For example, if Crown owns the can plant, then Crown owns the cans produced there until Pepsi buys them. Furthermore, in bargaining over the sale of the cans, Crown can threaten to sell the cans to Coke (i.e., under nonintegration, the upstream party can threaten to consign the good to its alternative use). On the other hand, if Pepsi owned the can plant then Pepsi could prevent the can plant from dealing with outside customers.

Suppose also that the production equipment has been specialized to meet the downstream party's needs. For example, the can plant might have been configured to produce cans to Pepsi's specifications rather than Coke's. Then the good's value to the downstream party will exceed its value in the alternative use; that is, $Q > P$. The surplus that the upstream and downstream parties can jointly achieve by transacting with each other is thus $Q - P$, but each party would like to capture all of this surplus. For example, Crown would like to sell its cans to Pepsi for Q, but Pepsi would like to pay only P.

This model may seem rather distant from the contemporary and international concerns of Powell, Stark, and Westney, but I believe it is actually quite closely related. First of all, there are many direct applications of this model beyond soda cans in the 1950s. For example, suppose that the upstream party is an inventor, the downstream party is a manufacturer, and the asset is the inventor's invention. Rather than discuss ownership of a physical asset like a can plant, we now consider ownership of intellectual property—the invention. If the manufacturer will own any inventions that the inventor might produce, then the inventor can be thought of as an employee working in the manufacturer's R&D lab. Alternatively, if the inventor will own the inventions then he or she can sell them either to the manufacturer or to an alternative user. This second example (which can be

---

in somewhat more detail below, their paper is on a par with Coase (1937) and Williamson (1975, 1985) in its impact on the emerging field of organizational economics.

enriched to include issues such as licensing, alliances, and so on) is quite close to some of Powell's discussions of the biotech and pharmaceuticals industries.

In addition to expanding the list of direct applications of this model, one can also reinterpret the model more broadly, along the following lines. Organizational sociologists have long emphasized the distinction between formal and informal aspects of organizational structure. Formal aspects include the job descriptions and reporting relationships described in an organization chart, as well as formal contracts and ownership stakes; informal aspects include norms and mutual understandings, as well as networks of nonreporting relationships among individuals. In the model presented earlier, asset ownership is the formal aspect of organizational structure (and relational contracts will be the informal aspect, as discussed later). I believe that close cousins of the model sketched here can be used to analyze other formal aspects of organizations—not just ownership rights to physical or intellectual property, but also job design, reporting relationships, formal contracts, and share ownership.[4] Throughout this family of models, the common question will be how formal aspects of organizations support or constrain informal aspects, such as the relational contracts to which we turn next.

AN ONGOING SUPPLY RELATIONSHIP

In the 1950s and '60s, the metal can industry looked horrible: suppliers were strong (such as U.S. Steel), customers were strong (such as Pepsi, Coke, and Campbell's Soup), and entry into the industry was cheap (a used production line cost only $150,000 and could be set up in a small space close to an important customer). Industry giants such as American Can and Continental Can were losing money and diversifying out of the industry, but Crown Cork and Seal made money by specializing in customer service. That is, Crown not only began a relationship with a customer by tailoring the specifications of the cans and the schedule for deliveries to the customer's requirements, but (more importantly) Crown stood ready to modify

---

[4] There may seem to be an inconsistency here: I argued above that the semi-autonomy of Powell's project teams is backed by informal promise and reputation rather than formal contract, yet here I argue that the job designs and reporting relationships in an organization chart can be viewed as formal structure. But what is formal and what is informal depends on the level of analysis. If the CEO can redesign the organization at a moment's notice then *for relationships involving the CEO*, the organization chart is informal—it is backed by promise rather than law. But in analyzing, say, the relationship between a middle manager and her subordinate (assuming that neither can affect the organization structure), the organization chart can sensibly be viewed as formal—it is backed by something more like law than by the promises of either the middle manager or her subordinate.

can specifications and delivery schedules when unusual circumstances arose. Of course, Crown did not make these modifications for free; to the contrary, Crown was able to charge a premium because of its reputation for flexibility and service. In short, in the terminology of this essay, Crown had an important relational contract with its customers: Crown would make reasonable modifications under the terms of the existing formal contract; substantial modifications could also be made, but would create the expectation of fair compensation, either on a one-shot basis or by revising the terms of the formal contract for the future.

Crown's customer service illustrates both of Williamson's (1975) ideas. First, formal contracts are almost always incomplete—they often do not specify important future events that might occur, not to mention what adaptations should be made if a particular event does occur. Second, relational contracts may overcome some of the difficulties with formal contracts—relational contracts may allow the parties to utilize their detailed knowledge of their situation to adapt to new contingencies as they arise. Of course, the irony in this illustration is that Crown was not integrated with Pepsi. That is, the motivation for and benefits of relational contracts are as Williamson (1975) described, but the transaction is occurring between firms instead of within. A useful model of relational contracts must therefore be applicable both within and between firms.[5]

To see why the theory of repeated games may help in developing such a model, recall that the drawback of any relational contract is that it cannot be enforced by the courts: having a contract that utilizes the parties' specific expertise makes it prohibitively expensive for the courts to adjudicate disputes. Therefore, relational contracts must be "self-enforcing," in the sense that each party's concern for its reputation must outweigh that party's temptation to renege on the relational contract.[6] This kind of logic—in

---

[5] Williamson (1985, ch. 3) pays greater attention to relational contracts between firms, but construes them as features of "hybrid" forms of organization, lying on a continuum between markets and hierarchies. In contrast, the model in Baker, Gibbons, and Murphy (2001) suggests that the set of governance structures is at least two-dimensional (integrated vs. not and relational governance vs. spot), in which case it is not possible to array all governance structures on a line between markets and hierarchies. This two-dimensional view of governance is consistent with Powell's (1990) assertion that networks are "neither market nor hierarchy."

Williamson (1996, ch. 4) devotes still greater attention to relational contracts between firms, recognizing the prevalence and longevity of these relationships and their associated "hybrid" organizational forms. The contributions of the Baker-Gibbons-Murphy model are to ask and answer how and why relational contracts between firms might differ from those within, and consequently when one might outperform the other.

[6] Powell's chapter observes that a "dense, transactional infrastructure of lawyers, financiers, and venture capitalists has emerged to facilitate, monitor, and adjudicate network relationships." This observation is completely in keeping with the model developed here, because the model can readily be extended to involve more than two parties. As an example of such a

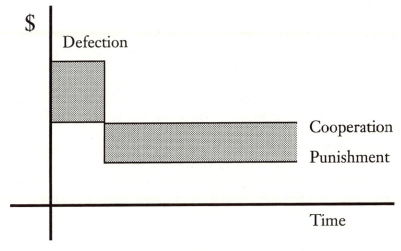

Figure 7.2. Time-paths of possible payoffs from trigger strategy.

which the shadow of the future subdues the temptations of the present—
is widely known outside economics from Axelrod's (1984) analysis of Tit-
for-Tat strategies in the Prisoners' Dilemma. In economics, however, many
analyses of repeated games focus on "trigger" strategies, in which defection
ruins the relationship forever. Trigger strategies can be applied in a very
broad class of repeated games, including the repeated game based on the
one-shot supply model above.[7]

To illustrate a trigger strategy, consider a repeated Prisoners' Dilemma.
A player's current options are to "Cooperate" or "Defect," but defection
will be discovered and result in "Punishment" forever after, whereas cooperation today will create the same choice between cooperation and defection tomorrow. As suggested by figure 7.2, cooperation is the optimal
choice today if the present value of the current and future payoffs from
cooperation exceeds the present value of the higher current payoff from
defection followed by the lower future payoffs from punishment.

To analyze trigger strategies in a repeated-game model of an ongoing
supply relationship, recall the model of a one-shot supply transaction described previously, but now suppose that the transaction is to be repeated

---

multi-player relational contract (where some of the players are monitors and adjudicators),
see Greif, Milgrom, and Weingast's (1994) model of a merchant guild. The key feature of
both the basic model presented here and all such extensions is that the courts would find it
prohibitively expensive to engage in such monitoring and adjudication. That is, the game
may include more than two players, but it is still a game rather than a formal contract.

[7] For a more detailed but still fairly nontechnical motivation and analysis of trigger strategies in repeated games, see Gibbons (1997).

indefinitely, with the outcome of each transaction observed by both parties before the next transaction occurs. Crown's promise of customer service is an important relational contract between firms. In the model, think of Crown's promise as the upstream party's pledge to deliver a high value of Q to the downstream party. Of course, the same promise might also be quite important within a firm. That is, if Pepsi bought the can plant from Crown, Pepsi might well expect and desire its new can division to provide the same modifications to can specifications and delivery schedules that Crown had previously provided.

The key result in this repeated-game model of an ongoing supply relationship is that the size of the incentive to renege on a relational contract (i.e., the extent to which the payoff from defection exceeds the payoff from cooperation in figure 7.2) depends on who owns the asset. Consequently, implementing the best feasible relational contract requires making the right choice about integration. In certain settings, integration supports a better relational contract than nonintegration can; in other settings, the reverse holds. The remainder of this section is devoted to explaining this key result.

To begin, suppose that the upstream party owns the asset. This case gives rise to the classic "hold-up" problem because the upstream party can threaten to consign the good to its alternative use unless the downstream party pays a high price. That is, Crown could threaten to sell the cans to Coke. In the model, Pepsi's value for the cans is Q and Coke's is only P < Q. Thus, Crown's threat to sell the cans to Coke should not be carried out, because Pepsi is willing to pay more than P for the cans. Instead, after such a threat, suppose that Crown and Pepsi agree on some price between P and Q. The key point is that Crown will receive at least P, and this in turn gives Crown an incentive to take actions that increase P: Crown will pay attention to Coke so as to improve its bargaining position with Pepsi. But actions that increase P may have no (or even negative) effect on Q. Thus, Crown may find it privately optimal to take actions that give it a larger share of a smaller total surplus in its relationship with Pepsi. Such actions are inefficient: both Crown and Pepsi could be made better off if those actions were stopped.

Pepsi's instinctive reaction to this hold-up problem might be the one often prescribed in the transaction-cost literature: buy the can plant in order to decree that the plant cannot sell cans to Coke. In this sense, vertical integration could indeed prevent one hold-up from occurring, as argued by Klein, Crawford, and Alchian (1978) and Williamson (1979). The insight of Grossman and Hart (1986), however, is that using formal instruments to eliminate one hold-up problem typically creates another. As an example of this conundrum, consider Klein, Crawford, and Alchian's account of the events preceding the acquisition of Fisher Body by General Motors. GM asked Fisher to invest in a new technology to produce closed metal auto bodies rather than the then-standard open wood bodies. Both parties understood that GM could hold up Fisher after such an investment, such as by offering to pay only marginal rather than average cost. Consequently, the parties signed a contract that gave Fisher certain protections, including a formula specifying the price as a markup of Fisher's variable costs. But this contract created ways for Fisher to hold up GM, such as by threatening to overstaff its plants so as to pad variable cost. Grossman and Hart's abstract model is similar: using asset ownership (another formal instrument, akin to a formal contract) to solve one hold up problem inevitably creates another.

Ultimately, GM bought Fisher, but at a high price. The price had to be high because Fisher had to be persuaded to give up its strong bargaining position created by the pricing formula in the formal contract. But the reason that it was efficient for GM to buy Fisher does not hinge on this acquisition price, which is merely a transfer between the parties and so has no effect on the efficiency of operations. Instead, the reason for GM to buy Fisher (according to Klein, Crawford, and Alchian) was to stop Fisher's inefficient actions, such as overstaffing. Analogously, it might be efficient for Pepsi to buy the can plant from Crown if, under nonintegration, Crown has a strong incentive to take inefficient actions that increase the cans' value to Coke (P) but distract Crown from providing service to Pepsi (i.e., reduce Q).

The striking feature of this long-standing and sensible account of the Fisher Body acquisition (see also Klein 1991) is that it never mentions life in the Fisher division of GM after the acquisition. But without considering the difference between life as a division and life as an independent firm, the analysis cannot ascertain whether the Grossman-Hart conundrum applies. That is, if vertical integration stopped Fisher's hold up of GM, might it also have created a new way for GM to hold up Fisher? In keeping with Grossman and Hart, I will argue that integration probably did create such a reverse hold up. But I will then argue that this conundrum arises because of the reliance on *formal* instruments (such as formal contracts or asset ownership) to eliminate individual hold-up problems, and that a potential solution to the conundrum is to use *informal* instruments (namely, relational contracts) in tandem with formal instruments to ameliorate all hold-up problems simultaneously. To make these arguments concrete, I return to the Crown-Pepsi example and the model above.

Imagine that Pepsi bought the can plant from Crown. That is, the downstream party owns the asset. The upstream party is then an internal division rather than an external supplier, but the downstream party is still interested in receiving high-quality service. The downstream party could try to create an incentive for the upstream party to supply high-quality service by promising to pay a bonus to the upstream party if the latter produces a sufficiently high value of Q. Unfortunately, like all relational contracts, this promise is vulnerable to reneging: when the downstream party owns the asset, the downstream party can simply take the intermediate good without paying the upstream party anything.[8]

Reneging on a promised bonus is just one example of possible hold-ups within organizations. Richer models could capture reneging temptations concerning promotions, task allocation, capital allocation, internal auditing, transfer payments, and so on. Lawler (1971), Bower (1970), Dalton (1959), Eccles (1985), and many others offer evidence that such varieties of reneging are alive and well in many organizations. The key feature of all of these examples is that one party with authority makes a promise to another party without. In each case, the temptation to renege on such a promise can again be analyzed using figure 7.2.

We are now ready to revisit the key result in this section: that the incentive to renege on a relational contact depends on who owns the asset. Suppose the parties would like the upstream party to deliver quality Q^* and the downstream party to pay upstream a fee F^*. Under nonintegration, the upstream party is tempted to renege, by taking actions that increase P so as to collect a fee greater than F^*, even if the resulting quality is $Q < Q^*$. Under integration, it is the owner (here, the downstream party) who is tempted to renege, by simply taking the good and not paying the fee F^*. Thus, not only the size of the incentive to renege but also the identity of the party tempted to renege depends on who owns the asset.

We therefore have a situation dear to an economist's heart: a trade-off. Upstream ownership offers the upstream party some recourse should the downstream party renege, and hence decreases the downstream party's temptation to renege, but upstream ownership also encourages the upstream party to consider the interests of other parties, and hence may create a temptation for the upstream party to renege. In some settings, the first of these considerations is more important, so integration is optimal; in others, the second dominates, so nonintegration is preferred. In all settings, however, the guiding principle is to induce efficient actions (and discourage inefficient actions) by implementing the best possible relational contract. The integration decision is merely an instrument in this quest.

This section's equal-opportunity analysis of reneging on relational contracts within and between firms is related to Granovetter's (1985) observa-

---

[8] In case such reneging is not immediately plausible, recall the inventor-invention-manufacturer example sketched above. Imagine that the inventor is an employee in the R&D lab of a large pharmaceutical firm, and suppose the firm has promised to share the profits from inventions fifty-fifty with the inventor. If the inventor creates a drug worth ten billion dollars,

tion that Williamson's (1975) treatment of markets is undersocialized but his treatment of hierarchy oversocialized. In the repeated-game model, the possibility of relational contracting between firms makes markets less undersocialized, and the possibility of reneging on relational contracts within a firm makes hierarchy less oversocialized. Similarly, Dow (1987) argues that authority within a firm that is strong enough to restrain opportunistic bargaining may also be strong enough to engage in its own novel forms of opportunism. Dow's argument is a cousin of the Grossman-Hart conundrum: making one party the owner may stop hold-ups by the non-owner, but it may also create hold-up opportunities for the owner. This section's repeated-game model extends Dow's argument by noting that an appropriate relational contract may discourage the owner from engaging in the latter hold-ups, but also that the power and effectiveness of such a relational contract is limited by reneging temptations. Finally, Sako and Helper (1998) analyze supplier relationships in the auto industry and find that reported levels of trust and opportunism are independent of whether the parties were integrated or not—consistent with the spirit of Granovetter, Dow, and the repeated-game model.

In the model I have presented, I interpret a relational contract between nonintegrated parties as a hand-in-glove supply relationship. But there are many other relational forms of organization discussed in the business and organizational literatures, including joint ventures, strategic alliances, networks, and business groups, as well as the structures described by Powell, Stark, and Westney. Although the model I have discussed has only two stages of production with one party at each stage, richer models could add both parties and stages. For example, one could begin to model a joint venture in which two parties at one stage create an asset at another stage, which they control by both formal and informal means. Similarly, one could begin to model a business group in which several parties at several stages of production are linked by both cross-ownership and relational contracts, possibly through a central party. Formal structures such as fifty-fifty ownership in joint ventures or minority stock holdings in business groups may be better understood using models that study the interplay between these formal structures and informal relational contracts between the parties.

CONCLUSION

In summary, I have tried to say four things about relational contracts and the boundary of the firm. First, following Klein, Crawford, and Alchian (1978) and Williamson (1979), ownership can stop hold-up. Second, fol-

---

do we expect the firm to keep its promise? How would the situation differ if the inventor had worked in her own independent research firm?

lowing Grossman and Hart (1986), the use of formal instruments (such as formal contracts or asset ownership) to stop one hold-up problem typically creates another. Third, following Barnard ([1938] 1975), Simon (1951), Macaulay (1963), Macneil (1978), and many others, relational contracts offer important advantages over formal contracts and ownership structures, but relational contracts are vulnerable to reneging. Finally, following Baker, Gibbons, and Murphy (2001), implementing the best feasible relational contract requires optimizing the boundary of the firm. Combining these ideas produces a new perspective: the parties' relationship is the central issue; the integration decision should be made in the service of that relationship.

To conclude, let me return to the Powell, Stark, and Westney chapters. In particular, I will consider three overarching themes: contingency, efficiency, and path dependence. For each theme, I find encouraging agreement and complementarity between the economic model and the sociological accounts.

First, contingency: Powell argues that rapid technological change places a premium on relational forms of organization, and Westney suggests that the Japanese employment system was premised on continuous growth. Using the model just discussed, one can interpret these two observations as claims about the value and the feasibility of relational contracts, respectively. Recall that the role of relational contracts is to utilize the parties' detailed knowledge of their situation to adapt to new contingencies as they arise. Surely this role is more valuable in settings of rapid change (but just as surely, formal contracts cannot be abandoned in these settings, or else change may too easily cause reneging temptations to exceed the value of continuing the relationship). Whether rapid or gradual, change may cause a relational contract that is feasible and valuable today to become infeasible and valueless tomorrow. For example, the market shift from mainframe to personal computers can be seen as causing IBM to abandon its no-layoffs policy. The end of decades of continuous growth in Japan can be interpreted similarly.

Second, efficiency: Stark claims that even relational forms of organization have their problems, such as "problems of accountability that accompany the relentless pursuit of flexibility." This is an important point, and is again consistent with the economic model. Relational forms of organization may offer advantages over purely formal organizations, but this does not imply that relational forms of organization can or will be perfect. In Gibbons (1999) I say more about this distinction between the best imaginable (first-best) and the best feasible (second-best) organizational forms. For the purposes of this essay, the central idea is that relational forms of organization are most useful in difficult environments, such as Powell's world of rapid technological change. Thus, saying that relational forms may outperform purely formal organizations in such difficult environments is by no means a guarantee that relational forms can perform perfectly. Furthermore, there is abundant evidence that relational contracts often hurt rather than improve organizational performance; see, for example, Roethlisberger and Dickson (1939) and Roy (1952). Thus, even if relational forms could perform perfectly, there is some doubt about whether they will. This indeterminacy appears in the economic model as the existence of multiple equilibria in the repeated game. I believe that an economic theory of leadership can and should be developed around the idea that leaders try to move organizations to new equilibria. Hermalin (1998) has already made a nice start in this direction.

Finally, path dependence: Stark and Westney predict that the relational forms of organization that come into existence and flourish will depend on the history of prior relationships. I agree. Unfortunately, if economics has only started to make progress on the concept of leadership, it has done even less in examining such path dependence. From an economic perspective, the two problems are similar: both involve creating a new equilibrium from the understandings and expectations of actors with different (or even conflicting) experiences. Understanding this interplay between history and incentives seems a daunting task, but I will close on a happy note: Granovetter (1999, 162) not only agrees that the task is important, but suggests that this is where "the true potential lies for interdisciplinary cooperation."

CHAPTER 8

Welcome to the Seventeenth Century

Charles Tilly

WELCOME TO the seventeenth century! As you enter the twenty-first century, in some respects you will be moving back in time. Back, in fact, two or three centuries. Throughout most of the world over most of human history, including the seventeenth century, people have undertaken risky long-term enterprises chiefly by relying on what we might call networks of trust. Under various names such as trade diasporas, lineages, and sects, such networks combine strong ties, considerable extent, many triads, and significant barriers to entry or exit.

Risk is threat multiplied by uncertainty. People frequently confront short-term risk without creating elaborate social structure; on their own they leap raging rivers, engage in unsafe sex, drive while drunk, or bet a thousand dollars. When it comes to the long-term risks of reproduction, cohabitation, investment, migration, or agricultural enterprise, however, people generally embed those risks in durable, substantial social organization. To that extent, they trust others—they make the reduction of threat and/or uncertainty contingent on the performance of other people when they cannot entirely control. Such sets of relations to others constitute networks of trust.

In most circumstances, participants in networks of trust have shielded them zealously from governmental intervention, with powerful participants working out protected accommodations such as indirect rule and powerless participants employing what James Scott calls "weapons of the weak" (1985). The chief exceptions to that insulation of trust networks from government have occurred in cases where members of the networks in question ran their own governments; ruling dynasties, for example, have often used intermarriage as cement among interacting regimes. For most people over the bulk of history, however, viable visions of the future have relied far less on performance of governments or autonomous economic organizations than on access to sturdy networks of trust.

The eighteenth to twentieth centuries stood out from all others in these (and in many other) regards. Beginning in Western Europe, entrepreneurs and officials started to work out contingent compacts in which government and risky enterprise depended on each other. (To some extent, these Europeans were adapting models discovered in Asia and expanding experiments initiated earlier by government-backed trading companies.) Through an interplay that we still do not fully understand, two sorts of organizations acquired power in the capitalist world: bounded firms, on one side; consolidated states, on the other. Durable, autonomous, legally constituted firms controlling considerable fixed capital became increasingly prominent sites of production and distribution. They reduced (but never eliminated) the relative importance of households, kin groups, and temporary coalitions of merchants as instruments of production and distribution. At the same time, relatively centralized, differentiated, and territorially delimited states, which exercised substantial control over stocks and flows of resources within their territories, achieved great priority over other forms of government.

Both sorts of organizations created institutions of circumscription (monitoring their boundaries and flows across them) and of central control (creating direct links between coordinating agencies and routine life on the small scale). Locked gates, assembly lines, graded pay scales, and foremen exemplify these institutions on the side of firms. Passports, censuses, cadasters, and income taxes exemplify them on the side of states. James Scott calls these projects of bounding, central control, and uniformity "high modernism" (1998).

Although states and firms never worked together in perfect harmony, they established cooperation, or at least a modus vivendi over a wide range of circumstances. States licensed firms, created patent systems, built infrastructure, standardized legal tenders, and otherwise stabilized conditions for capitalist production. Firms, for their part, paid taxes, helped war efforts, and submitted to governmental intervention on behalf of their workers. Despite incessant haggling over the details, firms and states took each other's continued existence for granted—so much so that disruptions of one by war, revolution, disaster, or international financial crisis shook the other fundamentally.

In the process, an unprecedented share of risky, long-term enterprises and their associated trust networks came to depend on the survival of both sorts of organization. Household investments, security in old age, long-distance trade, access to information, acquisition of skills, subsistence, and cohabitation lost much of their reliance on autonomous trust networks as firms and states became the means of their realization. Within limits, people even began entrusting life, health, physical security, and collective survival to armies, police forces, hospitals, and transportation systems operated by others with whom they had no direct personal ties.

Of course firms and states present their own problems of trust. As other chapters in this volume argue (with backing from a large literature on risk control), a significant portion of firm activity and organization embodies efforts to render the actions of workers, agents, contractors, and other firms more predictable and/or less threatening to the enterprise at hand. All political regimes rely on at least a modicum of trust, and capitalist democracies fail without extensive trust—trust in governmental agents to meet their commitments, trust in other political actors to take losses without destroying the system, trust in the regime to survive long enough for the maturing of individual and collective projects undertaken on the assumption that existing institutions would stay in place.

Shocks such as Russian and Italian losses in World War I, German hyperinflation of the 1920s, and foreign-backed mayhem during the Spanish Civil War of 1936 to 1939 recurrently dissolved democracy-sustaining systems of trust. Yet the astonishing feature of the period after 1700 is the great increase in the intersection between (1) the sorts of networks in which most people have historically invested their life-chances while shielding them from the influence of large economic organizations and governments, and (2) the firms and states that became the world's dominant organizations during the nineteenth and twentieth centuries.

During the twentieth century, the intertwining of trust networks, firms, and states followed different trajectories in capitalist and state socialist regimes. Capitalist regimes reinforced conditions for the existence of firms, but generally held them at arm's length. State socialist regimes absorbed most firms into governmental structure. Significant differences followed. Under capitalism, long-term personal welfare generally continued to depend on the accumulation of property by kin-based units, while commercial enterprises relied on state-backed stabilization of property, credit, money, and access to markets. Under state socialism a remarkable bifurcation of risk-absorption occurred: governments provided a widely available minimum access to goods and services required for mere survival; beyond that minimum no one acquired reliable access to superior goods, services, personal protection, and influence without deploying clandestine interpersonal networks and/or achieving significant state office. Some of postsocialism's largest problems emerged from the fact that the first sort of risk-absorption started to collapse while the second became the basis of widespread rent-seeking.

My account obviously lacks nuance. Among capitalist regimes, analysts commonly stress variation in the involvement of states with various sorts of risk-reduction, puzzling for example over differences between the relatively thick welfare provisions of Scandinavia and the starkly thinner provisions that prevail in the United States. Close students of capitalist economies have also identified remarkable variation from industry to industry, period to period, and place to place in how much of production and distribution occurs within neatly bounded firms, and how much economic activity relies on shifting contracts among temporary clusters of producers and distributors. Their studies have, indeed, provided important inspiration for analyses in this very volume. To students of state socialist regimes, further-more, differences among China, Czechoslovakia, and Albania virtually obliterate whatever properties they shared in the days before the Warsaw Pact collapsed. One can hardly think of them as specimens of a single variant of capitalism in which the state incorporates firms. Seen in the perspective of centuries, nevertheless, the eighteenth to twentieth centuries display a startling convergence and interdependency overall of states, economic organizations, and trust networks—with capitalist and state socialist regimes merely marking some of the larger variations on a common theme.

That brief historical era now seems to be ending. Deep changes are occurring in all four elements of our basic formula: firms, states, trust networks, and interactions among them. As the essays by Walter Powell, Eleanor Westney, and David Stark document abundantly, production structures in North America, East Asia, and Eastern Europe are emerging that bear little resemblance to classic twentieth-century models of well-bounded, autonomous, maximizing firms. (To what extent firms ever corresponded to those models is, of course, a second question raised urgently by these reports and the literatures on which they draw.) As the essays also imply but do not say very explicitly, states are also changing fundamentally; they are losing some of their capacity and propensity for circumscription and central control while ceding influence over a considerable range of activities to transgovernmental and nongovernmental organizations.

As the essays fail to say, networks of trust are likewise mutating. Partly as a consequence of alterations in firms and states, the late twentieth century is witnessing expansion of people's efforts to create trustworthy solidarity within networks defined chiefly by shared religion, ethnicity, locality, or cultural preference. People are again trying strenuously to shield such networks from disruptive intervention by governments and economic organizations—except where those networks control their own governments and economic organizations. Finally and inevitably, interactions among economic structures, governmental organizations, and trust networks are shifting in ways that forecast significantly different qualities of life during the twenty-first century. In some regards, those interactions are returning our world to the seventeenth century.

To the degree that today's changes are reversing those of two or three centuries ago, a clearer analysis of the earlier transition should help us frame the right questions about what is happening now. Just as most people look with dread at the short-run consequences of today's changes, few seventeenth-century people welcomed what they actually experienced of changes in governmental structure, economic organization, and networks of trust. The expansion of European-style warfare and of European-style capitalist property relations interacted to yield enormous long-term advantages for those few who controlled (or were acquiring control over) combinations of the following:

- effective procedures, organizations, and personnel for extracting the means of war from ever-reluctant populations
- states that would and could protect their riskier long-term economic enterprises without diverting their major returns to state activities
- substantial blocs of commercially viable agricultural land
- major concentrations of merchant capital
- relatively immobile landless labor
- access to world markets

People who exercised none of these sorts of control—the vast majority of the world population—generally avoided or resisted short-run consequences of such control by the powerful. The general population continued to shield trade diasporas, lineages, sects, and other networks of trust from such disruptive activities as taxation, military recruitment, and conversion of common lands to private use. Hence in Europe and regions of European conquest, the prevalence of rebellion. Yet, like the rest of us weak opportunists, the people also adapted to changes that they could not block. They engaged in what Asef Bayat (1997) felicitously calls "the quiet encroachment of the ordinary"—seizing their shares of crumbling estates, converting temporary evasions of feudal dues into permanent exemptions, generating desperately needed money-income through cottage manufacturing, and so on. They took on commitments of courtship, marriage, childbearing, inheritance, apprenticeship, migration, agricultural investment, military service, and religious affiliation whose long-term payoffs tacitly assumed survival of rising institutions. People thus committed themselves unwittingly but inexorably to the emerging order.

Such accommodations doubly compromised existing autonomous networks of trust, first by weakening their connections and effectiveness, second by integrating what remained of them increasingly into firms and states. State-backed churches, for example, gained increasing control over sexual pairing and reproduction. Access to land came to depend much more heavily on state registration of claims to property. Firms began to accumulate exclusive means of production and distribution. The range of everyday problems for which trust networks could offer effective solutions diminished radically. Capitalization, proletarianization, and governmental appropriation of coercive means reduced the scope of autonomous trust networks to sentimental attachment, niche-protection within the capitalist state system, and mutual aid in times of crisis.

Obviously I am again riding roughshod across variation. Within Europe alone I am ignoring differences among the extensive kin-, religion-, and language-linked trust networks of the Balkans, the tight subordination of

Lutheran churches to war-making states in Scandinavia, the oligarchic seg-
mentation of Swiss cantons, and the extraordinary short-term capacity of
the fissiparous Dutch Republic to coalesce for commercial and military
efforts. For the sake of illuminating what may be happening as we move
from the twentieth to the twenty-first century, nevertheless, it helps to
draw two simple conclusions from all the earlier transition's tangled complexity: (1) in historical perspective, the rise to world organizational dominance of sharply bounded firms and consolidated states established an ut-
terly exceptional era; (2) one fundamental consequence of that transition
was the partial destruction and partial integration into firms and states of
previously autonomous trust networks and the risky activities embedded
in them.

In this light, the analyses of Walter Powell, Eleanor Westney, and David
Stark take on new meaning. For in those two regards they are documenting
momentous reversals: diminution of firms' and states' organizational dominance and reemergence of autonomous trust networks. When Powell
speaks of firms as networks, industries as capabilities, and work as projects,
when Westney speaks of network organizations, and when Stark speaks of
recombinant property, all are speaking of ruptures in previous boundaries
and central controls. They are also observing how capital markets, those
quintessentially far-reaching networks of trust, are emerging as primary
links among the world's powerful people and as major determinants of
local economic activity. Along with other recent analysts, they imply that
world-spanning capital markets are gaining autonomy with respect to firms
and states. To some degree, non-firm networks among institutional investors and venture capitalists create their own firms as temporary interfaces
with existing organizations and acquire their own instruments of government in the form of such institutions as the World Bank. Mostly, however,
they connect over, under, and through existing firms and states, evading
and eroding their control.

Outside the assigned scope of the essays by Powell, Westney, and Stark,
international networks, some with their own bounded organizations, link
elite activists on behalf of environmental conservation, human rights, in-
digenous peoples, and other state-spanning causes. Meanwhile, relatively
powerless and power-seeking people are investing in religious, ethnic, racial, and taste-based trust networks whose autonomy from bounded firms
and grasping states they are attempting to secure—except where they can
establish their own bounded firms and grasping states. Thus a new division
between uses of trust networks by powerful and powerless people is emerging as a parody of the seventeenth-century distinction between agents and
objects of indirect rule.

Why are these changes occurring? Powell refers broadly to the coevolution of technology and organization, implying that under changing condi-

tions new network-based organizational forms are driving out their self-contained predecessors. But why and how? Powell raises doubts whether the expansion of global markets in capital and commodities is dissolving the old bounded entities, and whether American capital's search for cheap labor outside the United States is driving changes in American corporate organization. He points instead to the speed, volume, and reduced cost of information flow. Technological change figures centrally in his causal account.

Analyzing Japanese experience, Westney attributes far more influence to political decisions on the part of national authorities than Powell does for the United States. She also allows some room for the international diffusion of models (notably Japanese-inspired models of flexible specialization) and for pressures from international competitors. Concentrating on what makes Japan different rather than what makes Japan change, however, ultimately Westney declares herself agnostic with respect to the how and why of long-term organizational change.

Examining organizational changes in East Central Europe, Stark concedes some causal significance to international agencies, foreign financiers, and national governmental policies, but focuses on improvisation by domestic entrepreneurs within constraints set by existing institutions, resources, understandings, and networks. Without developing the argument, Stark also invokes a set of evolutionary adaptations that recall Powell's references to coevolution. Thus if we were to draw from the analyses of Powell, Westney, and Stark a causal model of organizational changes from the twentieth to the twenty-first centuries, we would no doubt include alterations of information technology, governmental intervention, demands of international agencies, diffusion of organizational models, actions by agents of international capital, and improvisation by domestic entrepreneurs, all operating within broader processes of coevolution mediated most directly by competition of producers and distributors within world markets. Such a compendious model would leave urgent questions unanswered concerning interactions among the elements, priorities among them, and causal mechanisms producing their effects.

Yet the roster of elements may still be incomplete. Think back to the historical interdependence of states and firms. Considering how the transition from the seventeenth to nineteenth centuries occurred, it might be worth examining yet another factor that rarely figures in current discussions. The war-driven formation of national military forces strongly promoted the emergence and world dominance of consolidated states (Burke 1997; Porter 1994; Tilly 1992). The formation of consolidated states in turn increased the viability of bounded, autonomous firms (North 1998). The collapse of the Soviet Union, the Cold War's end, and the spread of democratic regimes are combining to transform war and military organization. Mass warfare among great powers becomes less likely as civil war, genocide, and guerrilla warfare become more prevalent (Ausenda 1992; Beissinger 1996; Creveld 1991; Dawisha 1997; Fein 1993; Foran 1997; Gurr 1993; Gurr and Harff 1994; Lupher 1996; Mansfield and Snyder 1995; Ward and Gleditsch 1998). Great powers have, to be sure, held to visions of past conflict by sustaining national armed forces and such international organizations as NATO. Yet military doctrine, practice, and organization are gradually moving away from mass armies toward low-intensity conflict involving multilateral forces.

Even single-country interventions now require multilateral authorization. Although Britain still felt free to send its own military forces into its disputed colony of the Falklands/Malvinas in 1983, it did so only after invoking sanctions from the United Nations Security Council and the European Community. The United States called out the Association of Eastern Caribbean States to join its 1990 invasion of Grenada. Even the American-dominated Gulf War of 1990 brought together forces from Saudi Arabia, the United Kingdom, Egypt, Syria, Niger, Kuwait, Oman, Bahrain, Senegal, Morocco, Qatar, and the United Arab Emirates under cover of United Nations resolutions. As compared with Bosnia or Somalia, furthermore, the Falklands, Grenada, and Persian Gulf episodes represent exceptionally unilateral interventions. Reduction of mass national armies and an emphatic shift toward multinational intervention in dispersed, small-scale conflicts are reversing the military processes that reinforced bounded, centralized, autonomous, high-capacity states during the eighteenth and nineteenth centuries. If such states lose power relative to other organizations and networks, we have every reason to expect decline in forms of organization that depend on the presence of bounded, centralized, autonomous, high-capacity states. Perhaps the alteration of governmental organization should occupy a larger place in our causal story than the concentration on firms and their antitheses alone leads us to recognize.

How might such a causal connection work? We can imagine at least two plausible processes. The first is geographic fragmentation of economic interests in coercion. The eighteenth and nineteenth century nationalization of economic interests subjected capitalists increasingly to the authority of single, unified states, but it also made those states' coercive capacities increasingly available as backing to any firm's domestic and international interests. The multiplication of enterprises and capital-based coalitions that operate in many states' jurisdictions simultaneously reduces capital's advantage from aligning with any single state—unless perhaps it is a superstate capable of coercing all the rest. At the same time, dispersion of control gives regional agents of large enterprises more opportunities and incentives to draw on local agents of coercion, whether state-backed, dissident, or purely mercenary. The interplay among diamond merchants, oil merchants, arms merchants, and military entrepreneurs (governmental and otherwise) in recent African conflicts gives some weight to the speculation.

The second plausible causal connection between low-intensity warfare and changes in state-capital relations runs through the declining capacity of states to draw resources, including military manpower, from their subject populations. Margaret Levi has made a strong case that citizens' compliance with governmental demands rests on what she calls contingent consent. Levi's model of "contingent consent" (1997, 21) states that individual citizens are more likely to comply with costly demands from their governments, including demands for military service, to the degree that (1) citizens perceive the government to be trustworthy; (2) the proportion of other citizens complying (that is, the degree of "ethical reciprocity") increases; and (3) citizens receive information confirming governmental trustworthiness and the prevalence of ethical reciprocity.

More loosely, Levi argues that citizens consent to onerous obligations when they see their relations to governmental agents and to other citizens as both reliable and fair. Her evidence from the United States, Canada, the United Kingdom, France, New Zealand, Australia, and Vietnam concerns differential compliance with demands for military service according to period, population segment, and character of war. Observed differentials confirm Levi's empirical generalizations summarizing contingent consent: on the whole, compliance with conscription was greater in such situations as those of relatively high trust.

More important for present purposes, Levi makes the case that all three of her proximate causes—trust in government, compliance of others, information about governmental trustworthiness and prevalence of ethical reciprocity—depend significantly on governmental capacity and performance. Any visible weakening of governmental capacity to meet commitments and/or to enforce obligations therefore diminishes compliance. To the extent that current decoupling of states and firms undermines state capacity, according to such an argument, it also tends to weaken nationally recruited military forces. In yet another regard, the world could be returning to the mercenary armies that waged seventeenth-century wars. European rulers turned massively away from mercenaries and toward nationally recruited armies when they could because mercenaries were greedy, predatory, autonomous, and inclined to banditry when discharged (Thomson 1994).

Notice the further implications of any such causal connection for networks of trust. The historically exceptional overlap of trust networks with economic organizations and governmental institutions could well be diminishing, especially for the power-seeking and the powerless. If that were the case, we might expect increasingly strenuous efforts by powerful, power-seeking, and powerless populations to insulate their own trust networks from intervention by firms and governments. Not only private military forces, but also mafias, drug-distribution networks, and clandestine flows of currency illustrate the possibility of insulating such networks, even in a world of extensive surveillance. The implications for democracy are chilling; a world in which each population makes private, exclusive, and hence unequal provision for its own long-term high-risk enterprises threatens any democratic collaboration whatsoever.

I am not claiming that these elaborations, extrapolations, and contextualizations of Powell's, Westney's, and Stark's well-informed observations on changing economic forms are true. I am claiming they deserve serious investigation. When it comes to anticipating twenty-first-century qualities and textures of life, the stakes are high.

CHAPTER 9

Conclusion: The Futures of Business Organization and Paradoxes of Change

Paul DiMaggio

THE CHAPTERS in this volume have taken us from Silicon Valley to Budapest, and from Budapest to Tokyo; from the advanced-technology companies of the new millenium to the kinship-based enterprises of the seventeenth century; and from the frameworks of institutional sociology and network analysis to the variform precincts of economics, history, and evolutionary theory. Observing different worlds through different lenses, the authors have not surprisingly reached somewhat different conclusions. At the same time, there are substantial areas of agreement. My purpose in this chapter is to identify points of consensus and divergence and, above all, to articulate the questions that we—authors and readers, scholars and policymakers and business managers—must keep in mind as the twenty-first century firm evolves from an object of speculation to one of ongoing study and practice.

Students of the corporation today are in a position similar to their counterparts a century ago, witnessing institutional transformation and, without benefit of hindsight, only modestly equipped to differentiate fundamental from transitory elements of change. Authors who focus, as did Marx, upon a system logic that transcends the management of particular companies, may arrive at quite different conclusions from those who, as did Weber, emphasize the organizational logic of the firm. Those who study the most dynamic sectors of the economy may reach different conclusions than those who study older industries with saturated markets and mature product lines. And, at a time in which university-based scholars are drafting legal codes for newly capitalist economies and consulting with large firms as experts on corporate strategy and structure, what scholars believe to be true may actually influence the shape of change.

Nearly all of the authors represented here believe that change is occurring. Many expect this change to be discontinuous, even radical. And they agree upon many of the same facts, especially that business firms are becoming flatter, relying more on teamwork and less on narrow job de-

I am grateful to Frank Dobbin, Peter Marsden, Walter Powell, David Stark, and Charles Tilly for helpful comments on an earlier draft of this conclusion.

scriptions and elaborate hierarchies, and interacting in complex and cooperative ways. At the same time, the interpretations they give their observations are quite different and, taken together, confront the reader with a series of questions. How can it be, for example, that a period of intense merger activity is characterized by the apparent efflorescence of small, entrepreneurial firms, spin-offs, and outsourcing arrangements? How is it that a tightening of the market's grip around companies facing more intense competitive pressures and more assertive forms of investor control appears to be associated with a loosening of the organizational form of bureaucracy, which emerged in response to past market competition? How is it that the workplace can at once be described as more engaging and less alienating, on the one hand, and more demanding, less secure, and more spatially dispersed on the other?

Such are the paradoxes of rapid change. In some cases, the paradoxes dissolve upon close inspection, and ones sees that the future may belong to quite different kinds of firms, with distinctive characteristics, suited to different environments and developing along different trajectories. In other cases, apparent contradictions represent inchoate possibilities within the contemporary firm, and which of these possibilities are realized will depend both on managerial choices and public policies. Still other paradoxes take us down dimly lit passageways terminating in conundrums.

It would be premature to offer dispositive predictions about the future of corporate enterprise, but it is not too early to identify the questions that researchers should ask in order to build on the excellent work that has already been done. I address four such questions in the rest of this chapter. First, what are the new organizational forms that the authors have identified, how are they related to the classic models of markets and hierarchies, and how are they related to one another? Second, if we divide the emerging forms into their smallest components, what changes are most important and most widespread? What factors are likely to promote or to stand in the way of their continued diffusion? Third, are such trends traceable to different if concurrent causal processes or do they cohere into new organizational logics at both the firm and the system level? Finally, what role do ideas play in the perception and diffusion of change? To what extent have firms changed, and to what extent have we acquired a conceptual apparatus that permits us to see modes of organizing that the cultural power of bureaucracy once made invisible; and, to the extent the latter is the case, how might this altered vision itself induce structural change?

NETWORKS OF CHANGE

The image of the "networked" high-technology firm has become a powerful model for the rest of industry, an inspiration to entrepreneurs and a specter haunting executives of mature firms. A 1999 advertisement for a major international business-consulting firm (Anderson Consulting) in the *New York Times* captures the model's essential features: new technology, customer service, flexibility, and networks.

> You're real, they're virtual. You build, they collaborate. You're product-driven, they're customer-driven. Face it. You're still trying to make money the old-fashioned way. . .you'll have to change your ways. The business model you're after isn't the massive, vertically integrated marketing machine you've worked so hard to create. It's a fluid network of alliances, acutely attuned to the needs of its customers. . . . Are you nimble enough to keep your people, process and technology focused on strategies that shift frequently and suddenly?

Today, the network is the central trope of organizational change, just as the assembly line was at the beginning of the twentieth century. Indeed, networks figure prominently in each of the first three chapters. Walter Powell (and later Charles Tilly) write of "network forms of organization," and Powell describes the rise of lateral task-based networks within the firm, and collaborative networks of companies engaged in cooperative efforts at technical and product innovation. David Stark describes informal networks of cooperating firms throughout Eastern Europe. Eleanor Westney describes the vertical and horizontal networks that link Japanese companies into informally but durably connected *keiretsu*. Moreover, in each region, the interfirm network is not just a metaphor: researchers have used formal methods of network analysis to model and graphically depict the structure of these ties (Powell et al. 1996; Stark 1996; Gerlach 1992).

The term "network" elides much, however. As Reinier Kraakman puts it, "there are networks and there are networks. . . .. The substance, durability and legal character of the relationships matter." David Bryce and Jitendra Singh distinguish between interfirm networks designed to compete in R&D or production, and those that exist to hedge financial or political risk. In organization studies, the term "network" no longer connotes simply a set of nodes and the connection among them—one can, after all, use network notation to map the formal hierarchical links of a traditional bureaucracy (organization charts were normative efforts to do just that) or patterns of exchange on a spot market—but rather a particular kind of connection characterized by some combination of informality, equality, and commitment.

The particular mix of these qualities varies from business network to business network. Japan's vertical *kereitsu* are high on informality but low on equality; task groups in United States firms are formal (people are usually assigned to them by bureaucratic superiors) but high on equality. Czech hierarchical interfirm networks are informal but they are durable because the companies at the top own those at the bottom. In the United States, biotech networks and customer-supplier webs in the apparel industry (Uzzi 1997) are both informal and nonhierarchical. But whereas the former are fast-moving learning machines that entail intense, focused relationships that can be abandoned when partners' interests shift (Powell et al. 1996), the latter constitute a diversified portfolio, mixing arms-length business dealings with some relationships so perduring that firms will jeopardize economic advantage to protect their partners' interests (Uzzi 1997).

One may ask whether a term as versatile as "network" deserves a place in social science's conceptual armory; to be sure, these examples suggest the importance of dimensionalizing the notion and developing a precise and common terminology. But I think there are more important lessons to be drawn from the variety of network-like forms that the authors in this volume describe.

Following Oliver Williamson (1975), economists and many sociologists have identified markets and hierarchy (bureaucracy) as the two major organizational forms between which executives and entrepreneurs must choose. More recently, Williamson (1985) has acknowledged that there are "hybrid" forms, and still others have posited the existence of a third species based on prebureaucratic sources of solidarity—"clans" (Ouchi 1980)—or on trust nurtured through ongoing interaction— "network organizations" (Powell 1986). Robert Gibbons, in this volume, argues that contemporary firms no longer face the classic Coasian choice of "make or buy," so much as a "make or cooperate" decision with its own distinct set of criteria.

When one places the organizational forms described in this volume side by side, the taxonomy appears considerably more complex. (See figure 9.1.) Rather than a two-form model with hybrids, or a three-species typology, one sees several forms arrayed on a two-dimensional space defined by the extent of explicit coordination among partners and the degree to which some actors are capable of dominating others. For the most part, coordination and domination are positively correlated, so that five of the forms appear along a downward-sloping diagonal. But two off-diagonal forms— oligopolistic markets and long-term relational contracts—demonstrate that the association is not absolute.[1]

From the standpoint of organizational analysis, each of these forms is suited to carry out different functions and entails different bases of solidarity. From an economic perspective, each requires different types and amounts of transaction-specific investment and occasions different forms of risk. From the standpoint of law and economics, each type has different implications for system efficiency and may require different forms of legal regulation. And from the vantage point of evolutionary theory, as Bryce

---

[1] For a somewhat similar typology, see Campbell and Lindberg (1991).

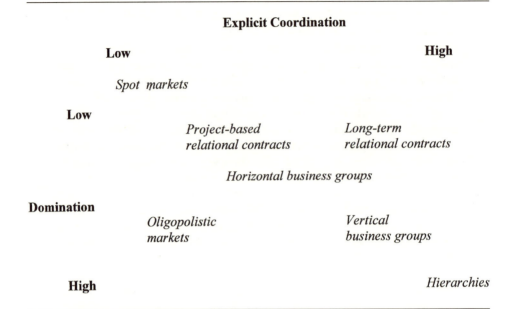

Figure 9.1. A typology of organizational forms.

and Singh point out in this volume, each is likely to thrive in different environments.

Several questions follow from these observations. First, for what purposes does it make sense to view the stations between market and hierarchy as "hybrids" or, in Kraakman's phrase, "half steps from the firm to the market," and for what purposes should we conceive of them as distinct organizational alternatives? As an empirical matter, one might document transition rates between each pair of forms: if rates do not vary significantly with proximity on the continuum, then a stronger case may be made for the view that each type is a distinct species. If rates do vary, then documenting and understanding the transition processes that underlie changes in the prevalence of different organizational forms should be a central research priority.

Second, to what unit of analysis do these characterizations apply? Transaction-cost economics maintains the useful fiction that its unit of analysis is the transaction, but, in practice, studies that use transaction-cost language often aggregate transactions into systems of governance far more extensive than a single form of exchange. Organization theorists usually analyze firms, but a firm can be a member of a vertical business group, participate in horizontal associations that seek to influence government policies, and use spot markets to acquire some inputs, long-term relational contracts to deal with customers, project-based relational contracts for research and development, and rigid hierarchy to manage offshore production facilities. Perhaps we should ask questions about the organizational forms not of businesses but of business functions, with the expectation that within any one firm (or group of cooperating companies), many organizational forms will coexist.

How Broadly Is Organizational Change Occurring?

The cases for some kinds of change are stronger than those for others. Some differences—for example, the flattening of management structures—appear to be widespread. Others—for example, the externalization of product innovation into multifirm networks or the substitution of contingent workers for internal labor markets—appear to characterize particular industries. In this section we take stock of the fates of the Weberian bureaucratic firm and of the neo-Marxian synthesis that described postwar capitalist systems as a whole (see chapter 1).

This effort is necessarily speculative, because the social-science community has failed to generate the kind of evidence one needs to track organizational change with confidence. Whereas most advanced societies regularly collect survey data on individuals in order to chart trends, comparable repeated measures of organizational structure and strategy are virtually nonexistent (Kalleberg et al. 1996). Consequently, we must rely primarily on broad overviews based on government statistics (good for employment trends but less useful for describing organization-level change) or on case studies of particular companies or industries. Because most researchers are attracted to firms or industries that are undergoing visible and interesting transformation, a review of such literature may overestimate the extent of change. A major priority for the research community should be to establish systems that collect trend data on the structure, governance, and behavior of organizations comparable to that now collected routinely from human beings.

Bureaucracy

We see evidence of change of several kinds in the internal logic of organizations, but the most dramatic is the decline of hierarchy, in two senses. First, hierarchy is flattening out, as changes in communications technologies increase the number of employees that supervisors can manage effectively; and, second, the nature of management is itself changing as more tasks are being assigned to horizontally organized teams with substantial discretion to select work processes to achieve their assigned goals. The latter, potentially liberating, mechanism has spread to many high-tech white-collar workplaces with highly skilled staff, and to many blue-collar workplaces, as well (Committee on Techniques for the Enhancement of Human Performance 1999). The former approach, in which enhanced surveillance capacity serves as a functional equivalent to bulky hierarchies, operates in low-skill service settings as well as in some blue-collar workplaces.

Evidence for the flattening of hierarchies comes largely from the United States and Western Europe: Japanese firms have been "unbureaucratic" in this sense for a long time, and workplaces in Eastern Europe (in so far as Hungary, which experimented with semi-autonomous work teams in the socialist era, is typical [Stark 1990]) are in a period of experimentation and thus heterogeneity. In the West, however, the shift appears to be real.

The second major change in the bureaucratic firm is a decline in formalization—that is, in the number and inhibiting force of rules—especially rules about work roles and task assignments. At the shop-floor level, many observers refer to this as the "reintegration of conception and execution," a reference to Braverman's (1974) classic analysis of capitalism's tendency to "de-skill" workers by separating the work of hand and mind (Sabel 1990). More broadly, Powell suggests that United States and European companies are increasingly likely to tell managers (or project teams) what they want and let them accomplish it by whatever means are most useful. Consistent with his argument, Kelley's (1990) study of computerized machine operations in one thousand plants reported that companies with more recently implemented systems were more likely than others to place information and authority in the hands of shop-floor employees, as opposed to concentrating it among engineers and managers.

As Powell points out, change is most evident in newer and more innovative industrial sectors. White-collar teams in high-tech workplaces get to shape proximate goals, as well as means. Blue-collar teams have much control over tools and methods, but narrow goals are imposed by management. And in service industries like banking, teams and similar debureaucratizing approaches are barely used at all. Nonetheless, the overall trend, in both white- and blue-collar workplaces, is toward broader, more supple job descriptions, fewer rules prescribing how work should be done and who should do it, and a less differentiated occupational structure (Committee on Techniques for the Enhancement of Human Performance 1999). These changes are most marked in the advanced Western economies: once again, the Japanese have had fewer formal rules and have used teams for years, and the situation in the Eastern European situation appears to be in flux.

A third way in which contemporary firms are said to deviate increasingly from the Weberian model is in the attenuation of ties between workers and firms. In contrast to the first two, this trend appears in all of the regions described in the preceding chapters. Powell documents downsizing in the blue-collar ranks, and a sharp decline in middle-managerial employment in large United States firms (though not in the managerial share of the economy overall), either through job elimination or through outsourcing and use of contingent workers. Moreover, he presents suggestive evidence that employees, especially managers, have considerably less long-term job security than in the past and are accordingly less loyal to their employers (on these trends see also Committee on Techniques for the Enhancement of Human Performance 1999). Such trends are not limited to the West: Westney depicts the Japanese system of lifetime employment as under siege. Change has been even sharper in the former socialist systems that Stark describes: whereas work under socialism was a right, now workers must trust their fates to fickle labor markets.

Will these trends hold in the long run? Powell warns that the future is fluid, but also points out that new forms of organization are most visible in new, economically dynamic industries. This is a powerful indicator because, as Stinchcombe (1965) argued, dramatic change in organizational forms has regularly occurred more through dynamic succession than through the transformation of existing entities. Indeed, since 1980, many manufacturing operations structured along conventional bureaucratic lines have been shipped offshore, at the same time that entrepreneurs have founded new research-intensive firms designed according to novel specifications (Baron, Burton, and Hannan 1999). The diffusion of management philosophies favoring flatness, collaboration, and teamwork for almost two decades (Kanter 1983; Hammer and Champy 1993) means that today's entrepreneurs often build such philosophies into the organizations they design (Baron, Hannan and Burton 1999). Other things being equal, then, as old companies fail and new ones join business's top ranks, we should see less hierarchy, fewer rules, more diffuse roles, and less long-term commitment in employment relationships.

Of course other things are rarely equal. Bryce and Singh's evolutionary perspective leads us to ask if the environment is changing in a way that favors network-centered forms over more hierarchical, rule-centered bureaucracies. Three features appear conducive to such change. First, the work-force is increasingly educated. Educated workers do better than those with less education in situations that demand initiative, and worse in jobs that are repetitive and require taking lots of orders. Second, women have come to constitute an ever larger proportion of work-force entrants, and there is some evidence that women are better than men at working in groups (Baron, Hannan, and Burton 1999). Third, and most important, as Powell and Bryce and Singh emphasize, new information technologies make collaborative work more productive than hierarchically organized processes (see also Hammer and Champy 1993; Zuboff 1995).

If we grant that the changes in work organization to which I have called attention are likely to continue, do they represent a major shift away from legal-rational bureaucracy—either toward a new type of "network organization" or, as Tilly suggests, to premodern, trust-based entities? Here caution is in order. For one thing, no one is seriously proposing that even the most exemplary reengineered forms are more similar to prebureaucratic administrative systems than to the Weberian model. The key battles over the separation of person from position and of home from workplace, the legitimacy of universalistic norms governing the application of rules and standards of evaluation, and systems of control that tether employees to the goals of their superiors, were joined and won (in publicly owned Western corporations, at least) a long time ago. Even the startup firms of Silicon Valley adopt most of the standard bureaucratic means of "formalizing, standardizing, and/or documenting employment practices" within a few years of founding (Baron, Burton, and Hannan 1999). Residues of patrimonialism, however, can be found more readily in the kinship-based business groups of East Asia (Orrù, Biggart, and Hamilton 1997) or Latin America (Zeitlin et al. 1976), or in small businesses everywhere, than in big firms in the most advanced economies. What we see, then, is an evolution or loosening of bureaucratic structure, and not its replacement by something else.

Nonetheless, evolution, if sufficiently persistent, can culminate in radical change. Do current changes spell the end of bureaucracy later on? Bureaucracy relies on redundant features—many rules, clear lines of command, well-defined roles conducive to accountability, careful record-keeping, reward systems that bind employees to the firm—that all serve as mechanisms of control. This redundancy makes bureaucracy resilient, so that one can relax many elements of bureaucracy without losing the control advantages of the system as a whole. In Japan, for example, tenure-in-place in a sharply segmented labor market with little mobility between primary sector firms created strong enough incentives that firms avoided the hyperdivision of labor and atrophy-inducing rules that once characterized many Western firms. Similarly, machine production (in which rules are embedded in the design of person-machine interactions) or the use of a professional work force (in which rules are embedded in highly trained and socialized people) sometimes permit relaxation of rules and reduction (other things being equal) in supervisory effort.

Yet bureaucracy is not infinitely flexible. One cannot substitute its features for one another indefinitely, like so much corn syrup for beet sugar, without losing its control advantages; nor can one relax them indefinitely, either. Three questions, in particular, confront current efforts at organizational redesign.

First, how much autonomy can project groups be given before they begin to pursue interests other than those of the company's top management? Students of network forms of organization and, even more so, advocates of workplace reform, at times appear to neglect the truism that nearly everyone involved with organizations tries to use them for their own ends (Perrow 1986, ch. 1). The annals of technical work, for example, are chock full of tales of technical professionals who use company money to work on projects of primarily scientific interest.

On the one hand, well-designed task forces and project teams enhance control by removing work from contexts in which departmental agendas can subvert corporate goals (see, e.g., Thomas 1994, for excellent examples of the latter). On the other hand, the dissolution of formal roles, and the accountability that is built into them, deprives management of a critical basis for evaluating employee performance, especially when the results of a project cannot be judged until long after the project group has been dissolved. Organizations are not very good at measuring complex task performance under the best of conditions, much less when individuals work in interdepartmental teams. Stark reports that members of Hungarian work teams he studied held each other accountable "in multiple registers," but these inside-contracting groups had relatively stable membership over time, and their members were principals as well as agents [1990]. Whether team self-evaluation works as well, even with clear criteria, when membership is temporary and members have their eyes on their next assignment, is questionable.

Moreover, we cannot assume that project-based systems of work *will* be properly designed, for large corporations often design and implement systems poorly. It seems likely that work-process redesign that relaxes rules and blurs interunit boundaries and responsibilities can be highly effective if well executed. But such innovations may raise the stakes of failure, by eliminating the safety net of accountability and direct control that formal job descriptions and well-defined roles and responsibilities provide when things go wrong. Studies of popular workplace innovations often find a substantial difference between models and their implementation (Osterman 1994; Hackman and Wageman 1995). Even Frederick Winslow Taylor ([1911] 1947) lamented that no company had ever implemented scientific management faithfully enough to give it a true test.

These observations suggests the importance, first, of constructive skepticism as to the potential for wide diffusion of organizational models that require exceptional selflessness and dedication from managers and technical professionals; and, second, of research into the circumstances under which such models *are* implemented successfully. For example, in theory, project teams are supposed to possess the power to acquire the resources they need internally or externally. But studies of the methods companies use to administer buy-and-sell transactions among their subunits suggests that administrative details often stand in the way of competitive pricing and autonomous choice (Eccles and White 1988). How have the companies about which Powell writes overcome this dilemma? More generally, under what conditions does a company gain more from organizing a function horizontally than it risks by rendering staff less accountable, and therefore capable of using their enhanced autonomy to pursue parochial agendas.

Second, for the majority of employees—workers, managers, and professional staff—who *do* want to do their jobs conscientiously, the new order of team-based work may prove psychologically demanding in two senses. For one thing, some evidence suggests that "reengineered" companies demand such extraordinary commitment of time and energy from project-team members that employees, especially those with families to which they would like occasionally to attend, often burn out (Perlow 1998). For another, people respond poorly to uncertainty: without clear mandates, work teams and their members may be paralyzed by doubt, as Kunda (1991) documented in his ethnography of an exemplary, team-based, horizontally organized, computer firm that ultimately exchanged its postmodern organizational structure for a more conventional design.

To be sure, jobs in project-based, horizontal, work organizations have many attributes that students of work redesign have shown to increase worker commitment and satisfaction (Hackman and Oldham 1980): employees are responsible for and have knowledge of the results of their labors; they are responsible for whole tasks, work autonomously, and get to do many types of work; and they receive clear feedback from internal "clients." But as research has also shown, for these characteristics to produce positive outcomes, workers must feel confident about more mundane parts of the employment contract, especially job security and compensation. Employees who are poorly paid or who worry that their jobs are constantly on the line, may find horizontally organized work teams to be sources not of challenging stimulation but of unendurable pressure.

Third, relaxation of rules and formal job descriptions has traditionally been associated with strong firm-based career incentives, as in Japan. If firms abandon rules and shift from jobs to projects at the same time that they rely more on contingent workers and consultants, they may indeed reach the limits to which Weberian bureaucracy can be pushed. It remains to be seen whether the result will be the emergence of a genuinely alternative organizational form, or if lack of controls and incentives capable of regulating principal-agent relationships will only produce even less effective bureaucracies.

Of course, it is not clear that these several modifications of the bureaucratic model are taking place in the same firms. Powell makes an important point when he warns that new forms of organizing present two possibilities:

a high road of challenging work, fairly rewarded; and a low road of exploited workers and contingent work, technically monitored and controlled. In effect, these represent two variants on legal-rational bureaucracy, one emphasizing the reward system as a way to control labor, the other emphasizing direct supervision, digitally enhanced. Clearly documenting the prevalence of these types (as well as more conventional bureaucratic variants) across business functions in a representative sample of enterprises in different industries and in different national societies should be a research priority. Until such research indicates otherwise—and the evidentiary bar should be high—we should assume that bureaucracy will be a permanent, albeit protean and polymorphic, fixture of the corporate landscape.

The System Level

The authors of the first three chapters also note that fundamental changes have occurred in the system of relations among firms (and in the relationships between firms and states). Again the changes differ from place to place. In the United States, Western Europe, and Japan, companies work more closely with their suppliers and customers, and much innovation is organized around strategic, task-focused alliances among collaborating firms. In Eastern Europe, the privatization of formerly state-run firms generated dense webs of cross-ownership, within which one can discern both vertical and horizontal groups of companies whose ties defend them against political and economic volatility. Once again, structures that are new or inchoate in the west are well developed in Japan, which has had strong supplier relations, task-focused R&D alliances, and defensive business groups for decades.

Powell, Stark, Westney, and Tilly emphasize the extent to which task-oriented collaborations and defensive groups share a common foundation of relational contracting and how they diverge sharply from conventional models of market and hierarchy. By contrast, Kraakman, Bryce and Singh, and (implicitly) Gibbons, emphasize differences between task-based collaborations and defensive groups in both function and structure. Here I consider each of these two forms of alliance in turn.

RELATIONAL CONTRACTS AND STRATEGIC ALLIANCES

Most knowledgeable observers believe that firms are engaging in more long-term collaborations—especially close information-sharing relationships with suppliers and collaborations around product development—now than during most of the twentieth century. Whereas managers used to be taught to keep suppliers at arm's length, maintain sufficient inventories to avoid hold-ups, and avoid entangling alliances, now they are urged to invest in long-term relationships with their suppliers, use just-in-time delivery to keep inventories low, and establish shared computer systems to facilitate exchange. Similarly, companies externalize more functions than in the past. Research and development, in particular, is more likely to entail cooperation among companies, and between companies and universities and other public or nonprofit entities (Powell and Owen-Smith 1998; Mowery 1999, 7–8; Merrill and Cooper 1999, 111–12).

Although comparable over-time data from large samples of firms would be welcome, the evidence for these trends is strong. Skeptics point out that there have always been relational contracts between producers and suppliers of goods and services (Macauley 1963). But Powell and Westney describe something different, in which a far greater and more systematic functional burden is placed on relationships than was customary in the recent past. Whereas Macauley's firms' ties were used more for lubricating and mediating, today's collaborations often entail organizing and innovating, with firms making substantial investments in shared information systems, placing engineers in one another's workplaces, and assigning staff to joint task groups. Of course, one could point to even more pervasive "relational contracting" in the nineteenth-century world of family firms (Chandler 1977); but here, to an even greater extent, contemporary "relational contracts" differ strikingly in their structural basis, scope, and function.

At the same time, such collaborations are new primarily in the West. As with other current developments, Japan was there first; and, as Stark points out, informal inter-enterprise collaboration was endemic under socialism—not in the interest of product innovation, but because the absence of reliable markets forced managers to rely on barter networks to find the inputs they required.

Whereas writers of popular management texts have elevated relational contracting, close customer relations, and just-in-time deliver to the status of orthodoxy, scholars studying Western firms have actually been much more cautious. Gibbons argues that firms decide whether or not to establish relational contracts based on cost factors that are highly situation-specific. And Powell suggests that alliances are likely to occur only under carefully specified conditions: "the more rapidly knowledge develops, and the more diverse its sources, the more firms will turn to relational contracting and collaboration."

It follows from this that we should see relational contracting and research alliances proliferate in fast-moving, high-technology industries, especially those in which "the sources of knowledge are disparate and the pathways of technological development uncharted," which is, of course, precisely where Powell and others have studied them (Powell et al. 1996, 143). We would anticipate finding them as well in competitive, style-dependent consumer industries like apparel—which has long had complex forms of interfirm alliance (Doeringer and Watson 1999)—and in industries, like banking, under-going innovation in marketing methods. In a study of relations between small firms and banks, Uzzi (1999) argues that although relational con-tracting is crucial to success, such ties represent a minority share of firms' transactional portfolio, with many exchanges still conducted at arm's length. Weak ties, he suggests, help firms (and the banks that lend to them) scan the environment and monitor innovations in lending; but firms ultimately return (with the information they have acquired) to their relational partners, who use the information to structure new deals. Uzzi's argument that suc-cessful firms maintain a balanced portfolio of business relationships is broadly applicable, and Powell's argument about the role and sources of knowledge enables one to predict the optimal balance in different industries.

Powell notes that contemporary versions of relational contracting and product-development alliances have significant system-level implications for at least two reasons. First, company boundaries are becoming more porous as firms share information, technology, staff, and even office space to unprecedented degrees. Second, such changes foretoken a shift in agency, as strategic alliances rather than firms become key actors in com-petitive rivalry.

Kraakman argues that strategic alliances, rather than indicating the ob-solescence of the corporation, are possible *because* the corporate form con-stitutes accountable allies. Kraakman is undoubtedly right on this point, but he may nonetheless dismiss the significance of alliances too quickly, for they appear to emerge when competitive pressures for prompt action make impractical the formal contracting for which the corporate form is so well suited. Rather than watch opportunities evaporate as lawyers negotiate deals, companies rely on trust and reputation to take advantage of opportu-nities as they arise. Corporations remain important less due to their legal agency than because they are the entities to which reputation adheres (a role that is itself possible because of the other advantages Kraakman so lucidly enumerates).

Powell alerts us to the centrality of the information revolution to these new developments, a position that Bryce and Singh strongly endorse. It seems clear that United States companies would collaborate less closely with their customers and suppliers were it not for high-speed digital net-works (Tapscott 1999); and that flexible production, teamwork, and decen-tralized organizational structures work better with well-functioning and accessible information systems (O'Mahony and Barley 1999, 143).

At the same time, information technology is less central to apparently similar relationships in non-Western business systems. As Westney notes, interfirm collaborations serve to promote two different things—technical flexibility and trust—and these two functions, while undoubtedly related, are analytically distinct. Whereas United States networks are often based on information technology, Japanese collaborations are more often based on interpersonal relationships. Clearly, another research priority for students of the corporation is to understand better the balance between trust and technical flexibility as both antecedents and results of relational contracts and strategic alliances (and how and why this balance varies across industries and cultures).

The United States high-tech collaborations that Powell describes are ordinarily limited in time and function. Trust is important, and relations among participants may entail warmth and reciprocity, but for the most part cooperation is restricted to particular projects and joint interests. Accounts of United States firms suggest that long-term, multiplex relationships are relatively infrequent and rarely aggregate to enduring business groups. By contrast, small companies in the industrial districts of Europe and Japan, where governments have long been permissive in their stance toward collaboration among competitors, collaborate on a regular basis over many years and across many types of exchange (Lazerson 1995). The role of the state in shaping such patterns is significant. The increased visibility of interfirm collaborations in the United States doubtless reflects the liberalization (some would say the evisceration) of federal antitrust policy after 1980, just as their relatively limited scope reflects the U.S. federal government's peculiar (by international standards) concern with the negative impact of business collusion. Nonetheless, even in the United States, the new business model entails the externalization of functions and affords small companies a larger role in the product-development process than they once held.[2]

Kraakman is incredulous. He points out that there is "no hard evidence about where the economy as a whole is moving on the Coasian spectrum of firms-to-networks-to-markets" and argues that we should not witness a dramatic rise in the economic importance of small, nonbureaucratic enterprise during a "decade of unprecedented merger activity." From an evolutionary perspective, however, the two trends may be mutually supportive. According to "niche partitioning theory" (Carroll 1985), increased industrial concentration creates new opportunities for small firms to thrive. When, in a given industry, firm sizes are normally distributed, so the argument goes, small firms have little chance against their middling competitors. When a few giants (for example, the handful of major breweries that survived the consolidations of the 1960s and 1970s) dominate, they leave plenty of crumbs for small firms (for example, the microbreweries that became popular in the 1980s and 1990s) to pick up. In some cases, this process results in giant and small firms with complementary interests: the

---

[2] I am indebted to Frank Dobbin for reminding me of the importance of state policy in shaping patterns of collaboration at the national level.

largest pharmaceutical companies have partnered actively with small biotech firms, which have skills that they themselves lack (and might extinguish if they tried to internalize them through acquisition); and similar patterns of large-firm/small-firm partnership are visible in the semiconductor and software industries (Mowery 1999, 3). Ironically then, industrial concentration and vital small firms may go hand in hand, so long as the giants find subcontracting a useful approach to some key business functions.

THE MIGRATION OF AGENCY FROM COMPANIES TO BUSINESS NETWORKS

For years, business firms have been the dominant corporate actors in capitalist economies. It has been the corporation, pursuing goals set, in principle at least, by its investors and shareholders, that has created new products and processes, built new plants, developed new markets, and issued most people's paychecks. The notion that corporations have and continually employ agency is built into our language, our culture, and our law.

It is significant, then, that the chapters on the West, the former socialist world, and East Asia *all* describe a migration of agency from firms to networks or groups (see also Castells 1996, 171). Given companies' "growing involvement in an intricate latticework of collaborations," writes Powell of the United States, it may be appropriate to "regard the interorganizational network as the basic unit of analysis." Stark describes the "relatively discrete business groupings based on interorganizational-ownership ties constructed across boundaries of enterprises" in the new economies of Eastern Europe and writes that strategy and structure are "emergent properties of groups" rather than of firms. Writing of Japan, Westney states that the vertical business group "rather than the individual incorporated company" is "the appropriate level of analysis for benchmarking exercises, or for international stock analysts interested in assessing investments, and probably for comparative organizational analysis." For all of the differences in the organizational forms that these authors describe, they agree that these networks and not the firms they comprise are the key actors for many important economic purposes.

To be sure, the similarity of language elides significant differences. Westney's claims are perhaps most limited because she writes of the vertical *keiretsu*, which is firm-like insofar as it possesses a central executive capable of exercising considerable authority over subordinate members. Her key point is a comparative one: certain functions that are usually integrated into companies in the West are spread out among them in Japan, making comparison between large United States firms and the lead company in a Japanese vertical *keiretsu* misleading. In other words, we see in Japan a dispersion of activity and of assets, but not necessarily of authority.

Powell's account of the analytic centrality of interfirm networks is also delimited, though in a different way. As in Japan, the network is the site of some key business functions as companies employ one another's resources in order to achieve common goals. Also as in Japan, valuation of companies increasingly must take into account the worth of assets held outside the firm. Finally, Powell's networks add a third dimension that, following Stark, might be called "asset interdependence": certain assets (knowledge, creative potential, even proprietary processes that must be combined to yield marketable products) acquire value only in the context of collaboration among companies.

Asset interdependence is at the heart of Stark's account of Hungarian networks' agency. Moreover, the Hungarian networks are, in effect, strategic units, establishing different (but always highly diversified) asset portfolios suited to that country's uncertain and heterogeneous business environment. The vertical, within-industry groups appear similar in structure and function to Japan's vertical *keiretsu*; by contrast, the amorphous, horizontal networks may represent a more distinctive species.

Kraakman resists attributing agency to networks. The corporate legal form has so many advantages, he argues, that any diffusion of agency into amorphous networks or company groups exacts substantial penalties, reducing efficiency and raising the cost of capital. Four possibilities follow from this. First, such claims may be empirically false. Second, the networks may be imperatively coordinated under the control of a lead actor (Japanese vertical *keiretsu*, some Hungarian groups, and some U.S. alliances). Networks may represent, third, an inefficient form of managerial rent-seeking (Japanese and perhaps Hungarian cross-shareholding arrangements) or, fourth, a short-term adaptation to institution failure (Hungary's underdeveloped securities law and capital markets)—in which cases they are bound, in the fullness of time, to yield to centralized corporations with clear legal boundaries. Bryce and Singh are likewise skeptical about the long-term adaptive qualities of interfirm networks, arguing that "the risks that come with network membership are understated, even poorly understood." Indeed, Tilly is alone among the commentators in endorsing the view of networks as agentic, and that is because he takes a much longer view. Tilly agrees with Kraakman that the modern state and the corporation are thoroughly interdependent. But whereas Kraakman appears to regard this partnership as the stable terminus of evolution. Tilly, who believes that the modern state's days are numbered, views it as ephemerally contingent. And whereas Kraakman argues that networks are viable only so long as legal corporations sit at their foundation, Tilly suggests that corporations may one day be viable only if they are draped over a latticework of informal social relations.

Three questions are central to assessing the viability of the multicompany group or network as an economic actor. First, how can such an entity *aggregate the interests* of its members into something approximating a single objective function? Second, how can capital markets *value* networks when their assets are spread across several legal entities? Third, how can networks be made *accountable*, so that they can enter into contracts with other entities (e.g., investors, business partners, agencies of the state)? If the "network form" is to supplant or even complement the firm as an economic actor, it must be able to solve each of these three problems: interest aggregation, valuation, and accountability.

Let us begin with the dilemma of interest aggregation. There are at least three possible solutions. First, some networks, like the vertical *keiretsu*, are dominated by a lead firm with powers of *imperative coordination* comparable (though exerted through different instruments of authority and persuasion) to those of an executive. A second solution, employed by many of the high-tech alliances that Powell describes, is a combination of *focused objectives and limited scope*. Such alliances are ad hoc, forming around acknowledged shared interests, rather than seeking such interests after formation. Focus is sustained through ongoing interaction aimed at achieving well-specified results within a brief time horizon. A third solution is *distributed intelligence*, which Stark suggests characterizes Hungarian interfirm networks, permitting them to generate strategic behavior as an emergent phenomenon. The problem with "distributed intelligence" as a mechanism of strategy formation is that the term ordinarily refers to the capacity of well-structured systems with known goals (for example, a ship's crew steering their vessel safely through a treacherous channel) to generate effective behavior when no single participant possesses an overview of the environment (Hutchins 1994). The notion that systems can employ "distributed intelligence" to create structure and set goals bears an affinity to work in the natural sciences on self-organizing complex systems—a tantalizing connection that raises more fruitful questions than it can yet be expected to answer.

There is no guarantee that any of these solutions will work in specific instances, and there is always the risk that once partners invest in shared assets—a form of Williamson's (1985, 55) "fundamental transformation" from spot market to constrained exchange (see also O'Mahony and Barley 1999, 151)—one or more will attempt to take advantage of the others' commitments—either successfully, thus exploiting their partners, or unsuccessfully, paralyzing the venture. Under such conditions, a fourth mode of interest aggregation, *organizational design*, comes into play. Mechanisms familiar to game theorists—shared interest in continuing the interaction, giving and taking hostages, and so on—may align interests sufficiently to sustain cooperation (Dyer and Singh 1999). Consistent with Gibbons' argument in this volume, empirical analyses informed by game theory of how intercompany groups identify shared objectives when the scope of collaboration is broad would seem an important research priority.

Economic valuation is a second central dilemma that must be solved if interfirm groups can emerge as significant economic actors. Like other enterprises, the companies in business networks require investment. But as Kraakman points out, in so far as their assets are interdependent with those of the network entity, they may be difficult to value. If so, in order to raise capital they may have to pay a steep premium over what a more strongly bounded firm would spend.

Solutions to the valuation problem appear more readily available than solutions to the interest-aggregation dilemma, though the issue is still a difficult one. First, analysts with detailed local knowledge—for example, Silicon Valley's venture capitalists—can assess the value of companies' business relationships through a variety of soft measures. Second, investors may use the reputation of executives and participating firms as signals to evaluate the quality of lesser known partners and to assure themselves that shared assets will be fully exploited (Stuart et al. 1999). Certainly, financial institutions that have learned to value such intangibles as human capital, goodwill, and intellectual property find no insuperable barrier to placing an approximate dollar value on shared assets and social capital.

Of course, the capacity to value shared assets will depend to a great extent on the third dilemma of multifirm networks, that of accountability. If firms are accountable to one another for their stewardship and use of shared assets, then investors may have some confidence that such assets will ultimately generate shareholder returns. Without such accountability, it is far more difficult to make inferences about how a network-level surplus will be distributed among the network's component firms, leading the assets of each to be undervalued. Indeed, although they disagree on many other points, both Kraakman and Stark identify accountability as the critical problem of intercorporate networks. As the latter argues (in chapter 3, this volume), the "acute flexibility" that facilitates adaptiveness and innovation is no "unmixed blessing":

> The same opportunistic blurring of boundaries that leads to a recombination of assets and a decomposition and reintegration of organizations also . . . erodes (or in the postsocialist case, retards) accountability. . . . To be accountable according to many different principles becomes a means to be accountable to none.

How can companies in horizontally organized interfirm networks cope with the dilemma of accountability? First, they must recognize it as a dilemma. Whether by intent or in effect, cross-shareholding—the most important form of linkage in Hungary and the Czech Republic and a key form, as well, in Japan—tends to augment managers' power, insulating them from shareholder pressure and stymieing the development of a market for corporate control. Some managers may be willing to sacrifice a great deal in the cost of capital or corporate performance to retain this autonomy.

For managers who are unwilling or unable to make such sacrifices—and from the standpoint of the economy as a whole—finding solutions to the accountability dilemma is a top priority. The precise nature of the dilemma depends on the scope and functions of the intercompany network, of course. Where the group is entirely defensive, the problem is to increase the accountability of the firm. Where the group itself acts through joint projects—R&D consortia, creating new enterprises, and so on—the problem is to assure investors that peripheral companies' assets will not, in effect, be looted by more central firms.

Kraakman points out that many features of corporate and securities law are designed to make autonomous firms accountable to their shareholders. The effect of their transnational diffusion (for example, to France) has been to weaken the power of groups as firms have become more accountable. Similarly, in 1999 Japan reformed its accounting standards to make large firms more readily comparable to their Western counterparts. For example, lead firms must now report on the performance of their majority-owned subsidiaries, making it more difficult for them to hide economic reversals by exporting them down the vertical interfirm network (Gao 2000, ch. 8).

But such reform may not work everywhere. Stark argues that adopting Western legal forms is a poor solution for the postsocialist world, precisely because the optimal design for such economies' firms depends on as yet unpredictable institutional developments for which companies must remain prepared by keeping their options open. Therefore, making firms fully accountable to investors, and therefore beyond the influence of communities, workers, and the state, may not be in the enterprise's, or the system's, long-term interest.

A similar argument can be made about the role of *kigyo shudan* in Japan's economy, but with an ironic twist. Hungarian networks serve to hedge risk through ambiguity, which makes them flexibly adaptive but ill-equipped to engage in synoptic planning. By contrast, for Japan, the ability to ignore quarterly reports and pursue long-term strategies was the positive flip side of the short-run inflexibility that horizontal *keiretsu* networks entailed.

Kraakman argues that one cannot have it both ways, and that only the current structure of corporate and securities law is capable of providing the assurance investors require to create efficient capital markets. He may well be correct. But, of course, the current structure was constructed arduously over many decades in order to serve an economic system built around autonomous corporations. Other scholars have pointed to small variations in property law (for example, California's refusal to enforce noncompetition covenants between employers and their employees) that conduce to the vitality of network forms (Gilson 1999). Might an alternative legal regime just as effectively constitute interfirm networks as agents—and provide as stable a framework for their governance, valuation, and accountability—as the current framework has done for the free-standing corporation? Perhaps so, but as Bryce and Singh point out, only if environmental change renders the competitive advantages of such networks so overwhelming as to provide impetus to a difficult, costly, and conflictive process of legal innovation. Stark suggests that the weakness of state structures have stimulated the beginnings of such a process in parts of the former socialist world. If Tilly is correct, perhaps the worldwide decline of the modern state that he envisions will provide exactly the impetus required for more broad-ranging institutional change.

In the short run, however, concerns about accountability are least relevant to the United States, where the big news at the system level has been the shareholders' counter-revolution against management control (Useem 1996). Here, horizontal alliances have a different, and less defensive, function than in Japan or the socialist world, serving the practical ends of combining assets to achieve identifiable short-run objectives. Such alliances, and the enterprises they spin off, often externalize high-risk, high-payoff activities and enhance the role of specialist venture capitalists with detailed local knowledge. In so doing, they may actually improve investors' ability to value companies and hold managers accountable for their performance.

Do Observed Changes Cohere into a New System Logic?

To be sure, change—significant change—is occurring in the structure, governance, and strategic behavior of the corporation throughout the world; and, just as surely, many of these changes bear a family resemblance. Affinities among changes within economic systems and apparent similarities in innovations between them have caused many observers to ask whether we are witnessing the emergence of a new system logic—a "network form of organization"—comparable to the rise of the legally autonomous business corporation more than a century ago.

What Is a Logic?

This is a momentous claim, so it is important to analyze both the reasoning behind it and the evidence in its favor. The term "system logic" is used in many different ways, but all of them refer both to specific structural elements (types of management structures, employment contracts, consumer relations, types of interfirm networks and so on) *and* to factors that create an affinity among these elements. Such factors include structural incentives (adopting one element in the system leads to changes that induce companies to adopt additional mutually enhancing elements) and ideational features: a story that explains why the parts fit together, or a central value orientation that the elements reflect (Biggart 1992; Boltanski and Thévenot 1991; Friedland and Alford 1991).

The balance between structural incentives and ideational features varies among approaches to organizational logics, though almost all entail some combination of the two. Of the chapters in this volume, Powell's account, like Weber's "ideal-type model" of bureaucracy, emphasizes structural incentives the most. He begins with market conditions—shorter product cycles, regionally differentiated markets, competition in markets for sophisticated technologies—that dictate certain strategic choices. In order to accomplish these goals, firms are induced to adopt such techniques as flexible production, just-in-time delivery, high-speed digital communication networks, and the use of subcontracting and alliances to gain information. Such innovations emerge together not only because they address common problems, but because they are mutually supportive, with adoption of one (for example, leveling vertical control structures) necessary to reap the rewards of another (for example, implementing advanced communications technology).

By contrast, Stark emphasizes variation in regimes of valuation that underlie organizational forms. For Stark, a "logic" comprises forms of discourse and understanding that are also principles of exchange (long-term reciprocity versus short-term profit-focus, narrowly firm-centered objective functions versus those that include the welfare of workers or communities) associated with particular institutional sectors. These cultural forms in turn have implications for how firms conduct their business and justify their decisions.

How Logics Cohere

The question, in any case, is this: Are the changes in the organization of the firms and economic systems that the authors describe merely temporally concurrent, related only by the coincidence of co-incidence? Or are these trends integrated with one another, functionally and ideally, to a degree that one should treat them as constitutive of a new organizational logic, a coherent and organic whole?

In its simplest form, one can think of an "organizational logic" as a simple machine, the parts of which (the structural elements) must be present if the machine is to work properly. If so, then the test of whether the reforms and practices described in chapters 2 through 4 cohere into a new "logic" is to see if they tend to occur in the same companies and economic systems. If the presence of a structural element is correlated highly with that of other elements, it is presumably part of the new form. If several elements are always, or almost always, found together, the claims for a new form are plausible. If the correlations among structural elements are low and statistically insignificant, then the claims must be rejected.

Such statistical analyses are a research priority that could reveal a lot, if only by requiring scholars to think hard about anomalous results they would doubtless produce. But statistical approaches to taxonomy are only a starting point, because the world is almost always more complicated than the "simple machine model" of organizational logic implies, for several reasons.

CAUSAL HETEROGENEITY AND UNEVEN DEVELOPMENT

The components that eventually cohere into new logics are ordinarily present in some firms long before environmental change makes them more broadly attractive. They arise for many reasons (not necessarily related to those that drive their later diffusion) and become popular at different rates. Therefore, early in the process through which a new "organizational logic" emerges, we cannot expect to find an overwhelmingly strong empirical association among its components, although such an association may emerge as the system matures. Thus Powell describes the rise of the "new logic of network production" as a matter of incremental "fits and starts," with components that are not yet "tightly coupled."

FUNCTIONAL EQUIVALENCE OF PARTS AND SYSTEM MATURATION

Once a system has emerged, however, functional equivalence may also reduce the extent to which elements of it are observed in the same firms. For example, a consumer-product company may improve its responsiveness to the market and develop new products that consumers find attractive either by maintaining strong, interactive, relationships with clients or by entering into product-development networks with its collaborators. Although both strategies are part of the "network form" of organization—insofar as that form is defined by an intensification of external working relationships aimed at enhancing competitive fitness through ongoing change in products and processes—companies that do one may not need to do the other. Early in the diffusion of the new form, "network-model" firms may be so strikingly different from vertical, highly differentiated, conventional bureaucracies that their similarity to one another will be evident. Should the "network form" ever become as widespread as the vertical, differentiated bureaucracy, however, differences among "network firms" that adopt variations on a common theme will be more salient (both intellectually and in their influence on the results of formal classification analyses).

DIFFERENT CONTEXTS FOR SIMILAR PRACTICES

Related to this, as practices diffuse, they often take on different meanings in different contexts (Westney 1987). The Japanese production system emerged in conjunction with lifelong employment security. A functional affinity is easy to perceive: Workers can risk more to achieve company goals, and enterprises can safely invest more in workers with the expectation of benefiting from their expertise, if workers and companies stick together. Yet as Westney notes, United States companies have adopted key aspects of the Japanese production system at the same time that employment security has declined and the prevalence of contingent work has increased. The elements that United States companies borrowed are the same, but what results from their adoption is not a "Japanese production system" in the United States, but rather "a distinctive organizational form shaped by a very different social and economic context."

CHANGE OVER TIME IN PRINCIPLES OF SYSTEM INTEGRATION

Finally, elements that are essential parts of a new organizational logic at one time, may not be central to it at a later point in its evolution. As many have noted, technological developments that enable firms to embed production rules and routines in machinery permit them to reduce the number of such rules to which workers are subject, without overturning the logic of bureaucracy. Similarly, Westney suggests that although the Japanese production system was built on the Japanese employment system, including lifelong employment security, the production system can now function adequately without it.

Logics, Diversity, and Convergence

The fact that a single underlying organizational logic can generate a wide variety of concrete forms has important implications. For it suggests that the rise of a new organizational logic, if indeed that is what we are observing, is unlikely to lead to cross-national convergence of organizational forms and strategies, any more than the success of the bureaucratic model of organization led to a single approach to organizing enterprise, or the success of capitalism led to a single formula for the organization of market economies (Orrù et al. 1997; Biggart and Guillén 1999).

This volume's authors are in rare agreement on this point. Powell argues that change will occur everywhere, but that "distinctive national ensembles of practices, institutions, and political cultures" will channel change in different ways. Westney notes that American companies have incorporated "the most effective elements" of Japanese management as they restructured at the end of the twentieth century; and that Japan, under pressure from poor economic performance and demographic change, may selectively incorporate aspects of United States capital markets and even of Western employment systems. But she also notes that such innovations are actively transformed in the process of adoption (see also, Westney 1987).

Like Powell and Westney, Stark heralds the increasing role of networks at every level of corporate enterprise, emphasizing the similarity between emerging Eastern European intercompany alliances and East Asian business systems, and finding "heterarchy" present, albeit varying in origin, throughout the world. Stark believes that systems will converge to the extent that they must all respond to "the challenge of building organizations that are capable of learning" by being able "to redefine and recombine assets." But he also believes that "heterarchy" will vary cross-nationally depending on historical antecedents, legal frameworks, and the resources that businesses have available to them.

Ultimately, as Bryce and Singh argue, the extent to which organizational structure and strategy converge depends on the extent to which firms face similar environments. Environmental variation is patterned primarily by industry (which determines the nature and extent of competition as well as basic technology and cost structures) and nation-states (which create legal environments, institutional contexts, and cultural particularities). Indeed, states have played a major role (either actively or by omission) in the emergence of all the systems described in this volume. The trajectories of Eastern Europe's former socialist economies reflects both their organization under socialism and policy choices by successor states (Stark and Bruszt 1998). The Japanese state has long shaped its economy. And the growth of interfirm alliances in the United States followed on the relaxation of antitrust policies under President Reagan and his successors, the Bayh-Dole Act of 1980 (which fueled universities' interest in the commercial exploitation of basic research), and other changes in regulatory, trade, and intellectual-property policy during this period (Mowery 1999). When different local mechanisms lead to similar outcomes across national cases, either the diversity of proximate antecedents masks broader similarities in causal dynamics, or the very local forces that militate toward convergence today may lead to divergence tomorrow.

Several authors note that diffusion of the "network model" is likely to occur both through organizational learning and through the influence of Western management schools, accounting firms, legal scholars, and consulting companies, the latter of whom package a single version of the "network firm" for distribution around the world. Kraakman alone among the authors predicts that one form will dominate: because of advantages associated with Western corporate and securities law, he believes that the Western model of the corporation will be adopted by states throughout the world. But the difference between his view and those of the other authors may be less than it appears, because Kraakman predicts convergence in property rights and governance, whereas the other authors focus upon divergence in organizational structure and strategy, a great deal of which is possible within a Western corporate legal regime.

Logics or Meta-Logics?

Stark presents the most complex view of organizational logics because he locates them in the environment and views organizations as sites at which these logics intersect. Stark contends that different "principles of organization" compete within Hungarian firms and that this rivalry is useful because it makes firms more complex, which, in turn, engenders extensive search behavior and enhanced adaptive capacity. In other words, "heterarchy" is both an organizational form and a framework for navigating among competing organizational logics. Heterarchy provides flexibility—not the flexibility-within-market-competition that Powell's product-development alliances and Westney's vertical *keiretsu* offer, but an opportunity to trade off economic sleekness in return for legitimacy in a system that has not fully committed itself to the market. In other word, "heterarchy" is less a single logic, than a meta-logic, a means by which businesses can oscillate among several principles of organization at once.

Stark's view of "logics" bears a strong affinity to the evolutionary tradition's notion of "selection regimes," in that the former are tied to particular institutions that influence the firm's chances for survival and growth. It also bears a close affinity to John Meyer and W. Richard Scott's notion that environmental heterogeneity is mirrored by structural differentiation (and decoupling of parts) within organizations (Meyer et al. 1987). From an evolutionary perspective, the coexistence of multiple "logics of organization" should reflect environmental heterogeneity: heterarchies should outcompete smaller, specialized firms so long as state, market, and informal networks all provide vital resources according to different principles of selection. This is the case in Eastern Europe, where institutions are being negotiated and "the winnowing forces of selection," as Bryce and Singh put it, blow "simultaneously from many different directions." In such an environment, enterprises must be able to play at once in several games, as organizational forms coevolve with principles of selection that themselves compete for legitimacy. From a comparative standpoint, one must ask if heterarchy is a generic response to uncertainty and change, a new meta-logic of organizing likely to spread throughout the world, or a specialized and perhaps evanescent response to the sudden profusion of selection regimes peculiar to the former socialist world.

In the end, whether the new developments described by the essays in this volume, cohere into a distinctive organizational model or logic may depend on the level at which one seeks coherence. There are notable affinities among many of the ways that companies reduce hierarchy, interdepartmental and interfirm boundaries, and the number and scope of formal rules in order to compete more effectively in rapidly changing markets. It is less clear that there is any logical affinity between such task-focused networks and the market-buffering alliances defined by cross-shareholding that we find in Japan and the former socialist world. To be sure, as Stark suggests, the latter may provide a space necessary for innovation that leads to the former, as well as an informal regulatory framework for task-based relations among firms. On the other hand, many observers of the United States "network form" attribute responsibility for its emergence to precisely the opposite development: the antimanagerial counterrevolution and the rise of effective markets for corporate control, in combination with *more intense* competitive pressures. If there is a new "logic of organizing," it seems at this point relatively independent of—and articulated in different ways and in different contexts to—concurrent changes at the system level.

As Manuel Castells (1996, 167–68) has noted, changes in the corporate form during the last quarter of the twentieth century reflected less the emergence of a single best model than a failure of the old "powerful but excessively rigid model associated with the large, vertical corporation, and with oligopolistic control over markets." Despite the diversity of forms, he argues

> Recent historical experience has already provided some of the answers concerning the new organizational forms of the informational economy. Under different organizational arrangements, and through diverse cultural expressions, they are all based in networks. *Networks are the fundamental stuff of which new organizations are and will be made* [emphasis in original].

Many of the authors of this volume would agree with Castells on this point. Yet it raises a significant question, which is the last I shall address here. Given the diversity of forms that networks can take and the vast range of relationships the term is used to denote, should we not wonder that networks are being discovered in so many locations and in so many forms more or less at once? To what extent is the attention devoted to "the network enterprise" a reflection of organizational change, and to what extent is it a by-product of changes in the perceptual apparatus we use to apprehend the world?

Changing Organizations or Changing Schemata?

Large business corporations are heterogeneous in composition, spatially dispersed, structurally complex, and hard to visualize. When entities are difficult to fathom in their entirety, we employ synecdoche in order to reduce complexity to manageable proportions. It has been conventional to understand business institutions in terms of the dominant technology of the day. In the nineteenth century, this was the railroad: the "locomotive" became a central metaphor for power and force, and the system of tracks and schedules became an important way to conceive of order and discipline. In the twentieth century, the automobile factory was the epitome of enterprise, its assembly line the paradigm case that represented the firm. As we enter the twenty-first century, the high-speed computer plays a similar role, making it natural to think of enterprises in terms of networks and flows.

Indeed, the language of networks suffuses this volume. Most of the authors agree that bureaucracy has been supplanted in businesses throughout the world by networks of various shapes and sizes. As we have seen, they are in good company, developing (with unusual sophistication and knowledge) intuitions about the increasingly important role of "networks" that are visible from the humblest precincts of management consulting to the loftiest aeries of social theory.

Our Schemata Affect What We Perceive

I have argued that as particular technologies grip observers' imaginations, they provide powerful schemata—sets of conceptual categories and intuitions about the relations among them. Cognitive psychologists and intellectual historians have demonstrated that schemata influence both the aspects of reality we perceive and how we interpret those perceptions (Fleck [1935] 1979; DiMaggio 1997; Zerubavel 1998).

The imagery of the network provides a powerful family of schemata for observing the world of business. It is easy to forget that the notion of "network" is less a description of any particular form of association than it is an analytic convenience, a means of describing systems as consisting of a set of actors (units, nodes, objects) connected by a set of relations or flows. In this sense, any organization—from the military units of ancient Rome to the Fordist bureaucracies of the mid-twentieth-century United States to the lean, flat enterprises of contemporary Silicon Valley—can be described in network terms. What is an organization chart (that ultimate artifact of corporate bureaucracy), if not a diagram of a network? Considered in this light, the discovery that business is organized and carried out by networks seems a little bit like M. Jourdain's recognition that he had been "speaking in prose" (Molière 1670).

This is too flippant, of course, because the networks to which contemporary students of business call attention share a certain relational openness, a tendency to crosscut formal organizational or subunit boundaries, and modes of accommodation more fluid and consensual than hierarchical authority or formal contract. It is reasonable, however, to ask to what extent our ability to notice networks of this kind has been enhanced by our ability to theorize them, just as the ability of previous generations of scholars to apprehend bureaucracy was cultivated by the well-crafted lenses that bureaucratic theory provided. In a telling aside, after noting that current enterprises "bear little resemblance to classic twentieth-century models of well-bounded, autonomous, maximizing firms," Tilly wonders "to what extent firms ever corresponded to these models." And that is precisely the point. Social-science models of what a corporation is and should be have quite clearly changed. Is the world of business keeping up with our models?

Contemporary students of the firm benefit from a quiet revolution that shook the social sciences during the 1960s and 1970s. On the one hand, this revolution was marked by a pervasive realism, a structuralist and often antinomian wish to look behind the veil of everyday appearance to identify underlying patterns that conventional wisdom obscures. In mainstream sociology this took the form of network analysis, which promised to use matrix algebra to lay bare the rules and logic of social organization (White, Boorman, and Breiger 1976). In organization studies, it expressed itself in neoinstitutional theory's apparent dismissal of formal organizational structure as a set of "rational myths" (Meyer and Rowan 1977) and in organizational ecology's privileging of selection over learning as a mechanism of organizational change (Hannan and Freeman 1977). Even economics, which has never valued formal network analysis, embraced network imagery in agency theory's view of the firm as a mere organizing node in a network of bilateral contracts (Jensen and Meckling 1976). These developments all portrayed formal organizational structures—bureaucracy and the organization chart—as epiphenomena that the analyst must penetrate in order to capture the essence of organizational life. And network analysis (made practical by improvements in computational power) provided both a language and a formal method for doing this.

The move toward realism, toward a suspicion of surface appearance, was a cultural shift visible far more widely than in academic social science. So is a ubiquitous infatuation with the notion of networks and fluidity, and the weakening of categorical boundaries in almost every institutional arena. We need not explain this larger sea change in order to acknowledge its influence on organizational studies. What is important is the powerful convergence between the broader culture and social-science theory and method that occurred after 1980. If cultural change inculcated the disposition to question formal representations of organization in a new generation of social scientists, the theoretical and methodological work of the 1970s gave them tools to do so legitimately and effectively. Once they did, broader cultural transformations rendered journalists and businesspeople eager to embrace and elaborate upon the insights their efforts yielded.

To point out that arguments about the "network form" are grounded in changes in both the social sciences and the broader culture is in no way to cast doubt upon the results of the research on which such arguments are based. It is always too easy to plunder history in order to argue that there is nothing new under the sun. With respect to changes inside the firm, one might note that Henry Ford wrote of "flexible production" (albeit mass production), advocated working closely with independent subcontractors, and foresaw a day when universal electrification would lead to "a complete decentralization in which most plants will be small," geographically dispersed, and independent (1930, 156–57). Consider Dalton's (1959) account of how informal networks honeycombed manufacturing firms in the 1950s, or Macauley's (1963) work on the ubiquity of relational contracting between firms and their suppliers a few years later. With respect to intercompany networks, consider the role of networks in nineteenth-century family enterprise (Chandler 1977; Hall 1982); the extensive coordination on many fronts among the railroad enterprises of the nineteenth century, and the cartelization of much of U.S. industry before the emergence of modern antitrust law in the late 1890s (Dobbin 1994); research on the intercorporate network in the United States, especially modes of coordination among financial institutions during much of the twentieth century (Mizruchi and Stearns 1994; Mintz and Schwartz 1985); the significant role of joint ventures (commercial *and* political) in the postwar oil industry (Blair 1976; Sampson 1975); or Zeitlin's stunning analysis of family-group control of the Chilean economy in the Allende era (Zeitlin et al. 1976).

The point is *not* that we've seen it all before. Rather the lesson is that in interpreting the present, we need to be alert to continuities with the past. The question is not merely "are there *more* networks (or are networks more important) now than before," but rather, *are there different kinds of networks, doing different things?* The authors of chapters 2 through 4, alert to these considerations, have avoided the pitfalls of much of the management literature. Powell traces the prehistory of the network form of organization and explicitly describes qualitative differences between business networks today and in the past. Westney and Stark likewise place the networks they discuss in historical perspective.

I would suggest, however, that scholars interested in the firm go even farther than this. Let us acknowledge that in assessing the nature and extent of organizational change at both firm and system levels, we cannot escape, to some extent, conflating change in the phenomena with change in the instruments (in this case, the theoretical apparatus) that we use to measure the phenomena. One solution to this problem, which the authors here employ to a praiseworthy degree, is reflexivity. A more systematic solution is recalibration: using current perspectives to reexamine the past, and looking at contemporary data through multiple lenses.

This means two things in practice. Before the late 1970s, most scholars gave short shrift to informal social organization in business organizations, and those that attended to it lacked the theoretical and methodological tools for studying networks that we now possess. Contemporary scholars (outside of the field of new institutional economics, in which empirical studies of contemporary corporate change have played a relatively minor role) have paid less attention than warranted to formal mechanisms of coordination and control. Earlier in this chapter, I emphasized the importance of focusing on the mechanisms by which successful intracompany teams and interfirm networks address the problems of interest aggregation, valuation, and comparability. Here I would add that we can gain much by reexamining the history of the business corporation with the new methodological and theoretical resources scholars have employed to study contemporary business networks. I doubt that such a reassessment would belie many of the specific claims of novelty for the developments that constitute the "network model" or "network form" of organization. But I am confident that it would enrich our comparative understanding of business enterprise by awakening us to much that was invisible to earlier generations of scholars.

What We Perceive Will Influence What Businesses Do

If science is influenced by cultural transformation outside the academy, social science is peculiar in its capacity to shape the culture and practices of the societies in which it operates (Giddens 1984). Weber's analytic model of bureaucracy informed normative ideas about management, in all likelihood making companies more bureaucratic than they might otherwise have become. The economic model of *homo economicus*—an analytic abstraction—is a normative model that justifies and quite possibly increases the prevalence of self-serving behavior (Marwell and Ames 1981; Miller 1999).

By the same token, social-science work on contemporary organizational change, and especially descriptions of the network form of organization, is likely to increase the rate at which companies adopt features of this form. In effect, the creative efforts of managers and entrepreneurs have intersected with the theoretical and empirical work of the scholars who have studied them to generate what, following Neil Fligstein (1990), we might call a "network conception of the firm." Powerful institutional forces may encourage that conception's diffusion. Such effects are likely to take place through at least three broad avenues, which Walter Powell and I (1983) have characterized, respectively, as mimetic, normative, and coercive isomorphic processes.

Mimetic processes are those that focus managers' attention on particular companies as exemplars, with the result that less successful firms attempt to imitate salient aspects of those companies' structures and practices, often with only hazy information about how these may be linked to the companies, business success. The widespread diffusion of "benchmarking" over the past two decades has rationalized this process to a great degree, making such imitation easier. The role of the business press and popular management writers, enthusiastic as they are about aspects of the "network model," should stimulate diffusion significantly by identifying exemplars,

Normative isomorphic processes reflect the adoption of particular practices and structures by professional bodies, consultants, and educational institutions to which firms or their staff look for guidance. Powell writes of the "growing institutional infrastructure of law, consulting, and venture capital firms" who "are potent carriers of new recipes." One may add to this list the organizational behavior and strategy courses taught in many management schools and elements of the human-resources profession.

Management consultants have always been in the business of distilling management wisdom into packages that can be sold to clients in digestible portions, a trade that makes them chronically susceptible to herdlike enthusiasms. Consultants are particularly taken with the network conception of the firm, I suspect, because it resonates so neatly with their own experience. Their work takes place in temporary project teams, often assembled from several geographically disparate offices, increasingly in collaboration with other firms. Their own organizational structures are flat and flexible, and their key staff routinely penetrate the boundaries of other large companies. Their success is governed by their principals' effectiveness at establishing and maintaining dense cooperative networks with both clients and collaborators. In effect, the network conception elevates their own experience to a paradigm for business writ large.

Finally, *coercive processes* entail the imposition of particular structures or practices through authority of the state or some other superordinate body. This form of diffusion is least likely to occur in the United States, but may influence developments in the former socialist world. Industry groups that form in reaction to uncertainty about the state's role in the economy may prove useful to states attempting to reach a rapprochement between capital and newly enfranchised workers (or between domestic capital and international lending agencies). Perhaps the networks Stark describes will become the sinews of a distinctly postsocialist brand of the corporatist governance systems that (in different ways) existed in Western Europe and Japan during much of the postwar era.

At the same time, diffusion of the network concept of the firm may be limited by at least two factors. First, as Fligstein (1990) argues, successful conceptions of the firm are ordinarily embodied in new categories of staff from whom corporate leadership is drawn (see also Ocasio and Kim 1999). Thus the "production concept" of the firm reflected the experience and skills of the engineers who founded many large corporations; the "marketing concept" took command once CEOs came to be recruited from sales departments; and the "finance conception" was embodied in the financial managers who rose to the top of many large companies during the 1960s. Without a comparable professional carrier class—some category of professional manager or functional specialist for whom a "network conception" of the firm resonates naturally—the network form may be slow to diffuse. The main candidates, at this point, are management consultants, information technology specialists (especially in firms with Chief Information Officer positions) and second-generation managers of entrepreneurial high-tech firms. It remains to be seen whether such jobs will become stepping stones to CEO positions outside the high-technology sector.

Second, key elements of the network conception of the firm stands in at least partial opposition to an even more powerful "rational myth"—the "finance conception" that views the company as a "nexus of contracts." From the microeconomic perspective, anything that smacks of an enduring relationship—from cross-ownership of securities to loyalty-infused relational networks to versions of corporate culture that identify employees as "stakeholders"—is highly suspect. As Kraakman explains, this perspective remains influential in the legal and financial communities and is embedded in corporate and security laws. As long as this is the case, it will at least constrain the development of the network model to those lines most consistent with the finance conception of the firm.

The contributors to this volume have given us much to think about. Like Marx, Weber, and others who tried to make intellectual sense of the industrial revolution, their goal has been to separate signal from noise, to distinguish the main lines of change from striking but ephemeral distractions. Professors Powell, Stark, and Westney examine kaleidoscopic data from three societies with business sectors at very different stages of development. Powell describes the results of the kaleidoscope's slow initial turns, as the first bits of glass begin their journey; his task has been to anticipate the patterns that will emerge once the cylinder rotates more vigorously. Stark, by contrast, describes the configuration of pieces *after* the kaleidoscope has been turned but before it has come to rest, while the pieces are in full tumble. No wonder that the insights of complexity theory seem especially well suited for the postsocialist case. Finally, Westney describes business in a society with a strongly institutionalized form that may be experiencing deinstitutionalization. The kaleidoscope turned, first in the Meiji era and then during the United States occupation, the pieces came to rest, and now at least some Japanese seek a way to set it turning again.

None of the contributors to this volume claims to provide a blueprint of the twenty-first century firm. No one has the global perspective to do that, and none of the contributors believes that a single model will prevail in every society and every industry. But by combining their perspectives and their expertise, they have illuminated the major lines of change and described the potential futures to which these lead. The union of their voices has yielded not the harmony of a single vision—at this point, who could trust a dialogue that produced that?—but rather an agenda for research and a shared framework within which to study, analyze, and argue about ongoing change in business organization at both the company and system level throughout the world.

References

Abegglen, James. C. 1958. *The Japanese Factory*. Glencoe, Ill.: Free Press.

———. 1973. *Management and the worker: The Japanese Solution*. Tokyo: Sophia University Press.

———. Abeggler, James C., and G. Stalk. 1985. *Kaisha: The Japanese Corporation*. New York: Basic Books.

Abrahams, Paul, and Gillian Tett. 1999. "The Circle Is Broken." *Financial Times*, 9 November, p. 18.

Alchian, Armen. 1950. "Uncertainty, Evolution, and Economic Theory." *Journal of Political Economy* 58:211–21.

Adler, P., M. Fruin, and J. Liker, eds., 1999. *Re-Made in America*. New York: Oxford University Press.

Aldrich, Howard. 1999. *Organizations Evolving*. Thousand Oaks, Cal.: Sage Publications.

Aldrich, Howard, and Peter V. Marsden. 1988. "Environments and Organizations." In *Handbook of Sociology*, edited by N. J. Smelser, 361–93. Chicago: Rand-Macnally.

Allen, Peter M., and J. M. McGlade. 1987. "Modeling Complex Human Systems: A Fisheries Example." *European Journal of Operational Research* 24:147–67.

Aoki, M. 1988. *Information, Incentives, and Bargaining in the Japanese Economy*. New York: Cambridge University Press.

———. ed. 1984. *The Economic Analysis of the Japanese Firm*. Amsterdam: North-Holland.

Applebaum, Eileen, and Rosemary Batt. 1994. *The New American Workplace: Transforming Work Systems in the United States*. Ithaca, N.Y.: ILR Press.

Arrow, Kenneth J. 1974. *The Limits of Organization*. New York: Norton.

Arthur, W. Brian. 1994. *Increasing Returns and Path Dependence in the Economy*. Ann Arbor: University of Michigan Press.

Ashkenas. Ron, Todd Jick, and Steve Kerr. 1998. *The Boundaryless Organization: Breaking the Chains of Organizational Structure*. San Francisco: Jossey-Bass.

Ausenda, Giorgio, ed. 1992. *Effects of War on Society*. San Marino: AIEP Editore for Center for Interdisciplinary Research on Social Stress.

Axelrod, Robert. 1984. *The Evolution of Cooperation*. New York: Basic Books.

Baker, George, Robert Gibbons, and Kevin J. Murphy. 2001. "Relational Contracts and the Theory of the Firm." Quarterly Journal of Economics.

Baran, Paul A., and Paul Sweezy. 1966. *Monopoly Capital: An Essay on the American Economic and Social Order*. New York: Monthly Review Press.

Barker, Kathleen, and Kathleen Christensen, eds. 1998. *Contingent Work: American Employment Relations in Transition*. Ithaca, N.Y.: ILR Press.

Barley, Stephen L., and Julian E. Orr. 1997. *Between Craft and Science: Technical Work in U.S. Settings*. Ithaca, N.Y.: ILR Press.

Barnard, Chester. [1938] 1975. *The Functions of the Executive*. Cambridge: Harvard University Press.

Baron, James N., Frank R. Dobbin, and P. Deveraux Jennings. 1986. "War and Peace: The Evolution of Modern Personnel Administration in U.S. Industry." *American Journal of Sociology* 92:350–83.

Baron, James N., M. Diane Burton, and Michael T. Hannan. 1999. "Engineering Bureaucracy: The Genesis of Formal Policies, Positions, and Structures in High-Technology Firms." *Journal of Law, Economics, and Organization* 15:1–41.

Baron, James N., Michael T. Hannan, and M. Diane Burton. 1999."Determinants of Managerial Intensity in Organizations." *American Sociological Review* 64:527–47.

Bartlett, Christopher, and Sumantra Ghoshal. 1993. "Beyond the M-Form." *Strategic Management Review* 14:23–46.

Baum, Joel A. C., and Christine Oliver. 1992. "Institutional Embeddedness and the Dynamics of Organizational Populations." *American Sociological Review* 57:540–59.

Baum, Joel A. C., and Jitendra V. Singh. 1994a. *Evolutionary Dynamics of Organizations*. New York: Oxford University Press.

———. 1994b. "Organizational Hierarchies and Evolutionary Processes: Some Reflections on a Theory of Organizational Evolution." In *Evolutionary Dynamics of Organizations*, edited by Joel A. C. Baum and Jitendra V. Singh, 3–20. New York: Oxford University Press.

Bayat, Asef. 1997. *Street Politics. Poor People's Movements in Iran*. New York: Columbia University Press.

Bebchuk, Lucian, Reinier Kraakman, and George Triantis. Forthcoming. "Stock Pyramids, Cross-Ownership, Dual Class Equity: The Agency Costs of Separating Control from Cash Flow Rights." In *Concentrated Ownership*, edited by Randall Morck, 295–315. Chicago: University of Chicago Press.

Bebchuk, Lucian, and Mark Roe. 1999. "A Theory of Path Dependence in Corporate Ownership and Governance." *Stanford Law Review* 52:127–70.

Beissinger, Mark R. 1996. "How Nationalisms Spread: Eastern Europe Adrift the Tides and Cycles of Nationalist Contention." *Social Research* 63:97–146.

Bendix, R. 1967. "Preconditions of Development: A Comparison of Japan and Germany." In *Aspects of Social Change in Modern Japan*, edited by Ronald P. Dore, 27–68. Princeton: Princeton University Press.

Benner, Chris. 1996. "Shock Absorbers in the Flexible Economy: The Rise of Contingent Employment in Silicon Valley." Manuscript, Deptartment of City and Regional Planning, University of California, Berkeley.

Berger, Suzanne, and Ronald P. Dore, eds. 1996. *National Diversity and Global Capitalism*. Ithaca: Cornell University Press.

Berle, Adolph, and Gardiner C. Means. 1932. *The Modern Corporation and Private Property*. New York: Macmillan.

———. 1968. *The Modern Corporation and Private Property*. Rev. ed. New York: Harcourt, Brace & World.

Bernhardt, Annette, Martina Morris, Mark Handcock, and March Scott. 1998. "Summary of Findings: Work and Opportunity in the Post-Industrial Labor Market." Report to the Russell Sage and Rockefeller Foundations, New York.

Besley, Timothy. 1995. "Nonmarket Institutions for Credit and Risk Sharing in Low-Income Countries." *Journal of Economic Perspectives* 9:169–88.

Biggart, Nicole. 1992. "Institutional Logic and Economic Explanation." *In Reworking the World: Organizations, Technologies and Cultures in Comparative Perspective*, edited by Jane Marceau, 29–54. Berlin: Walter de Gruyter.

Biggart, Nicole, and Mauro F. Guillén. 1999. "Developing Difference: Social Organization and the Rise of the Auto Industries of South Korea, Taiwan, Spain, and Argentina." *American Sociological Review* 64:722–47.

Black, Bernard S., and Ronald J. Gilson. 1998. "Venture Capital and the Structure of Capital Markets." *Journal of Financial Economics* 47:243–77.

Blair, John. 1976. *The Control of Oil.* New York: Pantheon Press.

Blau, Peter M. 1955. *The Dynamics of Bureaucracy.* Chicago: University of Chicago Press.

Blau, Peter M., and W. Richard Scott. 1962. *Formal Organizations.* San Francisco: Chandler.

Blumberg, Phillip. 1987. *The Law of Corporate Groups: Substantive Law.* Boston: Little, Brown.

Boltanski, Luc, and Laurent Thévenot. 1991. *De la justification: Les économies de la grandeur.* Paris: Gallimard.

Bound, John, and Richard B. Freeman. 1992. "What Went Wrong? The Erosion of the Relative Earnings of Young Black Men in the 1980s." *Quarterly Journal of Economics* 107:201–33.

Bound, John, and George Johnson. 1995. "What Are the Causes of Rising Wage Inequality in the United States?" Federal Reserve *Bank of New York Economic Policy Review* (January).

Bower, Joseph. 1970. *Managing the Resource Allocation Process.* Boston: Harvard Business School Press.

Boyer, Robert. 1996. "The Convergence Hypothesis Revisited: Globalization but Still the Century of Nations?" In *National Diversity and Global Capitalism*, edited by Suzanne Berger and Ronald P. Dore. Ithaca: Cornell University Press.

Braverman, Harry. 1974. *Labor and Monopoly Capital.* New York: Monthly Review Press.

Brom, Karla, and Mitchell Orenstein. 1994. "The 'Privatized' Sector in the Czech Republic: Government and Bank Control in a Transitional Economy." *Europe-Asia Studies* 46:893–928.

Brown, John Seeley, and Paul Duguid. 1998. "Organizing Knowledge." *California Management Review* 40 (3): 90–111.

Brynjolfsson, Erik, Thomas Malone, Vilay Gurbaxani, Ajit Kambil. 1994. "Does Information Technology Lead to Smaller Firms?" *Management Science* 40, 12:1628–44.

Buck, Andrew. 1999. "Organizing for the Market: Financial-Industrial Groups in Russia." Unpublished manuscript, Department of Sociology, Columbia University.

Burke, Victor Lee. 1997. *The Clash of Civilizations. War-Making and State Formation in Europe.* Oxford: Polity Press.

Burnham, James. 1941. *The Managerial Revolution: What is Happening in the World.* New York: John Day Company.

Burns, Tom, and G. S. Stalker. 1959. *The Management of Innovation.* London: Tavistock.

Burt, Ronald S., and Marc Knez. 1995. "Kinds of Third-Party Effects on Trust." *Rationality and Society* 7:255–92.

Buxbaum, Richard M. 1993. "Is 'Network' a Legal Concept?" *Journal of Institutional and Theoretical Economics* 149 (4): 698–705.

Cairncross, Frances. 1997. *The Death of Distance: How the Communications Revolution Will Change Our Lives.* Boston: Harvard Business School Press.

Callahan, Raymond. 1962. *Education and the Cult of Efficiency.* Chicago: University of Chicago Press.

Camic, Charles. 1989. "Structure after 50 Years: The Anatomy of a Charter." *American Sociological Review* 95:38–107.

Campbell, Andrew, and Michael Goold. 1999. *The Collaborative Enterprise: Why Links Across the Corporation Often Fail and How to Make Them Work.* Cambridge, Mass.: Perseus Publishing.

Campbell, Donald T. 1969. "Variation and Selective Retention in Socio-Cultural Evolution." *General Systems* 16:69–85.

Campbell, John L., and Leon N. Lindberg. 1991. "The Evolution of Governance Regimes." In *Governance of the American Economy,* edited by John L. Campbell, J. Rogers Hollingsworth, and Leon N. Lindberg, 319–55. New York: Cambridge University Press.

Capelli, Peter, with L. Bassi, H. Katz, D. Knoke, P. Osterman, and M. Useem. 1997. *Change at Work.* New York: Oxford University Press.

Carnoy, Martin, Manuel Castells, and Chris Benner. 1997. "Labor Markets and Employment Practices in the Age of Flexibility: A Case Study of Silicon Valley." *International Labour Review* 136 (1): 27–48.

Carroll, Glenn R. 1985. "Concentration and Specialization: Dynamics of Niche Width in Populations of Organizations." *American Journal of Sociology* 90:1262–83.

Carruthers, Bruce. 1996. *City of Capital: Politics and Markets in the English Financial Revolution.* Princeton: Princeton University Press.

Castells, Manuel. 1996. *The Rise of the Network Society.* Vol. 1 of *The Information Age: Economy, Society, and Culture.* Berkeley: University of California Press.

Chandler, Alfred A., Jr. 1962. *Strategy and Structure: Chapters in the History of the American Industrial Enterprise.* Cambridge: MIT Press.

———. 1977. *The Visible Hand: The Managerial Revolution in American Business.* Cambridge: Harvard University Press.

Chesbrough, Henry, and David Teece. 1996. "When is Virtual Virtuous? Organizing for Innovation." *Harvard Business Review* (January–February): 65–73.

Chew, D. H., ed. 1997. *Studies in International Corporate Finance and Governance Systems.* New York: Oxford University Press.

Clark, Andy. 1999. "Leadership and Influence: The Manager as Coach, Nanny, and Artificial DNA." In *The Biology of Business: Decoding the Natural Laws of Enterprise,* edited by John Clippinger, 47–66. San Francisco: Jossey-Bass.

Clark, R. 1979. *The Japanese Company.* New Haven: Yale University Press.

Clemons, E. K. 1991. "Corporate Strategies for Information Technology: A Resource-based Approach." *IEEE Computer* (November): 23–32.

Clippinger, John. 1999. "Tags: The Power of Labels in Shaping Markets and Organizations." *In The Biology of Business: Decoding the Natural Laws of Enterprise*, edited by John Clippinger, 67–88. San Francisco: Jossey-Bass.

Coase, Ronald. 1937. "The Nature of the Firm." *Economica* 4:386–405.

Coffee, John. 1996. "Institutional Investors in Transitional Economies: Lesson from the Czech Experience." In *Corporate Governance in Central Europe and Russia: Volume I. Banks, Funds and Foreign Investors*, edited by Roman Frydman, Cheryl W. Gray, and Andrzej Rapaczynski, 111–86. Budapest: Central European University Press.

Cohen, Wesley, and David Levinthal. 1989. "Innovation and Learning: The Two Faces of R&D." *Economic Journal* 99:569–96.

———. 1990. "Absorptive Capacity: A New Perspective on Learning and Innovation." *Administrative Science Quarterly* 35:128–52.

Cole, Robert E. 1971. *Japanese Blue Collar: The Changing Tradition*. Berkeley: University of California Press.

———. 1979. *Work, Mobility, and Participation: A Comparative Study of American and Japanese Industry*. Berkeley: University of California Press.

———. 1989. *Strategies for Learning: Small-group Activities in American, Japanese, and Swedish Industry*. Berkeley: University of California Press.

Committee on Techniques for the Enhancement of Human Performance, Commission on Behavioral and Social Sciences and Education, National Research Council. 1999. *The Changing Nature of Work: Implications for Occupational Analysis*. Washington, D.C.: National Academy Press.

Creveld, Martin van. 1991. *The Transformation of War*. New York: Free Press.

Cusumano, M. 1985. *The Japanese Automobile Industry: Technology and Management at Nissan and Toyota*. Vol. 122. Cambridge: Council on East Asian Studies, Harvard University.

Dalton, Melville. 1959. *Men Who Manage*. New York: John Wiley.

Danzinger, Sheldon, and Peter Gottschalk, eds. 1993. *Uneven Tides: Rising Inequality in America*. New York: Russell Sage Foundation.

———. 1995. *America Unequal*. Cambridge: Harvard University Press.

Davis, Gerald F., and Henrich R. Greve. 1997. "Corporate Elite Networks and Governance Changes in the 1980s," *American Journal of Sociology* 103:1–37.

Davis, Stanley M., and Paul R. Lawrence. 1977. *Matrix*. Reading, Mass.: Addison-Wesley.

Dawisha, Karen. 1997. "Democratization and Political Participation: Research Concepts and Methodologies." In *The Consolidation of Democracy in East-Central Europe*. Authoritarianism and Democratization in Postcommunist Societies, eds. Karen Dawisha and Bruce Parrott, vol. 1. Cambridge: Cambridge University Press.

Dawkins, Richard. 1996. *Climbing Mount Improbable*. New York: Norton.

DiMaggio, Paul. 1997. "Culture and Cognition." *Annual Review of Sociology* 23:263–87.

DiMaggio, Paul, and Walter W. Powell. 1983. "The Iron Cage Revisited: Collective Rationality and Institutional Isomorphism in Organizational Fields." *American Sociological Review* 48:147–60.

Dobbin, Frank. 1994. *Forging Industrial Policy: The United States, Britain, and France in the Railway Age*. New York: Cambridge University Press.

Doeringer, Peter, and Audrey Watson. 1999. "Apparel." In *U.S. Industry in 2000: Studies in Competitive Performance*, edited by David Mowery, 329–62. Report of the Board on Science Technology and Economic Policy, National Research Council. Washington, D.C.: National Academy Press.

Dore, Ronald P. 1973. *British Factory Japanese Factory: The Origin of National Diversity in Industrial Relations*. Berkeley: University of California Press.

———. 1983. "Goodwill and the Spirit of Market Capitalism." *British Journal of Sociology* 34:459–82.

———. 1986. *Flexible Rigidities: Industrial Policy and Structural Adjustment in the Japanese Economy, 1970–1980*. Stanford: Stanford University Press.

———. 1987. *Taking Japan Seriously*. London: Athlone Press.

Dore, Ronald P., and J. Ushio. 1999. "Nihonteki keiei Ronso [A debate on Japanese-style Management]." *Chuo Koron* No. 1375, pp. 84–97.

Dornisch, David. 1997. "The Project Life-Cycle: Local Initiative, Economic Restructuring, and Social Innovation in Post-Socialist Poland." Ph.D. diss., Department of Sociology, Cornell University.

Dow, Gregory. 1987. "The Function of Authority in Transaction Cost Economics." *Journal of Economic Behavior and Organization* 8:13–38.

Doz, Yves L., and Gary Hamel. 1998. *Alliance Advantage: The Art of Creating Value Through Partnering*. Boston: Harvard Business School Press.

Drucker, Peter F. 1971. "What We Can Learn from Japanese Management." *Harvard Business Review* 49 (2): 110–22.

———. 1976. *The Unseen Revolution: How Pension-Fund Socialism Came to America*. New York: Harper and Row.

Dyer, Jeffrey H. 1994. "Dedicated Assets: Japan's Manufacturing Edge." *Harvard Business Review* (November–December):174–78.

———. 1996a. "How Chrysler Created an American *Keiretsu*." *Harvard Business Review* (July–August): 42–56.

———. 1996b. "Specialized Supplier Networks as a Source of Competitive Advantage: Evidence from the Auto Industry." *Strategic Management Journal* 17, 4: 271–91.

Dyer, Jeffrey H., and W. G. Ouchi. 1993. "Japanese-style Partnerships: Giving Companies a Competitive Edge." *Sloan Management Review* 35:51–63.

Dyer, Jeffrey H., and Harbir Singh. 1999. "The Relational View: Cooperative Strategy and Sources of Interorganizational Competitive Advantage." *Academy of Management Review* 23:660–79.

Easterbrook, Frank, and Daniel Fischel. 1985. "Limited Liability and the Corporation." *University of Chicago Law Review* 52:89–117.

Eccles, Robert. 1981. "The Quasifirm in the Construction Industry." *Journal of Economic Behavior and Organization* 2:335–57.

———. 1985. *The Transfer Pricing Problem*. Lexington, Mass: D. C. Heath.

Eccles, Robert, and Harrison C. White. 1988. "Price and Authority in Inter-Profit Center Transactions." *American Journal of Sociology* 94 (Supplement): S17–S51.

The Economist. 1991. "Inside the Charmed Circle." 5 January, p. 54.

———. 1998. "Minority Shareholders: Local Heroes." 8 August, pp. 58–59.

———. 1999. "Japan's Growth Companies." 26 June–2 July, pp. 69–70.

Edwards, Richard. 1979.*Contested Terrain: The Transformation of the Workplace in the Twentieth Century*. New York: Basic Books.

Eisenhardt, Kathleen M. 1989. "Agency Theory: An Assessment and Review." *Academy of Management Review* 14:57–74.

Eisenhardt, Kathleen M., and Shona Brown. 1999. "Patching: Restitching Business Portfolios in Dynamic Markets." *Harvard Business Review* 77:72–82.

Engwall, Lars. 1997. "The Creation of European Management Practice." Research proposal, Deparment of Business Studies, University of Uppsala, Sweden.

Etzioni, Amitai. 1964. *A Comparative Analysis of Complex Organizations*. New York: Free Press of Glencoe.

Fama, Eugene F. 1980. "Agency Problems and the Theory of the Firm." *Journal of Political Economy* 8: 288–307.

Fama, Eugene F., and Michael Jensen. 1983a. "Agency Problems and Residual Claims." *Journal of Law and Economics* 26:327–349.

———. 1983b. "Separation of Ownership and Control." *Journal of Law and Economics* 26:301–25.

Farber, Henry S. 1996. "The Changing Face of Job Loss in the United States." Working paper 5596, National Bureau of Economic Research.

Faulkner, Robert R., and Andy Anderson. 1987. "Short-Term Projects and Emergent Careers: Evidence from Hollywood." *American Journal of Sociology* 92:879–909.

Feige, Edgar. 1998. "Underground Activity and Institutional Change: Productive, Protective, and Predatory Behavior in Transition Economies." In *Transforming Post-Communist Political Economies*, edited by Joan Nelson, Charles Tilly & Lee Walker. Washington, D.C.: National Academy Press.

Fein, Helen. 1993. "Accounting for Genocide after 1945: Theories and Some Findings." *International Journal on Group Rights* 1:79–106.

Finer, S. E. 1997. *The History of Government from the Earliest Times*. 3 vols. Oxford: Oxford University Press.

Fleck, Ludwik. [1935] 1979. *Genesis and Development of a Scientific Fact*. Chicago: University of Chicago Press.

Fligstein, Neil. 1990. *The Transformation of Corporate Control*. Cambridge: Harvard University Press.

Fontana, Walter, and Leo W. Buss. 1994. "The Arrival of the Fittest: Toward a Theory of Biological Organization." *Bulletin of Mathematical Biology* 56:1–64.

Foran, John. 1997. "The Future of Revolutions at the *fin-de-siècle*." *Third World Quarterly* 18:791–820.

Ford, Henry (in collaboration with Samuel Crowther). 1930. *Moving Forward*. Garden City: Doubleday, Doran, and Company.

Frank, Robert H., and Phillip J. Cook. 1995. *The Winner-Take-All Society*. New York: Free Press.

Freeman, Christopher. 1994. "The Economics of Technical Change." *Cambridge Journal of Economics* 18:463–514.

———. 1995. "The National System of Innovation in Historical Perspective." *Cambridge Journal of Economics* 19:5–24.

Freeman, Richard B. 1995. "Are New York Wages Set in Beijing?" *Journal of Economic Perspectives* 9:15–32.

Freeman, Richard B., and Lawrence F. Katz. 1994. "Rising Wage Inequality: The U.S. vs. Other Advanced Countries." In *Working Under Different Rules*, edited by Richard B. Freeman, 29–62. New York: Russell Sage Foundation.

Friedland, Roger, and Robert Alford. 1991. "Bringing Society Back In: Symbols, Practices, and Institutional Contradictions." In *The New Institutionalism in Organizational Analysis*, edited by Walter Powell and Paul DiMaggio, 232–63. Chicago: University of Chicago Press.

Fruin, W. M. 1997. *Knowledge Works: Managing Intellectual Capital at Toshiba*. New York: Oxford University Press.

Fruin, W. M., and T. Nishiguchi. 1993. "Supplying the Toyota Production System: Intercorporate Organizational Evolution and Supplier Subsystems." In *Country Competitiveness: Technology and the Organizing of Work*. edited by B. Kogut, 225–46. New York: Oxford University Press.

Fujimoto, T. 1997. "The Dynamic Aspect of Product Development Capabilities: An International Comparison in the Automobile Industry." In *Innovation in Japan*, edited by A. Goto and H. Odagiri, 57–99. New York: Oxford University Press.

Fukuda, Y. 1997. "Nihon-kei Kigyo Chushin Shakai no Kozo [The Structure of the Japanese Company-dominated Society]". *Hitotsubashi Daigaku Kenyu Nenpo: Keizaigaku Kenkyu* 38:53–117.

Galaskiewicz, Joseph. 1985. "Interorganizational Networks and the Development of a Single Mind-Set," *American Sociological Review* 50:639–58.

Galbraith, James R. 1973. *Designing Complex Organizations*. Reading, Mass.: Addison-Wesley.

Galbraith, John Kenneth. 1967. *The New Industrial State*. Boston: Houghton Mifflin.

Gambetta, Diego. 1993. *The Sicilian Mafia: The Business of Private Protection*. Cambridge: Harvard University Press.

Gao, Bai. 2000. *Japan's Economic Dilemma: The Institutions of Prosperity and Stagnation*. New York: Cambridge University Press.

Garratt, Bob. 1994. *The Learning Organization*. Rev. ed. New York: Harper Collins.

Gerlach, Michael. 1992. *Alliance Capitalism: The Social Organization of Japanese Business*. Berkeley: University of California Press.

Gibbons, Robert, 1997. "An Introduction to Applicable Game Theory." *Journal of Economic Perspectives* 11:127–49.

———. 1999. "Taking Coase Seriously." *Administrative Science Quarterly* 44: 145–57.

Giddens, Anthony. 1984. *The Constitution of Society*. Berkeley: University of California Press.

Gilson, Ronald J. 1999. "The Legal Infrastructure of High-Technology Industrial Districts: Silicon Valley, Route 128, and Covenants not to Compete." *New York University Law Review* 74:575–629.

Gilson, Ronald J. and Mark Roe. 1993. "Understanding Japanese *Keiretsu*: Overlaps Between Corporate Governance and Industrial Organization." *Yale Law Journal* 102:871–906.

Gomes-Casseres, Benjamin. 1996. *The Alliance Revolution: The New Shape of Business Rivalry.* Cambridge: Harvard University Press.

Gompers, Paul, and Josh Lerner. 1999. *The Venture Capital Cycle.* Cambridge: MIT Press.

Gordon, Andrew. 1985. *The Evolution of Labor Relations in Japan: Heavy Industry 1853–1955.* Cambridge: Council on East Asian Studies, Harvard University.

———. 1993. "Contests for the Workplace." In *Postwar Japan as History,* edited by A. Gordon, 373–94. Berkeley: University of California Press.

———. 1998. *The Wages of Affluence: Labor and Management in Postwar Japan.* Cambridge: Harvard University Press.

Gordon, David M. 1996. *Fat and Mean: The Corporate Squeeze of Working Americans and the Myth of Managerial Downsizing.* New York: Free Press.

Gordon, David M., Richard Edwards, and Michael Reich. 1982. *Segmented Work, Divided Workers.* Cambridge: Cambridge University Press.

Gordon, Karen, John Reed, and Richard Hamermesh. 1977. "Crown Cork and Seal Company, Inc." Harvard Business School Case #378–024.

Gouldner, Alvin. 1954. *Patterns of Industrial Bureaucracy.* Glencoe Ill.: The Free Press.

Gourevitch, Peter A. 1996. "The Macropolitics of Microinstitutional Differences in the Analysis of Comparative Capitalism." In *National Diversity and Global Capitalism,* edited by Suzanne Berger and Ronald P. Dore, 239–59. Ithaca: Cornell University Press

Grabher, Gernot. 1997. "Adaptation at the Cost of Adaptability? Restructuring the Eastern German Regional Economy." In *Restructuring Networks: Legacies, Linkages, and Localities in Postsocialism,* edited by Gernot Grabher and David Stark, 107–34. London and New York: Oxford University Press.

Grabher, Gernot, and David Stark. 1997. "Organizing Diversity: Evolutionary Theory, Network Analysis, and Postsocialist Transformations." In *Restructuring Networks: Legacies, Linkages, and Localities in Postsocialism,* edited by Gernot Grabher and David Stark, 1–32. London and New York: Oxford University Press.

Granovetter, Mark. 1985. "Economic Action and Social Structure: The Problem of Embeddedness." *American Journal of Sociology* 91:481–510.

———. 1993. "Business Groups." In *Handbook of Economic Sociology,* edited by Neil Smelser and Richard Swedberg, 453–75. Princeton: Princeton University Press.

———. 1995. "Coase Revisited: Business Groups in the Modern Economy." *Industrial and Corporate Change* 4:93–130.

———. 1999. "Coase Encounters and Formal Models: Taking Gibbons Seriously." *Administrative Science Quarterly* 44:158–62.

Grant, Robert M. 1996. "Toward a Knowledge-Based Theory of the Firm." *Strategic Management Journal* 17:109–22.

Greif, Avner. 1994. "Cultural Beliefs and the Organization of Society: A Historical and Theoretical Reflection on Collectivist and Individualist Societies." *Journal of Political Economy* 102:912–50.

———. Paul Milgrom, and Barry Weingast. 1994. "Coordination, Commitment, and Enforcement: The Case of the Merchant Guild." *Journal of Political Economy* 102:745–76.

Grimaldi, James V. 1998. "Analysis: Gates Takes His Rally to Wall Street—Industry Executives Show Support for Microsoft." *The Seattle Times*, 5 May, sec. C, p. 1.

Grossman, Sanford, and Oliver Hart. 1986. "The Costs and Benefits of Ownership: A Theory of Vertical and Lateral Ownership." *Journal of Political Economy*, 94:691–719.

Guillén, Mauro F. 1999. "Corporate Governance and Globalization: Arguments and Evidence Against Convergence." Working paper, The Wharton School, University of Pennsylvania, Philadelphia, PA.

Gulati, Ranjay. 1995. "Does Familiarity Breed Trust? The Implications of Repeated Ties for Contractual Choice in Alliances." *Academy of Management Journal* 38:85–112.

Gurr, Ted Robert. 1993. *Minorities at Risk. A Global View of Ethnopolitical Conflicts*. Washington, D.C.: U.S. Institute of Peace Press.

Gurr, Ted Robert, and Barbara Harff. 1994. *Ethnic Conflict in World Politics*. Boulder: Westview.

Haas, J. E., R. Hall and N. Johnson. 1966. "Towards An Empirically Derived Taxonomy of Organizations." In *Studies on Behavior in Organizations*, edited by R.V. Bowers, 157–180. Athens: University of Georgia Press.

Hackman, J. Richard, and Greg R. Oldham. 1980. *Work Redesign*. Reading, Mass.: Addison-Wesley.

Hackman, J. Richard, and Ruth Wageman. 1995. "Total Quality Management: Empirical, Conceptual, and Practical Issues." *Administrative Science Quarterly* 40:309–42.

Hadley, E. M. 1970. *Antitrust in Japan*. Princeton: Princeton University Press.

Hagedoorn, John. 1995. "Strategic Technology Partnering during the 1980s." *Research Policy* 24:207–231.

Hall, Peter Dobkin. 1982. *The Organization of American Culture, 1700–1900: Institutions, Elites, and the Origins of American Nationality*. New York: New York University Press.

Hall, Richard H. 1963. "The Concept of Bureaucracy: An Empirical Assessment." *American Journal of Sociology* 69:32–40.

Hamilton, G. 1993. "Civilization and the Organization of Economies." In *The Handbook of Economic Sociology*, edited by N. J. Smelser and R. Swedberg, 183–205. Princeton: Princeton University Press.

Hammer, Michael, and James Champy. 1993. *Reengineering the Corporation: A Manifesto for Business Revolution*. New York: Harper Collins.

Hannan, Michael T. 1986. "Uncertainty, Diversity, and Organizational Change." In *Behavioral and Social Sciences: Fifty Years of Discovery: In Commemoration of the Fiftieth Anniversary of the "Ogburn Report"*, edited by N. J. Smelser and Dean R. Gerstein, 73–94. Washington, D.C.: National Academy Press.

Hannan, Michael T., and John Freeman. 1977. "The Population Ecology of Organizations." *American Journal of Sociology* 82 (5): 929–64.

———. 1984. "Structural Inertia and Organizational Change." *American Sociological Review* 49:149–64.

———. 1989. *Organizational Ecology*. Cambridge: Harvard University Press.

Hansmann, Henry. 1996. "What Determines Firm Boundaries in Biotech?" *Journal of Institutional and Theoretical Economics* 152:220–25.

Hansmann, Henry and Reinier Kraakman. 2000a. What is Corporate Law? In *The Anatomy of Corporate Law: A Comparative and Functional Approach*, edited by Reinier Kraakman, Gerard Hertig, Henry Hansmann, and Hideki Kanda, working draft. Yale and Harvard Universities.

———. 2000b. "The Essential Role of Organizational Law." Working paper, Yale and Harvard Universities.

———. Forthcoming. "The End of History for Corporate Law." In *Are Corporate Governance Systems Converging?* edited by Jeffery Gordon and Mark Roe. Chicago: University of Chicago Press.

Harrison, Bennett. 1994. *Lean and Mean: The Changing Landscape of Corporate Power in an Age of Flexibility.* New York: Basic Books.

Harrison, Bennett. 1994. *Lean and Mean: The Changing Landscape of Corporate Power in an Age of Flexibility.* New York: Basic Books.

Hauser, W. B. 1974. *Economic Institutional Change in Tokugawa Japan: Osaka and the Kinai Cotton Trade.* Cambridge: Cambridge University Press.

Hayes, R. 1981. "Why Japanese Factories Work." *Harvard Business Review,* 59 (4): 56–66.

Head. Simon. 1996. "The New, Ruthless Economy." *New York Review of Books,* 29 February: pp. 47–52.

Health Care Advisory Board. 1997. *State of the Union for America's Health Systems: Payer Reform and Product Innovation at the Frontier.* Washington, D.C.: Advisory Board Company.

Hedlund, Gunnar. 1993. "Assumptions of Hierarchy and Heterarchy, with Applications to the Management of the Multinational Corporation." In *Organization Theory and the Multinational Enterprise*, edited by Sumantra Ghoshal and Eleanor Westney, 211–36. London: Macmillan.

Helper, Susan. 1993. "An Exit-Voice Analysis of Supplier Relations: The Case of the U.S. Automobile Industry." In *The Embedded Firm: On the Socioeconomics of Industrial Networks*, edited by G. Grabher, 141–60. London: Routledge.

Henderson, Callum. 1998. *Asia Falling.* New York: McGraw-Hill.

Hergert, Michael, and Deigan Morris. 1988. "Trends in International Collaborative Agreements." In *Cooperative Strategies in International Business*, edited by F. Contractor and P. Lorange, 99–109. Lexington, Mass.: Lexington Books.

Hermalin, Benjamin. 1998. "Toward an Economic Theory of Leadership." *American Economic Review* 88:1188–1206.

Higuchi, Y. 1997. "Trends in Japanese Labour Markets." In *Japanese Labour and Management in Transition: Diversity, Flexibility, and Participation*, edited by M. Sako and H. Sato, 27–52. London: Routledge.

Hofstadter, Douglas R. 1979. *Gödel, Escher, Bach: An Eternal Golden Braid.* New York: Vintage Books, Random House.

Holland, John. 1992. "Complex Adaptive Systems." *Daedalus* 121(1):17–30.

Horwitz, Morton. 1977. *The Transformation of American Law, 1780–1860.* Cambridge: Harvard University Press.

Hounshell, David. 1984. *From the American System to Mass Production 1900–1932: The Development of Manufacturing Technology in the U.S.* Baltimore: Johns Hopkins University Press.

Hutchins, Edwin. 1994. *Cognition in the Wild.* Cambridge: MIT Press.

Hutter, Michael, and Günther Teubner. 1993. "The Parasitic Role of Hybrids." *Journal of Institutional and Theoretical Economics* 149:706–715.

Ickes, Barry W., Randi Ryterman, and Stoyan Tenev. 1995. "On Your Marx, Get Set, Go: The Role of Competition in Enterprise Adjustment." Working paper, The World Bank.

Idei, N., and M. Tanaka. 1998. *"Sekai wa Degitaru Kakumei—Kigyo wa Senryaku Kakumei* [The World Digital Revolution, the Company Strategy Revolution]." *Ekonomisuto* 76 (14 [April]): 18–24.

Imai, K. 1988. "The Corporate Network in Japan." *Japanese Economic Studies*, 16: 3–37.

Imai, K., and R. Komiya. 1994. "Characteristics of Japanese Firms." *Business Enterprise in Japan: Views of Leading Japanese Economists*, edited by K. Imai and R. Komiya, 19–37. Cambridge: MIT Press.

Inkeles, Alex, and David H. Smith. 1974. *Becoming Modern: Individual Change in Six Developing Countries*. Cambridge: Harvard University Press.

Itagaki, H., ed. 1997. *Nihonteki Keiei. Seisan Shisutemu to Higashi Ajia: Taiwan, Kankoku, Chugoku ni okeru Haiburiddo Kojo* [The Japanese Management and Production System and East Asia: Hybrid Factories in Taiwan, Korea, and China]. Tokyo: Minerva Shobo.

Itami, H. 1984. *Nihontek keiei to wa nani ka?* [What Is Japanese-style Management?]. Tokyo: Nihon Keizai Shimbunsha.

———. 1994. "The "Human-Capital-ism' of the Japanese Firm as an Integrated System." In *Business Enterprise in Japan: Views of Leading Economists*, edited by K. Imai and R. Komiya, 73–88. Cambridge: MIT Press.

Jackall, Robert. 1988. *Moral Mazes: The World of Corporate Managers*. New York: Oxford University Press.

Jacob, François. 1977. "Evolution and Tinkering." *Science* 196 (4295 [10 June]): 1116–66.

Jaikumar, Ramchandran. 1986. "Postindustrial Manufacturing." *Harvard Business Review* 64:69–76.

Janoski, Thomas. 1998. *Citizenship and Civil Society. A Framework of Rights & Obligations in Liberal, Traditional, and Social Democratic Regimes*. Cambridge: Cambridge University Press.

Jensen, Michael, and William Meckling. 1976. "Theory of the Firm: Managerial Behavior, Agency Costs, and Ownership Structure." *Journal of Financial Economics* 3:305–60.

Johnson, Chalmers. 1982. *MITI and the Japanese Miracle: The Growth of Industrial Policy, 1925–1975*. Stanford: Stanford University Press.

Johnson, Juliet. 1997. "Russia's Emerging Financial-Industrial Groups." *Post-Soviet Affairs* 13 (4): 333–365.

Kagono, T., I. Nonaka, K. Sakakibara, and A. Okumura. 1985. *Strategic vs. Evolutionary Management*. Amsterdam: North-Holland.

Kahneman, Daniel, Paul Slovic, and Amos Tversky. 1982. *Judgment under Uncertainty: Heuristics and Biases*. New York: Cambridge University Press.

Kalleberg, Arne L., Jeremy Reynolds and Peter V. Marsden. 1999. "Externalizing Employment: Flexible Staffing Arrangements in U.S. Organizations." Working paper, University of North Carolina, Chapel Hill.

Kalleberg, Arne L., Ken Hudson, and Barbara Reskin. 2000. "Bad Jobs in America: Standard and Nonstandard Employment Relations and Job Quality in the U.S." *American Sociological Review* 65 (April): 256–78.

Kalleberg, Arne L., David Knoke, Peter Marsden, and Joe L. Spaeth. 1996. *Organizations in America: Analyzing Their Structures and Human Resource Practices*. Thousand Oaks, Cal.: Sage Publications.

Kanter, Rosabeth Moss. 1983. *The Change Masters: Innovation for Productivity in the American Corporation.*. New York: Simon & Schuster.

———. 1997. *Men and Women of the Corporation*. New York: Basic Books.

Kassarda, John D. 1995. "Industrial Restructuring and the Changing Location of Jobs." In *State of the Union: America in the 1990s*, vol. 7, edited by Reynolds Farley. New York: Russell Sage Foundation.

Katz, R. 1998. *Japan: The System that Soured*. Armonk, N.Y.: M. E. Sharpe.

Kauffman, Stuart A. 1989. "Adaptation on Rugged Fitness Landscapes." In *Lectures in the Science of Complexity*, vol. 1, edited by D. Stein, 527–618. Reading, Mass.: Addison-Wesley, Longman.

———. 1993. *The Origin of Order: Self-Organization and Selection in Evolution*. London: Oxford University Press.

Kelley, Maryellen R. 1990. "New Process Technology, Job Design, and Work Organization: A Contingency Model." *American Sociological Review* 55:191–208.

Kenney, Martin, and Richard Florida. 1993. *Beyond Mass Production: The Japanese System and Its Transfer to the U.S.* New York: Oxford University Press.

Kim, Taehwan. 2000. "Resisting the Market: The Politics of Hierarchies and Networks in Russian Fuel and Metallurgy Industries." Ph.D. diss., Department of Political Science, Columbia University.

Klein, Benjamin. 1991. "Vertical Integration as Organizational Ownership: The Fisher Body–General Motors Relationship Revisited." In *The Nature of the Firm: Origins, Evolution, and Development*, edited by O. Williamson and S. Winter. New York: Oxford University Press.

Klein, Benjamin, Robert Crawford, and Armen Alchian. 1978. "Vertical Integration, Appropriable Rents, and the Competitive Contracting Process." *Journal of Law and Economics* 21:297–326.

Knight, Frank H. 1921. *Risk, Uncertainty, and Profit*. Boston and New York: Houghton Mifflin.

Kobrin, Stephen J. 1997a. "The Architecture of Globalization: State Sovereignty in a Networked Global Economy." In *Governments, Globalization, and International Business*, edited by John H. Dunning. Oxford: Oxford University Press.

———. 1997b. "Electronic Cash and the End of National Markets." *Foreign Policy* 107 (Summer): 65–77.

Kogut, Bruce. 1989. "The Stability of Joint Ventures: Reciprocity and Competitive Rivalry." *Journal of Industrial Economics* 38:183–98.

Kogut, Bruce, Weijan Shan, and Gordon Walker. 1992. "The Make-or-Cooperate Decision in the Context of an Industry Network." In *Networks and Organizations*, edited by Nitin Nohria and Robert G. Eccles, 348–65. Boston: Harvard Business School Press.

Kono, T. 1984. *Strategy and Structure of Japanese Enterprises*. London: Macmillan.

Kornhauser, William. 1962. *Scientists in Industry: Conflict and Accommodation*. Berkeley: University of California Press.

Krackhardt, David, M. Lundberg, and L. O'Rourke. 1993. "KrackPlot: A Picture's Worth a Thousand Words". *Connections* 16:37–47.

Kumazawa, M. 1996. *Portraits of the Japanese Workplace: Labor Movements, Workers, and Managers*. Boulder: Westview Press.

Kunda, Gideon. 1991. *Engineering Culture: Control and Commitment in a High-Technology Corporation*. Philadelphia: Temple University Press.

Landa, Janet Tai. 1994. *Trust, Ethnicity, and Identity: Beyond the New Institutional Economics of Ethnic Trading Networks, Contract Law, and Gift-Exchange*. Ann Arbor: University of Michigan Press.

Landes, D. 1965. Japan and Europe: Contrasts in Industrialization. In *The State and Economic Enterprise in Japan*, edited by W. W. Lockwood, 93–182. Princeton: Princeton University Press.

Lane, David, and Robert Maxfield. 1996. "Strategy Under Complexity: Fostering Generative Relationships." *Long Range Planning* 29 (2): 215–31.

LaPorta, Rafael, Florencio Lopez-de-Silanes, and Andrei Shleifer. 1999. "Corporate Ownership around the World." *Journal of Finance* 54:471–517.

LaPorta, Rafael, Florencio Lopez-de-Silanes, and Andrei Shleifer, and Robert W. Vishny. 1998. "Law and Finance." *Journal of Political Economy* 106:1113–1150.

Lawler, Edward. 1971. *Pay and Organizational Effectiveness: A Psychological View*. New York: McGraw-Hill.

Lawrence, Paul, and Jay W. Lorsch. 1969. *Organization and Environment*. Homewood, Ill.: Richard Irwin.

Lazerson, Mark. 1995. "A New Phoenix? Modern Putting-Out in the Modena Knitwear Industry." *Administrative Science Quarterly* 40:34–59.

Lazonick, W. 1991. *Business Organization and the Myth of the Market Economy*. New York: Cambridge University Press.

———. 1993. "Industry Clusters versus Global Webs: Organizational Capabilities in the American Economy." *Industrial and Corporate Change* 2 (1): 1–24.

Ledford, G. E., Jr. 1993. "Employee Involvement: Lessons and Predictions." In *Organizing for the Future: The New Logic for Managing Complex Organizations*, edited by J. R. Galbraith, E. E. I. Lawler, and Associates, 142–71. San Francisco: Jossey-Bass.

Lenin, Vladimir. 1939. *Imperialism: The Highest Stage of Capitalism*. New York: International Publishers.

Leonard-Barton, Dorothy. 1995. *Wellsprings of Knowledge: Building and Sustaining the Sources of Innovation*. Boston: Harvard Business School Press.

Lerner, Josh. 1995. "Venture Capitalists and the Oversight of Private Firms." *Journal of Finance* 50:301–18.

Levi, Margaret. 1997. *Consent, Dissent, and Patriotism*. Cambridge: Cambridge University Press.

Levitt, Theodore. 1983. "The Globalization of Markets." *Harvard Business Review* (May–June): 92–102.

Levy, Frank, and Richard Murname. 1992. "U.S. Earnings Levels and Earnings Inequality: A Review of Recent Trends and Proposed Explanations." *Journal of Economic Literature* 30 (September): 1333–81.

Levy, Marion J., Jr. 1966. *Modernization and the Structure of Societies*. Princeton: Princeton University Press.

Lewontin, Richard C. 1982. *Human Diversity*. New York: Scientific American Books.

Lockwood, W. W. 1965. "Japan's 'New Capitalism.' " In *The State and Economic Enterprise in Japan*, edited by W. W. Lockwood, 447–552. Princeton: Princeton University Press.

Lundvall, Bengt-Ake, (ed.). 1992. *National Systems of Innovation: Towards a Theory of Innovation and Interactive Learning*. London: Pinter.

Lupher, Mark. 1996. *Power Restructuring in China and Russia*. Boulder: Westview.

Lynn, L. H., and T. J. McKeown. 1988. *Organizing Business: Trade Associations in the U.S. and Japan*. Washington, D.C.: American Enterprise Institute and University Press of America.

Lynn, L. H., and H. Rao. 1995. "Failures of Intermediate Forms: A Study of the Suzuki *Zaibatsu*." *Organisation Studies*, 16:55–80.

Macaulay, Stewart. 1963. "Non-Contractual Relations in Business: A Preliminary Study." *American Sociological Review* 28:55–67.

MacDuffie, John Paul. 1996. "Automotive White-Collar: The Changing Status and Roles of Salaried Employees in the North American Auto Industry." In *Broken Ladders*, edited by P. Osterman, 91–125. New York: Oxford University Press.

Macneil, Ian. 1978. "Contracts: Adjustments of Long-Term Economic Relations Under Classical, Neoclassical, and Relational Contract Law." *Northwestern University Law Review* 72:854–906.

———. 1995. "Relational Contracts: What We Do and Do Not Know." *Wisconsin Law Review* 3:483–526.

Malone, Thomas W., and John F. Rockart. 1991. "Computers, Networks, and the Corporation." *Scientific American* (September): 128–36.

Mansfield, Edward D., and Jack Snyder. 1995. "Democratization and the Danger of War," *International Security* 20:5–38.

March, James G. 1991. "Exploration and Exploitation in Organizational Learning." *Organization Science* 2 (1): 71–87.

March, James G., and Herbert Simon. 1958. *Organizations*. New York: John Wiley & Sons.

Marsh, R., and H. Mannari. 1971. "Lifetime employment in Japan: Roles, Norms, and Values." *American Journal of Sociology* 76:795–812.

Marwell, Gerald, and Ruth E. Ames. 1981. "Economists Free Ride: Does Anyone Else?" *Journal of Public Economics* 13:295–310.

Marx, Karl. [1867] 1887. *Capital: A Critical Analysis of Capitalist Production*. Translated by Samuel Moore and Edward Aveling. London: Sonnenschein, Lowrey.

———. [1852] 1973. *The 18th Brumaire of Louis Bonaparte*. Translated by Daniel DeLeon. New York: International Publishers.

Matsuura, H. 1994. *Amerika Kigyo ga 'Fukkatsu' shita riyu* [The Reasons for the Revival of American Enterprises]. Tokyo: Nihon Keizai Shimbunsha.

Maurice, Marc, François Sellier, and Jean-Jacques Silvestre. 1986. *The Social Foundations of Industrial Power*. Cambridge: MIT Press.

McDermott, Gerald A. 1997. "Rethinking the Ties that Bind: The Limits of Privatization in the Czech Republic." In *Restructuring Networks in Postsocialism: Lega-*

cies, Linkages, and Localities, edited by Gernot Grabher and David Stark, 70–106. Oxford: Oxford and New York University Presses.

McKelvey, Bill. 1982. *Organizational Systematics: Taxonomy, Evolution, Classification*. Berkeley: University of California Press.

McKelvey, Bill, and Howard Aldrich. 1983. "Populations, Natural Selection, and Applied Organization Science." *Administrative Science Quarterly* 28:101–28.

Merrill, Stephen A., and Ronald S. Cooper. 1999. "Trends in Industrial Research and Development: Evidence from National Data Sources." In *Securing America's Industrial Strength*, edited by National Research Council Board on Science, Technology, and Economic Policy, 99–116. Washington, D.C.: National Academy Press.

Meyer, John W., and Brian Rowan. 1977. "Institutionalized Organizations: Formal Structure as Myth and Ceremony." *American Journal of Sociology* 83 (2): 340–63.

Meyer, John W., W. Richard Scott, and David Strang. 1987. "Centralization, Fragmentation, and School District Complexity." *Administrative Science Quarterly* 32:186–201.

Miller, Dale. 1999. "The Norm of Self-Interest." *American Psychologist* 54:1053–60.

Miller, Gary J. 1997. "The Impact of Economics on Contemporary Political Science," *Journal of Economic Literature* 35:1173–1204.

Miner, Anne, Terry L. Amburgey, and Timothy M. Stearns. 1990. "Interorganizational Linkages and Population Dynamics: Buffering and Transformational Shields." *Administrative Science Quarterly* 35:689–713.

Mintz, Beth, and Michael Schwartz. 1985. *The Power Structure of American Business*. Chicago: University of Chicago Press.

Mishina, K., and T. M. Flaherty. 1997. "Intercon Japan." In *Global Operations Management*, edited by Therese Flaherty. New York: McGraw-Hill.

Mizruchi, Mark S., and Linda Brewster Stearns. 1994. "A Longitudinal Study of Borrowing by Large American Corporations." *Administrative Science Quarterly* 39:118–40.

Molière, Jean-Batiste. 1670. *Le Bourgeois Gentilhomme*. Act III, scene 4.

Morikawa, H. 1992. *Zaibatsu: The Rise and Fall of Family Enterprise Groups in Japan*. Tokyo: University of Tokyo Press.

Morin, Edgar. 1974. "Complexity." *International Social Science Journal*, 26 (4): 555–82.

Mowery, David C. 1999. "America's Industrial Resurgence?: An Overview." In *U.S. Industry in 2000: Studies in Competitive Performance*, edited by National Research Council Board on Science, Technology, and Economic Policy, 1–16. Washington, D.C.: National Academy Press.

Mowery, David C., and Richard R. Nelson, eds. 1999. *Sources of Industrial Leadership: Studies of Seven Industries*. New York: Cambridge University Press.

Mroczkowski, T., and M. Hanaoka. 1997. Effective Rightsizing Strategies in Japan and America: Is There a Convergence of Employment Practices? *Academy of Management Executive* 11:57–67.

Murakami, Y., and T. P. Rohlen. 1992. Social-Exchange Aspects of the Japanese Political Economy." In *Cultural and Social Dynamics*, Vol. 3 of *The Political Economy of Japan*, edited by S. Kumo and H. Rosovsky, 63–105. Stanford: Stanford University Press.

Murata, N. 1998 *Ichi-nen ato!? Risutora sareru hito.sarenai hito* [After One Year?! The Person Who Can Restructure, the Person Who Can't]. Tokyo: Dobunkan.

Murayama, K. 1994. *Denki Gyokai Hayawakari Mappu* [Easy-to-Understand Map of the Electronics Industry]. Tokyo: Ko Shobo.

Nakagawa, K. 1993. "Business Management in Japan—A Comparative Historical Study." *Industrial and Corporate Change*, 2:25–44.

Nakatani, Iwao. 1984. "The Economic Role of Financial Corporate Groupings." In *The Economic Analysis of the Japanese Firm*, edited by M. Aoki, 227–58. Amsterdam: North-Hollad.

———. 1997. "A Design for Transforming the Japanese Economy." *Journal of Japanese Studies*. 23:399–417.

Nelson, Daniel. 1980. *Frederick W. Taylor and the Rise of Scientific Management*. Madison: University of Wisconsin Press.

Nelson, Richard, ed. 1993. *National Innovation Systems: A Comparative Analysis*. New York: Oxford University Press.

Nelson, Richard, and Sidney G. Winter. 1982. *An Evolutionary Theory of Economic Change*. Cambridge: Harvard University Press.

Neumark, David. 2000. "Changes in Job Stability and Job Security: A Collective Effort to Untangle, Reconcile, and Interpret the Evidence." Working paper 7472, National Bureau of Economic Research, Cambridge, Mass.

Nisbett, Richard E., and Lee Ross. 1980. *Human Inference: Strategies and Shortcomings of Social Judgment*. Englewood Cliffs, N.J.: Prentice-Hall.

Nishiguchi, Toshihiro. 1994. *Strategic Industrial Sourcing: The Japanese Advantage*. New York: Oxford University Press.

Nishiguchi, Toshihiro, and Alexandre Beaudet. 1998. "Case Study: The Toyota Group and the Asian Fire." *Sloan Management Review* 40 (1): 49–59.

Nishiguchi, Toshihiro, and Jonathan Brookfield. 1997. "The Evolution of Japanese Subcontracting." *Sloan Management Review* (fall): 89–101.

Noble, G. 1998. *Collective Action in East Asia: How Ruling Parties Shape Industrial Policy*. Ithaca: Cornell University Press.

Nonaka, Ikujir. 1990. "Redundant, Overlapping Organizations: A Japanese Approach to Managing the Innovation Process." *California Management Review* 32:27–38.

———. 1995. *The Knowledge-Creating Company*. New York: Oxford University Press.

North, Douglass C. 1990. *Institutions, Institutional Change, and Economic Performance*. New York: Cambridge University Press.

———. 1998. "Understanding Economic Change," In *Transforming Post-Communist Political Economies*, edited by Joan M. Nelson, Charles Tilly, and Lee Walker. Washington, D.C.: National Academy Press.

Ocasio, William, and Hyosun Kim. 1999. "The Circulation of Corporate Control: Selection of Functional Backgrounds of New CEOs in Large U.S. Manufacturing Firms, 1981–1992." *Administrative Science Quarterly* 44:1–43.

O'Connor, James. 1973. *The Fiscal Crisis of the State*. New York: St. Martin's.

Okimoto, D. 1989. *Between MITI and the Market: Japanese Industrial Policy for High Technology*. Stanford: Stanford University Press.

Olmos, David R. 1995. "Early-Release Policy at HMOs Draws Fire; Health Care: Kaiser Decision to Send Some Mothers and Newborns Home after Eight Hours Raises the Debate to a New Level." *Los Angeles Times*, 16 June, see D, p. 1.

Olson, Mancur. 1982. *The Rise and Decline of Nations: Economic Growth, Stagflation, and Social Rigidities*. New Haven: Yale University Press.

O'Mahony, Siobhan, and Stephen R. Barley. 1999. "Do Digital Telecommunications Affect Work and Organization?: The State of Our Knowledge." *Research in Organizational Behavior* 21:125–61.

O'Rourke, Kevin, Alan Taylor, and Jeffrey Williamson. 1996. "Factor Price Convergence in the Late 19th Century." *International Economic Review* 37 (3): 499–530.

Orrù, Marco, Nicole Woolsey Biggart, and Gary G. Hamilton. 1997. *The Economic Organization of East Asian Capitalism*. Thousand Oaks, Cal.: Sage Publications.

Osterman, Paul. 1994. "How Common is Workplace Transformation and Who Adopts It?" *Industrial and Labor Relations Review* 47:173–88.

———. 1999. *Securing Prosperity*. Princeton N.J.: Princeton University Press.

———, ed. 1996. *Broken Ladders: Managerial Careers in the New Economy*. New York: Oxford University Press.

Ostroff, Frank. 1999. *The Horizontal Organization: What the Organization of the Future Looks Like and How It Delivers Value to Customers*. New York: Oxford University Press.

Ouchi, William G. 1980. "Markets, Bureaucracies, and Clans." *Administrative Science Quarterly* 25:120–42.

Padgett, John F., and Christopher K. Ansell. 1993. "Robust Action and the Rise of the Medici, 1400–34." *American Journal of Sociology* 98 (6): 1259–1319.

Palepu, Krishna, and Tarun Khanna. 1996. "Corporate Scope and Institutional Context: An Empirical Analysis of Diversified Indian Business Groups." Working paper 96–051, Harvard Business School, Boston, Mass.

Pasternack, Bruce A., and Albert J. Viscio. 1998. *The Centerless Organization: A New Model for Transforming Your Organization for Growth and Prosperity*. New York: Simon and Schuster.

Pedler, Mike, John Burgoyne, and Tom Boydell. 1991. *The Learning Company*. New York: McGraw-Hill.

Pempel, T. J. 1998. *Regime Shift: Comparative Dynamics of the Japanese Political Economy*. Ithaca: Cornell University Press.

Perlow, Leslie A. 1998. "Boundary Control: The Social Ordering of Work and Family Time in a High-Tech Corporation." *Administrative Science Quarterly* 43:328–57.

Perrow, Charles. 1967. "A Framework for Comparative Organizational Analysis." *American Sociological Review* 32:194–208.

———. 1986. *Complex Organizations: A Critical Essay*. 3d ed. Englewood Cliffs, N.J.: Prentice-Hall.

———. 1991. "A Society of Organizations." *Theory and Society* 20:725–62.

Pfeffer, Jeffrey, and Gerald Salancik. 1979. *The External Control of Organizations*. New York: Harper and Row.

Podolny, Joel, and Karen Page. 1998. "Network Forms of Organization." *Annual Review of Sociology* 24:57–76.

Pollert, Anna. 1988. "The 'Flexible Firm': Fixation or Fact?" *Work, Employment, and Society* 2 (3): 281–316.

Porter, Bruce. 1994. *War and the Rise of the State*. New York: Free Press.

Porter, Michael. 1980. *Competitive Strategy*. New York: Free Press.

———. 1990. *The Competitive Advantage of Nations*. New York: Free Press.

Portes, Alejandro, ed. 1998. *The Economic Sociology of Immigration: Essays on Networks, Ethnicity, and Entrepreneurship*. New York: Russell Sage Foundation.

Powell, Walter W. 1990. "Neither Market nor Hierarchy: Network Forms of Organization." In *Research in Organizational Behavior*, edited by Barry Staw and Lawrence L. Cummings, 295–336. Greenwich, Conn.: JAI Press.

———. 1996. "Inter-Organizational Collaboration in the Biotechnology Industry." *Journal of Institutional and Theoretical Economics* 120 (1): 197–215.

———. 1998. "Learning from Collaboration: Knowledge and Networks in the Biotechnology and Pharmaceutical Industries." *California Management Review* 40 (3): 228–40.

Powell, Walter W., Kenneth Koput, and Laurel Smith-Doerr. 1996. "Technological Change and the Locus of Innovation." *Administrative Science Quarterly* 44 (1): 116–45.

Powell, Walter W., Kenneth Koput, and Laurel Smith-Doerr, and Jason Owen-Smith. 1999. "Network Position and Firm Performance: Organizational Returns to Collaboration." In *Research in the Sociology of Organizations*, vol. 16, edited by David Knoke and Steven Andrews, 129–59. Greenwich, Conn.: JAI Press.

Powell, Walter W., and Jason Owen-Smith. 1998. "Universities and the Market for Intellectual Property in the Life Sciences." *Journal of Policy Analysis and Management* 17:253–77.

Powell, Walter W., and Laurel Smith-Doerr. 1994. "Networks and Economic Life." In *Handbook of Economic Sociology*, edited by N. J. Smelser and R. Swedberg, 368–402. Princeton: Princeton University Press.

Presser, Harriet B. 1995. "Job, Family, and Gender: Determinants of Nonstandard Work Schedules among Employed Americans in 1991." *Demography* 32 (4): 577–98.

Price, J. 1997. *Japan Works: Power and Paradox in Postwar Industrial Relations*. Ithaca: ILR Press and Cornell University Press.

Pugh, D. S., D. J. Dickson, C. R. Hinings, and C. Turner. 1968. "Dimensions of Organization Structure." *Administrative Science Quarterly* 13:65–91.

Purser, Ronald E., and Steven Cabana. 1998. *The Self-Managing Organization: How Leading Companies Are Transforming the Work of Teams for Real Impact*. New York: Simon and Schuster.

Ramseyer, J. Mark. Forthcoming. "Cross-Shareholding in the Japanese *Keiretsu*." In *Are Corporate Governance Systems Converging?* edited by Jeffery Gordon and Mark Roe. Chicago: University of Chicago Press.

Rao, Hayagreeva, Jitendra V. Singh. 1999. "Types of Variation in Organizational Populations: The Speciation of New Organizational Forms." In *Variations in Organizational Science: In Honor of Donald T. Campbell*, edited by Joel A. C. Baum and Bill McKelvey. Newbury Park, Cal.: Sage Publications.

———. 2001. "Organizational Speciation as New Path Creation: Institution-Building Activity in the Early Automobile and Bio-Tech Industries." In *Path as Process*, edited by Raghu Garud and Peter Karnoe. Hillsdale, NJ: Lawrence Erlbaum Associates.

Richardson, J. 1993. Parallel Sourcing and Supplier Performance in the Japanese Automobile Industry. *Strategic Management Journal* 14:339–50.

Ritti, Richard R., and Fred H. Goldner. 1979. "Professional Pluralism in an Industrial Organization." *Management Science* 16:233–46.

Roethlisberger, Fritz, and William Dickson. 1939. *Management and the Worker*. Cambridge: Harvard University Press.

Rohlen, T. P. 1983. "The Mazda Turnaround." *Journal of Japanese Studies* 9: 219–64.

Rohwer, Jim. 1995. *Asia Rising: The Economic Miracle in East and South East Asia and Why the West Will Profit*. New York: Simon and Schuster.

Romanelli, Elaine. 1999. "Blind (But Not Unconditioned) Variation: Problems of Copying in Socio-Cultural Evolution." In *Variations in Organizational Science: In Honor of Donald T. Campbell*, edited by Joel A. C. Baum and Bill McKelvey. Newbury Park, Cal.: Sage Publications.

Rose, Joan R. 1997. "In Defense of Drive-Through Deliveries." *Medical Economics* 74:26.

Rosenoer, Jonathan, Douglas Armstrong, and J. Russell Gates. 1999. *The Clickable Corporation: Successful Strategies for Capturing the Internet Advantage*. New York: Free Press.

Rosenbloom, Richard S., and William J. Spencer. 1996. "The Transformation of Industrial Research." *Issues in Science and Technology* 12 (3): 68–74.

Rosenkopf, Lori, and Michael L. Tushman. 1994. "The Coevolution of Technology and Organization." In *Evolutionary Dynamics of Organizations*, edited by Joel A. C. Baum and Jitendra V. Singh, 403–24. New York: Oxford University Press.

Rosenzweig, Philip, and Jitendra V. Singh. 1991. "Organizational Environments and the Multinational Enterprise." *Academy of Management Review* 16 (2): 340–61.

Roy, Donald. 1952. "Quota Restriction and Goldbricking in a Machine Shop." *American Journal of Sociology* 57:427–42.

Roy, William G. 1997. *Socializing Capital: The Rise of the Large Industrial Corporation in America*. Princeton: Princeton University Press.

Rubenstein, Moshe F., and Iris Rubinstein Firstenberg. 1999. *The Minding Organization: Connect the Brain, Heart, and Soul of Your Company to Creative Solutions*. New York: John Wiley and Sons.

Sabel, Charles F. 1990. "Moebius-Strip Organizations and Open Labor Markets: Some Consequences of the Reintegration of Conception and Execution in a Volatile Economy." In *Social Theory for a Changing Society*, edited by Pierre Bourdieu and James Coleman, 23–54. Boulder and New York: Westview Press and the Russell Sage Foundation.

———. 1992. "Studied Trust: Building New Forms of Cooperation in a Volatile Economy." In *Industrial Districts and Local Economic Regeneration*, edited by Frank Pyke and Werner Sengenberger, 215–50. Geneva: International Institute for Labor Studies.

———. 1994. "Learning by Monitoring: The Institutions of Economic Development." In *The Handbook of Economic Sociology*, edited by N. J. Smelser and R. Swedberg, 137–65. Princeton, N.J.: Princeton University Press.

Sabel, Charles F., and Michael C. Dorf. 1998. "A Constitution of Democratic Experimentalism." *Columbia Law Review* 98 (2): 267–529.

Sabel, Charles F., and Jonathan Zeitlin. 1996. *Worlds of Possibility: Flexibility and Mass Production in Western Industrialization*. Paris: Maison des Sciences de l'Homme.

Sakaguchi, Y. 1994. *Matsushita Okoku ga Abunai* [The Matsushita Giant Is in Danger]. Tokyo: Yell Shuppansha.

Sako, Mari. 1997. "Introduction: Forces for Homogeneity and Diversity in the Japanese Industrial Relations System." In *Japanese Labour and Management in Transition: Diversity, Flexibility, and Participation*, edited by M. Sako and H. Sato, 1–24. London: Routledge.

Sako, Mari, and Susan Helper. 1998. "Determinants of Trust in Supplier Relations: Evidence from the Automotive Industry in Japan and the United States." *Journal of Economic Behavior and Organization* 34:387–417.

Sampson, Anthony. 1975. *The Seven Sisters*. New York: Viking Press.

Samuels, R. J. 1987. *The Business of the Japanese State*. Ithaca: Cornell University Press.

Sayer, Andrew, and Richard Walker. 1992. *The New Social Economy: Reworking the Division of Labor*. Cambridge, Mass.: Blackwell.

Scher, Mark J. 1997. *Japanese Interfirm Networks and Their Main Banks*. New York: St. Martin's Press.

Schumpeter, Joseph. 1934. *The Theory of Economic Development*. Cambridge: Harvard University Press.

Scott, Elizabeth D., K. C. O'Shaughnessy, and P. Capelli. 1996. "Management Jobs in the Insurance Industry: Organizational Deskilling and Rising Pay Inequity." In *Broken Ladders*, edited by P. Osterman, 124–54. New York: Oxford University Press.

Scott, James C. 1985. *Weapons of the Weak*. New Haven: Yale University Press.

———. 1990. *Domination and the Arts of Resistance: Hidden Transcripts*. New Haven: Yale University Press.

———. 1998. *Seeing Like a State*. New Haven: Yale University Press.

Scott, John P. 1987. "Intercorporate Structures in Western Europe: A Comparative Historical Analysis." In *Intercorporate Relations: The Structural Analysis of Business*, edited by Mark Mizruchi and Michael Schwartz, 208–32. New York: Cambridge University Press.

Scott, W. Richard. 1965. "Reactions to Supervision in a Heteronomous Professional Organization." *Administrative Science Quarterly* 10:65–81.

———. 1992. *Organizations: Rational, Natural, and Open Systems*, 3d ed. Englewood Cliffs, N.J.: Prentice-Hall.

———. 1995. *Organizations and Institutions*. Thousand Oaks, Cal.: Sage.

Scott, W. Richard, Martin Reuf, Peter J. Mendel, and Carol Caronna. 2000. *Institutional Change and Health Care Organizations*. Chicago: University of Chicago Press.

Scranton, Philip. 1997. *Endless Novelty: Specialty Production and American Industrialization, 1865–1925*. Princeton: Princeton University Press.

Selznick, Philip. 1949. *TVA and the Grass Roots*. Berkeley: University of California Press.

Sennett, Richard. 1998. *The Corrosion of Character*. New York: Knopf.

Shapiro, Susan P. 1987. "The Social Control of Impersonal Trust," *American Journal of Sociology* 93:623–58.

Shibata, Masaharu 1998. *Naze Kaisha wa Kawaranai no ka?* [Why Aren't Companies Changing?]. Tokyo: Nihon keizai Shimbunsha.

Shishido, Zenichi. 1997. "Legal Monitoring Systems in Japan: Legal Possibilities and Current Practice." *Perspectives on Company Law*, edited by Fiona Patfield, 2:149–64.

Simon, Herbert. 1951. "A Formal Theory Model of the Employment Relationship." *Econometrica* 19:293–305.

Simonian, Haig. 1999. Germany to Abolish Tax on Disposal of Cross-Holdings. *Financial Times*, 24 December, p. 1.

Singh, J.V., D. J. Tucker, and R. J. House. 1986. "Organizational Legitimacy and the Liability of Newness." *Administrative Science Quarterly* 31:171–93.

Smitka, M. J. 1991. *Competitive Ties: Subcontracting in the Japanese Automotive Industry*. New York: Columbia University Press.

Spiers, Joseph. 1995. "Why the Income Gap Won't Go Away." *Fortune* 11 December, pp. 65–70.

Stark, David. 1989. "Coexisting Organizational Forms in Hungary's Emerging Mixed Economy." In *Remaking the Economic Institutions of Socialism: China and Eastern Europe*, edited by Victor Nee and David Stark, 137–68. Stanford: Stanford University Press.

———. 1990. "La valeur du travail et sa rétribution en Hongrie." *Actes de la recherche en sciences sociales* (Paris) 85 (3–19 November). Available in English as "Work, Worth, and Justice." *www.sociology.columbia.edu/faculty/stark/worth*.

———. 1996. "Recombinant Property in East European Capitalism." *American Journal of Sociology* 101:993–1027.

———. 1998. "Violating Parsons Pact: New Directions for Economic Sociology." Paper presented at the Conference on the Economics of Conventions, Bretesche, France.

———. 1999. "From Bureaucracy and Mass Communication to Collaborative Organization and Interactive Media: Organizational Innovation in Silicon Alley." Paper presented at the Annual Meeting of the American Sociological Association, August, in Chicago.

———. 2000. "For a Sociology of Worth." Conference on Economic Sociology at the Edge of the Third Millenium, January in Moscow.

Stark, David, and László Bruszt. 1998. *Postsocialist Pathways: Transforming Politics and Property in East Central Europe*. New York and London: Cambridge University Press.

Stark, David, Szabolcs Kemény, and Ronald Breiger. 1998. "Post-Socialist Portfolios: Network Strategies in the Shadow of the State." Paper presented at the 1998 Annual Meeting of the American Sociological Association, San Francisco.

Stinchcombe, Arthur L. 1959. "Bureaucratic and Craft Administration of Production." *Administrative Science Quarterly* 4:194–208.

———. 1965. "Social Structure and Organizations." In *Handbook of Organizations*, edited by James G. March, 142–93. Chicago: Rand-McNally.

———. 1968. *Constructing Social Theories*. Chicago: University of Chicago Press.

Streeck, Wolfgang. 1992. *Social Institutions and Economic Performance*. London: Sage Publications.

Streeck, Wolfgang, and Philippe C. Schmitter, eds. 1985. *Private Interest Government: Beyond Market and State*. Beverly Hills, Cal.: Sage Publications.

Stuart, Toby E., Ha Hoang, and Ralph Hybels. 1999. "Interorganizational Endorsements and the Performance of Entrepreneurial Ventures." *Administrative Science Quarterly* 44:315–49.

Sugayama, S. 1995. "Work Rules, Wages, and Single Status: The Shaping of the 'Japanese Employment System.' " *Business History* 37:120–40.

Sugeno, K., and T. Suwa. 1997. "Labour Law Issues in a Changing Labour Market: In Search of a New Support System." In *Japanese Labour and Management in Transition*, edited by M. Sako and H. Sato, 53–78. London: Routledge.

Szulanski, Gabriel. 1996. "Impediments to Internal Transfer of Best Practices." *Strategic Management Journal* 17:27–43.

Takeuchi, Yasuo. 1998. *'Nihon' no Owari* [The End of 'Japan']. Tokyo: Nihon Keizai Shimbunsha.

Tamás, Pál. 1993. "Inovációs teljesítmények és vallalati stratégiak [Achievement in Innovation and Company Strategies]." Working paper, Institute for the Study of Social Conflicts, Budapest.

Tapscott, Don, ed. 1999. *Creating Value in the Network Economy*. Boston: Harvard Business School Press.

Taylor, Frederick Winslow. [1911] 1947. *Principles of Scientific Management*. New York: W.W. Norton.

Taylor, William. 1991. "The Logic of Global Business: An Interview with ABB's Percy Bavenick." *Harvard Business Review* 69 (2): 91–105.

Teubner, Günther. 1991. "Beyond Contract and Organizational?: The External Liability of Franchising Systems in German Law." In *Franchising and the Law: Theoretical and Comparative Approaches in Europe and the United States*, edited by Christian Joerges, 105–32. Baden-Baden: Nomos Verlagsgesellschaft.

———. 1996. "Double Bind: Hybrid Arrangements as De-Paradoxifiers." *Journal of Institutional and Theoretical Economics* 152 (1): 59–64.

Tezuka, H. 1997. "Success as the Source of Failure? Competition and Cooperation in the Japanese Economy." *Sloan Management Review* (Fall/Winter).

Thomas, Robert. 1994. *What Machines Can't Do: Politics and Technology in the Industrial Enterprise*. Berkeley: University of California Press.

Thompson, E. P. 1971. "Time, Work, and Discipline." *Past and Present* (December): 56–97.

Thompson, James D. 1967. *Organizations in Action*. New York: McGraw-Hill.

Thomson, Janice E. 1994. *Mercenaries, Pirates, and Sovereigns: State-Building and Extraterritorial Violence in Early Modern Europe*. Princeton: Princeton University Press.

Tilly, Charles. 1992. *Coercion, Capital, and European States*. Rev. ed. Oxford: Blackwell.

Tilly, Chris, and Charles Tilly. 1998. *Work Under Capitalism*. Boulder: Westview Press.

Tomaney, J. 1994. "A New Paradigm of Work Organization and Technology?" In *Post-Fordism: A Reader*, edited by A. Amin. Oxford: Blackwell Publishers.

Toyo Keizai Shimposha, ed. 1994. *Zenzukai Nihon no Jimmyaku to Kigyo Keiretsu* [A Complete Graphic Guide to Japan's Enterprise Groups and Human Networks]. Tokyo: Toyo Keizai Shimposha.

Toyo, Keizai Shimposha, ed. 1995. *Nihon no Kigyo Guru-pu* [Japan's Enterprise Groups]. Tokyo: Toyo Keizai Shimposha.

Tsutsui, W. M. 1998. *Manufacturing Ideology: Scientific Management in Twentieth-Century Japan*. Princeton: Princeton University Press.

Turk, Herman. 1970. "Interorganizational Networks in Urban Society: Initial Perspectives and Comparative Research." *American Sociological Review* 35:1–19.

Udy, Stanley H. 1959. " 'Bureaucracy' and 'Rationality' in Weber's Organization Theory." *American Sociological Review* 24:791–95.

Upton, D. M., and A. McAfee. 1996. "The Real Virtual Factory." *Harvard Business Review* 74:123–33.

Useem, Michael. 1992. *Executive Defense: Shareholder Power and Corporate Reorganization*. Cambridge: Harvard University Press.

———. 1996. *Investor Capitalism: How Money Managers are Changing the Face of Corporate America*. New York: Basic Books.

Uzzi, Brian. 1997. "Social Structure and Competition in Interfirm Networks: The Paradox of Embeddedness." *Administrative Science Quarterly* 42:35–67.

Vallas, Stephen Y., and John P. Beck. 1996. "The Transformation of Work Revisited: The Limits of Flexibility in American Manufacturing." *Social Problems* 43 (3): 339–61.

Vogel, David. 1989. *Fluctuating Fortunes: The Political Power of Business in America*. New York: Basic Books.

Wada, K. 1995. "The Emergence of the 'Flow Production' Method in Japan." In *Fordism Transformed: The Development of Production Methods in the Automobile Industry*, edited by H. Shiomi and K. Wada, 11–27. New York: Oxford University Press.

Wagner, Gunter P., and Lee Altenberg, 1996. "Complex Adaptations and the Evolution of Evolvability." *Evolution*, 50 (3):967–76.

Waldinger, Roger. 1986. *Through the Eye of the Needle: Immigrants and Enterprise in New York's Garment Trades*. New York: New York University Press.

Ward, Michael D., and Kristian S. Gleditsch. 1998. "Democratizing for Peace." *American Political Science Review* 92:51–61.

Warren, Roland. 1967. "The Interorganizational Field as a Focus for Investigation." *Administrative Science Quarterly* 12:396–419.

Weber, Max. [1924] 1946. "Bureaucracy." In *From Max Weber: Essays in Sociology*, edited by Hans Gerth and C. Wright Mills, 196–252. New York: Oxford University Press.

———. [1910] 1978. *Economy and Society*. Translated and edited by G. Roth and C. Wittich. Berkeley: University of California.

Weick, Karl E. 1977. "Organization Design: Organizations as Self-Designing Systems." *Organizational Dynamics* 6 (2): 31–45.

Weidenbaum, Murray. 1996. "The Chinese Family Business Enterprise." *California Management Review* 38:141–56.

Westney, D. Eleanor. 1987. *Imitation and Innovation: The Transfer of Western Organizational Patterns to Meiji Japan*. Cambridge: Harvard University Press.

———. 1996. "The Japanese Business System: Key Features and Prospects for Change." *Journal of Asian Business*, 12:21–50.

Wheelwright, S. C. 1981. "Japan—Where Operations Really are Strategic." *Harvard Business Review* 59:67–74.

White, Harrison. 1993. "Values Come in Styles, Which Mate to Change." In *The Origins of Value*, edited by Michael Hechter, Lynn Nadel, and Richard E. Michod, 63–91. New York: Aldine de Gruyter

White, Harrison, Scott A. Boorman, and Ronald L. Breiger. 1976. "Social Structure from Multiple Networks: I. Blockmodels of Roles and Positions." *American Journal of Sociology* 81:730–80.

Whitehill, A., and S. Takezawa. 1968. *The Other Worker*. Honolulu: East-West Center Press.

Whitley, Richard. 1992. *Business Systems in East Asia: Firms, Markets, and Societies*. London: Sage Publications.

———. 1994. "The Internationalization of Firms and Markets: Its Significance and Institutional Structuring." *Organization* 1 (1): 101–24.

Williamson, Jeffrey. 1995. "The Evolution of Global Labor Markets since 1830: Background Evidence and Hypotheses." *Explorations in Economic History* 32: 141–196.

———. 1996. "Globalization, Convergence, and History." *Journal of Economic History* 56 (2): 277–306.

Williamson, Oliver E. 1975. *Markets and Hierarchies: Analysis and Antitrust Implications*. New York: Free Press.

———. 1979. "Transaction-Cost Economics: The Governance of Contractual Relations." *Journal of Law and Economics* 22:3–61.

———.1985. *The Economic Institutions of Capitalism*. New York: Free Press.

———. 1996. *The Mechanisms of Governance*. New York: Oxford University Press.

Wilson, William Julius. 1996. *When Work Disappears*. New York: Knopf.

Wong, R. Bin. 1997. *China Transformed: Historical Change and the Limits of European Experience*. Ithaca: Cornell University Press.

Woodward, Joan. 1958. *Management and Technology*. London: Her Majesty's Stationery Office.

Womack, James P., Daniel T. Jones, and Daniel Roos. 1990. *The Machine That Changed the World: The Story of Lean Production*. New York: Harper and Row.

Yamagishi, Toshio, and Midori Yamagishi. 1994. "Trust and Commitment in the United States and Japan," *Motivation and Emotion* 18:129–66.

Yoshino, M. Y. and T. B. Lifson. 1986. *The Invisible Link*. Cambridge: MIT Press.

Zeitlin, Maurice, W. Lawrence Neuman, and Richard E. Ratcliff. 1976. "Class Segments: Agrarian Property and Political Leadership in the Capitalist Class of Chile." *American Sociological Review* 41:1006–29.

Zerubavel, Eviatar. 1998. *Social Mindscapes: An Invitation to Cognitive Sociology.* Cambridge: Harvard University Press.

Zuboff, Shoshana. 1988. *In the Age of the Smart Machine: The Future of Work and Power.* New York: Basic.

———. 1995. "The Emperor's New Workplace." *Scientific American* 273:202–204.

Zucker, Lynne. 1986. "The Production of Trust: Institutional Sources of Change in the Formal Structure of Organizations, 1840–1920." *Research on Organizational Behavior* 8:53–111.

Index

Abegglen, James, 108, 109, 110, 133
accountability, 100–102, 228–30
accounts, 98–100
agency theory, 20–21
airline industry, 175n
Air Touch, 33
Alchian, A., 194–95
Allen, P. M., 72
alliance networks, 175n; change in, 221–25
Alliance of Motion Picture and Television
    Producers, 45
American Airlines, 175n
American Can, 191
American Management Association, 44
America Online, 33
Anderson Consulting, 212
Ansell, C. K., 101
antitrust legislation, 174–75
Aoki, M., 120, 125
Asea Brown Boveri (ABB), 47
asset ownership patterns, 189n, 195
associational networks, 130–33
AT&T, 40
authority relations, 167–68
automobile industry in the U.S., 172
Axelrod, R., 193

Barley, S. L., 57
Barnard, Chester, 15, 186
Baum, J.A.C., 176
Bayat, Asef, 204
Beck, J. P., 52
benchmarking, 116
Benner, C., 41, 45
Berle, Adolph, 123–24
Betamax-VHS race, 177
Blau, P. M., 186
Bound, John, 49
bounded firms, 201
Boyer, R., 66
Braverman, H., 216
Bridgestone, 117
British Airways, 175n
British Factory Japanese Factory (Dore),
    108–9

Bryce, D., 212
bureaucracy: compensation and, 9; files/re-
    cord keeping and, 9; roles/job descrip-
    tions and, 8–9; rules and, 8; Weber's
    model of, 7–10, 12, 13
bureaucratic firms, change in, 215–21
bureaucratic model, criticisms of: bureau-
    cracy and the market as alternatives,
    17–19; informal social relations, 14–16;
    transaction-cost approach, 17; variants in
    organizational structures, 16–17
business alliances, 5, 221–25

Campbell, D. T., 182
Canon, 116
capitalist firms, changes affecting, 33–35
capitalist regimes, 202–3
capitalist system, challenges to: interfirm al-
    liances, 23–25; reassertion of shareholder
    control, 20–22; social contract renegoti-
    ated, 22–23
capitalist system, Marx's views on, 7,
    10–13
Castells, Manuel, 236
chaebols, 155
Chandler, Alfred D., Jr., 18, 49
change: among and between firms, 221–30;
    in bureaucratic firms, 215–21; extent of,
    215–30; migration of agency from compa-
    nies to business networks, 225–30; net-
    works of, 211–15; new system logic and,
    230–36; paradoxes of rapid, 210–11; in re-
    lational contracts and strategic alliances,
    221–25; schemata versus organizations,
    236–42
Chase Manhattan, 43
Chemical Bank, 43
Chrysler Corp., 33, 49, 59, 178
Cisco Systems, 33–34
Citibank, 33
Clemons, E. K., 184
Coase, Ronald, 17, 148, 186
coercive processes, 241
Coffee, John, 95
Cole, Robert E., 111–12